Movies for Kids

UNGAR FILM LIBRARY

Stanley Hochman
General Editor

Academy Awards: An Ungar Reference Index,
edited by Richard Shale

American History / American Film: Interpreting the Hollywood Image,
edited by John O'Connor and Martin A. Jackson

The Classic American Novel and the Movies,
edited by Gerald Peary and Roger Shatzkin

The Blue Angel / *the novel by Heinrich Mann and the film by Josef von Sternberg*

Costume Design in the Movies / *Elizabeth Leese*

Faulkner and Film / *Bruce F. Kawin*

Fellini the Artist / *Edward Murray*

Film Study Collections: A Guide to their Development and Use / *Nancy Allen*

Hitchcock: The First Forty-Four Films / *Eric Rohmer and Claude Chabrol*

Loser Take All: The Comic Art of Woody Allen / *Maurice Yacowar*

The Modern American Novel and the Movies,
edited by Gerald Peary and Roger Shatzkin

Movies for Kids: A Guide for Parents and Teachers on the Entertainment Film for Children / *Ruth M. Goldstein and Edith Zornow*

On the Verge of Revolt: Women in American Films of the Fifties / *Brandon French*

Ten Film Classics / *Edward Murray*

Tennessee Williams and Film / *Maurice Yacowar*

OTHER FILM BOOKS

The Age of the American Novel: The film Aesthetic of Fiction between the Two Wars / *Claude-Edmonde Magny*

The Cinematic Imagination: Writers and the Motion Pictures / *Edward Murray*

Hollywood in the 1940s: The Stars' Own Stories, *edited by Ivy Crane Wilson, ed.*

A Library of Film Criticism: American Film Directors, *edited by Stanley Hochman*

Nine American Film Critics / *Edward Murray*

Saint Cinema / *Herman G. Weinberg*

1782 64

Movies for Kids

A Guide for Parents and
Teachers on the Entertainment
Film for Children

Ruth M. Goldstein and Edith Zornow

Introduction by Joan Ganz Cooney

REVISED EDITION

Frederick Ungar Publishing Co. New York

For David, Todd, Kim, Robin, and Sherri

Copyright © 1973, 1980 by Ruth M. Goldstein and Edith Zornow
Printed in the United States of America
Library of Congress Cataloging in Publication Data

Goldstein, Ruth M
  Movies for kids

  In the 1973 ed. E. Zornow's name appeared first on t.p.
  Bibliography: p.
  Includes indexes.
  1. Moving-pictures for children—Catalogs.
I. Zornow, Edith, joint author. II. Title.
PN1998.Z6 1980   791.43'088054   79-6149
ISBN 0-8044-2267-2
ISBN 0-8044-6194-5 (pbk.)

Acknowledgments

We are grateful to Rohama Lee, editor of *Film News,* for permission to include some annotations that originally appeared, in different form, in reviews in the magazine.

Many people have been most generous with help and information: Pauline A. Cianciolo; the staff of the Educational Film Library Association; Wendy Keys and Brooks Riley; Brenda Davies of the British Film Institute; Charles Silver of the film department of the Museum of Modern Art; Henry Geddes, director of the Children's Film Foundation; Audrey Ryan of the Miami-Dade Public Library; Nat Chediak, director of the Cinematheque of Coral Gables; Kathryn Cuskley of *Film & Broadcasting Review;* Ernest Parmentier of *Filmfacts;* Michael Linden of the Motion Picture Association of America; and Jerri Seiler.

Our thanks for their views on some of the movies, to Scheryl Christine Fair (15), Kimberly Ann Goldsmith (12), Robin Lyn Goldsmith (7), Lisa Betchia Morris (10), and Lonny Rex Morris (12).

For the index, and for more help than she knows she gives, we are grateful to Pearl Goldsmith, R.M.G.'s sister.

791.43
G01

Contents

Selections of stills from the films on pages 56–63, 100–107, 202–3

Preface to the Revised Edition

By a happy chance, this revised and greatly expanded edition of *Movies for Kids*, first published as a Discus/Avon paperback original in 1973, follows the celebration of the International Year of the Child. But for us it has been the year of the child and the movies for a long time.

We remember the children taken by their father to THE PUMPKIN EATER, hardly a Mother Goose tale, and the children bussed into an Adirondacks town by a camp director to see TOYS IN THE ATTIC, Lillian Hellman's turgid drama of violence and sexual rivalry.

Movies for Kids is based on the assumption that no adult needs to make that kind of mistake. Not a textbook, not a work on the art of film, not an introduction to film study, it is a guide for parents, teachers, and librarians—for everyone looking for good movies to entertain children.

The 430 features, featurettes, and documentaries described here, in full or capsule annotations, are all available in 16mm, for rental or sale, for non-theatrical showings in homes, schools, libraries, churches, synagogues, camps, and clubs. A few not yet in release non-theatrically may be seen on television or in theaters.

We could not, even if we would, offer a guide to films now in production which will be showing in theaters in the future. That Saturday afternoon when your kids want to go to the movies and you'd like to know what they're going to see, you have excellent advice waiting for you in movie reviews in newspapers or magazines or on TV. You even have the ratings, although they are likely to be less trustworthy guides than your own ethical and aesthetic convictions.

The parents, teachers, and librarians for whom we intend this book are those whose children make up the huge non-theatrical movie audience: the audience which discovers its movies on television, and the audience which discovers its movies in 16mm.

Today, in every school and community organization in the country, children are being shown movies for entertainment. We have tried to bring together a number of the best of these, the most entertaining and the most outstanding in quality.

What movies do children enjoy? Well, what turned *you* on? At twelve, one of the authors haunted a Brooklyn fleapit where they ran the old Emil Jannings pictures, and a friend went to every Joan Crawford movie three times. A junior-high student tells us that many of the kids in his class have seen STAR WARS many times. And of course they've seen every monster movie released this year. These are the movies the kids find for themselves, with or without "PG."

In this book we bring together movies you can help them discover and enjoy. You will be gratified by the catholicity of children; they are unique, quixotic, and full of surprises. Once, at a preview of Luis Buñuel's THE ADVENTURES OF ROBINSON CRUSOE, we were apprehensive about the effect on the younger kids of the Freudian nightmare sequence and the long, uneventful stretches, and so we asked for audience reactions. "What I liked best," one child wrote, "was the cat and the dog. What I liked least was, not enough of the cat, and the dog died." Another time, at a ballet film, we overheard a man ask a boy why he was there instead of at the ball game. "Who says I can't like both?" the boy said.

Since we do not feel dogmatic about children's tastes, we have approached this selection in the spirit of Robert Benchley's famous solution to a question on an international law exam. Asked to discuss the dispute between the United States and Great Britain on the Newfoundland fisheries and knowing nothing about it, he decided to answer the question from the point of view of the fish. Somewhere between the convictions of some parents, teachers, and film or television producers (that of course they know what's good for kids) and the convictions of most kids (that "parental guidance" is the kiss of death) we have taken our stand by the movies themselves. A movie of quality is a movie for kids. The exceptions are the films of brutality, of sadism, of cynicism, or of concepts which most youngsters will be able to handle better when they are more mature. Naturally, one thirteen-year-old's maturity is no more predictable than one thirty-year-old's; every list is flexible.

Our choices will not be everyone's. What criteria have we used in choosing movies of quality? The answer is to be found in every annotation. Taste, as Stanley Kauffmann has said, is a matter of instances, not precepts. We do not go by rules, but by our combined experience of more than fifty years with movies and with kids. Among these 430 movies there ought to be something for almost everybody—and quite a number of omissions and commissions for us to argue about.

Under the umbrella word *entertainment,* we hope you will find movies that make magic, that go on journeys, that spill over with laughter, that rouse wonder. There are even some movies that can do more. "We wander through this life together," said Albert Schweitzer, "in a semidarkness in which none of us can distinguish exactly the face of his neighbor. Only from time to time, through some experience we have of our companion, or through some remark he passes, he stands for a moment close to us, as though illuminated by a flash of lightning. Then we see him as he really is."

In the semidarkness of movie viewing, children receive vivid impressions of those like and unlike themselves. The best movies in our book are those which open the eye and the heart. We hope that youngsters who see them will enjoy many entertaining hours, illuminated by flashes of lightning.

Ruth M. Goldstein
Edith Zornow

Movies for Kids

Introduction

Joan Ganz Cooney
President, Children's Television Workshop

When I was a child growing up in Phoenix, Arizona, movies were often a delightful and memorable family occasion. My father took me to CAPTAINS COURAGEOUS; we both cried and cried, and I began my life-long love affair with Spencer Tracy. I went to LITTLE WOMEN three or four times with my mother and sister, and my brother and I were nobly politicized by MR. SMITH GOES TO WASHINGTON.

As critic Pauline Kael has written, "Movies are a past we share." Good movies are the source of something very special for both children and parents. They make a mockery of the generation gap; indeed, some movies that we enjoyed as youngsters are enjoyed even more by today's young. I was visiting recently with some friends in New York, and the grandmother, mother, father, and fourteen-year-old son were animatedly debating which was the "greatest Marx Brothers movie ever." Last summer, I attended a neighborhood party in the country where kids and their parents gathered at one of their homes to laugh, clap, and gasp with pleasure during a screening of SINGIN' IN THE RAIN. Does anyone doubt that this sharing of experience among the generations *is* education, and entertainment, for children in the best and truest sense?

Edith Zornow and Ruth M. Goldstein know their movies and they know their audience. *Movies for Kids* not only is a useful compilation but it makes delightful reading as well. The authors make their listings and comments with the kind of confidence that can come only from a lifetime of intimate knowledge of the subject matter. There is no trace of condescension nor of over-protection. Rightfully, a number of the films that are listed were

1

not even produced for young audiences, yet they have proved to be perfect for them.

I have known Ruth M. Goldstein only by reputation, but that reputation has been and is considerable. When many educators still considered movie-viewing as, at best, a diversion from the process of education, Ruth M. Goldstein was experimenting and exploring with the exciting interrelationship between film and the young. As a result of her pioneering, many of her former students are involved in teaching or working with film.

At the Children's Television Workshop we have the rare privilege of working on a day-to-day basis with Edith Zornow. She is one of film's most precious resources. There is hardly any factual information about movies and shorts that she does not know. Equally important, her cinematic judgment of what is good and what is bad, and why, is unfailing. At the Workshop, she is creating short-short films for *"Sesame Street"* and *"The Electric Company"* and her "little movies" are evolving into an exciting new film form. It is pure pleasure to know her as friend and colleague.

Films are beginning to take their rightful place within the complex process of educating our young. Edith Zornow and Ruth M. Goldstein in their *Movies for Kids* happily have accelerated the pace.

How to Look at a Movie

Tony Hodgkinson tells the story, in his UNESCO report on screen education, of the novice film teacher who was reproached by one of his pupils: "You know, sir, before I started your lessons I used to enjoy watching films. Now, when I go to the cinema, all I can do is count the shots!"

Overemphasis on technical analysis by teacher or parent runs counter to one of the basic attractions movies have for children. Remember? You didn't want to be told that you *had* to like a movie, as you had to like *The Scarlet Letter* in English literature courses. What was happening up there on the screen in the darkened theater was happening for you alone; you were eavesdropping on *now*, on the immediate and immensely personal experience.

We wouldn't want to straitjacket a child's response to the movies, any more than we'd want to restrain his enthusiasm for a poem by asking him to play the New Critics' game of symbol, symbol, who's got the symbol. It does help to ask, as John Ciardi does, "How does a poem mean?" And it can deepen one's pleasure in a moment of film to be able to recognize an image of visual poetry that has the richness of metaphor. "How does it work?" is a question that needn't spoil movie-watching.

Granted that an understanding of terms like *low shot, match cut, pan,* and *dissolve* should never be an end in itself, we can use knowledge of *film language* as a means to greater enjoyment and insight. "The most important element to me is always the idea that I'm trying to express," said director John Huston to an interviewer, "and everything technical is only a method to make the idea into clear form. I'm always working on the idea whether I am writing, directing, choosing music, or cutting."

Looking and listening intently, thinking about the movies they see, comparing their camera techniques subconsciously with those used in TV commercials—*slow motion, misty filters, focus-changing effects*—kids pick up many elements of film grammar. They realize that filmmakers communicate in a special language and that some movies may require as much planning as a moon shot. They are aware that certain things are selected for them to look at, lighted in a certain way, photographed from determined positions, arranged in a certain order, cut to a desired length, and matched with coordinated sounds. They know that there are more people involved in the making of a movie than meet the eye.

We do not have space to treat the art of the film, but many of the books in 100 *Good* Books About Film (pp. 255-59) provide an excellent introduction to the medium, its history and development, as well as treating film terms in expanded detail. What we should like to do here is to consider examples of film language as they appear in a few of the features and other films recommended in *Movies for Kids*.

A classic film for analysis is GREAT EXPECTATIONS. David Lean, writer of the screenplay as well as director, took Charles Dickens's opening chapter, in which Pip meets the convict Magwitch in the graveyard, and made a brilliant opening sequence which usually electrifies viewers. Here are some phrases in the language of the novel: ". . .the low leaden line beyond was the river. . .the distant savage lair from which the wind was rushing, was the sea. . .the small bundle of shivers growing afraid of it all and beginning to cry, was Pip."

And here is the film's language, in the screenplay:

> 4. VERY LONG SHOT OVER RIVER ESTUARY (WIND—FOOTSTEPS)
> *On* PIP *running right, camera trucking and panning. Movement stops at* PIP *toward foreground, glancing nervously at gallows pole at right as he exits right foreground.*
> DISSOLVE TO:
> CLOSE SHOT (SUNSET) (WIND—BRANCHES)
> PIP *as he appears above broken wall at left. Camera moves right and down with him as he climbs over wall to churchyard, glancing nervously about. He walks toward background, and stops at gravestone.*
> 5. CLOSE MEDIUM (WIND—BRANCHES)
> *On* PIP *as he tears weeds from grave and puts flowers on it.*
> 6. CLOSE SIDE ANGLE—PIP (WIND—BRANCHES)
> *As he lifts head. He faces camera looking up left.*
> 7. MEDIUM LONG UPWARD (WIND—BRANCHES)
> *On tree as it sways toward camera moved by wind.*
> 8. CLOSE-UP—PIP (WIND—BRANCHES)
> *As he reacts to off-shot noises.*
> 9. MEDIUM LONG (WIND—BRANCHES)
> *On heavy tree stump and bare stretching branches as they sway and creak in the wind.*

10. LONG MEDIUM (WIND—BRANCHES)
PIP *as he rises from grave and runs left, camera panning,*
bringing in CONVICT *in chains whom* PIP *bumps into sud-*
denly. CONVICT *grabs* PIP *by throat in close shot.*

PIP
Oh!. . .Oh. . .

11. CLOSE-UP—PIP
As he screams, shooting past CONVICT's *hands as they*
cover PIP's *mouth smothering scream.*
12. CLOSE-UP—CONVICT
WIND.

CONVICT
Keep still, you little devil, or I'll cut your throat.

No matter how few of the film terms used here one understands, the excitement of the scene builds up powerfully in the
mind's eye. How does Lean create this effect? In part, through
framing. A *frame* is one separate image on a strip of celluloid; it
is a unit of motion. By giving us a continuous flow of highly dramatic images, Lean works up to a climax in which we feel that we
are Pip, that *we* are running into the arms of a terrifying stranger—
while all the time sound intensifies image, the great tree creaks
in the wind, and we shiver with Pip.

Later on in the film, the camera tells us Pip is growing up. First
we see him in his blacksmith's clothes; then, through a *dissolve*
(gradual merging of the end of one shot into the beginning of the
next), we see him, several years afterward, dressed in the height
of fashion. The camera focuses on his feet and then *pans* (moves
from a fixed position) upward to reveal a young gentleman with
great expectations. A *montage* (superimposition of shots) shows
Pip getting lessons in dancing, boxing, and fencing. It's entertaining, but unless the viewer reads between the lines of film
language, to the actor's face and the point it makes—that Pip is
a self-satisfied fop—he will miss the director's idea. Pip is far more
foolish now than the boy in blacksmith's clothes.

Sometimes the camera does all our thinking for us. In 2001: A
SPACE ODYSSEY, there is a *match cut* (transition from one shot to
another that matches it in action or subject): we see a bone hurled
into the air by a prehistoric ape-man, then a space station pro-
jected into space by modern technologists. In the opening scene
of MODERN TIMES, a shot of a flock of sheep rushing through a
gate is immediately followed by a shot of a crowd of people rush-

ing out of the subway on their way to work. In each case, a simile is made visual.

Just as writers use syntax for their own purposes, film directors use the elements of film grammar to create their vision. Although Jean-Luc Godard once said, "Tragedy is close-up and comedy is long shot," Buster Keaton uses *close-shot* for one of the funniest moments in THE GENERAL, when he is trapped under a table and all we can see of him is one eye peering through a hole in the tablecloth. That one eye, reacting to the sight of his girl being brought in as a captive by the Union Army, is hilariously eloquent.

Slow and *fast motion* are familiar techniques. Slow motion, in the scene in A HARD DAY'S NIGHT when the Beatles, released from routine, are dancing in the field, gives us a dreamlike, lyrical feeling. The speed-up of fast motion, in THE LAVENDER HILL MOB, in the auto chase through London and the free-for-all at the police exhibition, gives us great Keystone fun. In the same movie, the camera surprises us and tips us off. Alec Guinness, drinking in a South American café with a representative of the law, rises from the table, and we see that he's handcuffed. Mr. Holland, it seems, is not going to get away with the gold-bullion caper.

In SHANE, director George Stevens conveys character and atmosphere through *angle shots, pans,* and *filmic symbols.* When Wilson shoots Torre so casually, the high and low camera angles show Wilson looming arrogantly, Torre looking up pathetically. Later on, at Torre's funeral, the camera angle is low from the coffin; Stevens pans from the gloomy hill (the scene is Jackson Hole, Wyoming) to the rough wooden box, the tumbleweeds frightening the horse, the dog trying to get back to his dead master, the valley leading to the town and the cause of the death. At this point, the musical score clinches the point; a single chord underlines the conflict.

Without sound and music, the impact of many film sequences would be greatly diminished. Pip's scream, in the opening scene of GREAT EXPECTATIONS, immediately silenced by the convict; the creaking of the tree in the wind and rain; Pip's feet crunching on the ground; the sharp single line of the convict's dialog—they create a mood of fear, enriching the power of the visual images. Sometimes sound is used as a kind of pun, making a transition from sequence to sequence, as in THE THIRTY-NINE STEPS when we switch from a woman shrieking to a train whistling, or in CITY LIGHTS when a pompous politician's speech turns into the ludicrous wail of a saxophone.

At other moments, sound can be the source of contrast. In SINGIN' IN THE RAIN, the contrast between what the actors are trying to say when they use dialog mikes for the first time and the actual sounds that come over the mikes is very funny, as is the sound of Jean Hagen's heartbeats when the mike is hidden inside her blouse. In HIGH NOON the ballad is a unifying theme for the action and lends the story a touch of legend. Kurt Weill said he could never forget the bittersweet melody at the end of Chaplin's THE CIRCUS, when the disillusioned tramp disappears in the distance, ready to face the world.

Color gets into the act, too. "Color beautifies everything and I never feel you get the conditions of people in color," said Peter Ustinov to explain why he made BILLY BUDD in black and white. That is not wholly accurate. Color beautifies MY FAIR LADY, true, but it also gives us "the conditions of people" at least once. When Eliza sings "The Rain in Spain," in the scene that marks her turning point, she is wearing a dark green dress with violets at the waist, which takes us back to Covent Garden where she started. WEST SIDE STORY uses color for many dramatic effects. In the dance-hall scene, Maria is the only girl in white, an obvious symbolism. At the end, when Tony is shot, the police car's revolving lamp flashes red on the members of the gang standing around him—a symbol of the violence which killed him, and a reminder of the sequence leading up to the rumble, when the whole screen was blood-red. Often the color of a movie is part of its enchantment; MOBY DICK is as beautiful as an old whaling print. Color may also provide contrast in the setting. In THE WIZARD OF OZ, the opening and closing Kansas scenes are in sepia and the Oz scenes in color; in THE RED BALLOON, the streets of Ménilmontant are gray or tan, the escaping balloon is scarlet.

Thus far we have been looking at the camera. But that is only part of the way a film works. We must look at the faces. "When you start a film," Federico Fellini has said, "you don't yet know what the faces will look like." The film can grow into meaning through the artistry of actors. SOUNDER is a case in point. Pauline Kael wrote of it, "One could do an iconography of smiles from this movie; often it is a smile that ends a scene, and it always seems the perfect end, just what was needed—an emblem of the spirit of a people, proof that they have not been destroyed." In the theater, the audience receives whatever it is the actor is projecting; in the film studio, the camera does—but if we do not understand what the camera is registering, or if the director has not edited the results skillfully, we may miss character, feeling, idea. Children prefer action to characterization in their movies, but that doesn't mean they are incapable of reading actors in depth. They can interpret "body language" with terrifying clarity.

In THE RED SHOES, for example, they see that Ludmilla Tcherina is as outrageous as she is beautiful, that Anton Walbrook loves himself more than the ballet, that Albert Basserman cries when a door sticks on opening night not because he is a fool but because he is a stage designer.

After asking how a film works, one asks about the human being who is behind it. Getting to know a director is one of the rewards of looking at movies. Take Alfred Hitchcock, whose speciality is showing us that there's nothing ordinary about the ordinary. How many moments of menace we can store up from THE LADY VANISHES: the accomplice disguised as a nun whose high heels we see all of a sudden, the train halting at a peaceful station in the Balkans and steaming in the cold until the shots ring out, and Miss Froy's *Horniman's Tea* label thrown out with the rubbish and pasting itself against the train window. And then there's Frank Capra, always good for a sight gag from the old silent comedy days. When Jean Arthur, in MR. SMITH GOES TO WASHINGTON, is telling James Stewart how you put a bill across in the Senate, she gets pretty long-winded, but Capra has her throwing a half-dollar up and catching it while she talks, then missing it and looking for it under the chair—the old sleight-of-hand, bound to keep the eye busy and safe if the main action falters.

Seeing what the director is doing, we may also ask what he is trying to tell us. In HIGH NOON, Zinnemann gives us not only images but a myth; this is not the historical West but an allegory, and we sort out the meaning of the marshal, the marshal's wife, the townspeople, in a moral drama of the frontier. In short films, especially, the director is often saying more than meets the eye. In LONELY BOY, about the teenage idol Paul Anka, he is raising questions about the nature of success, about the character of the "pop" singer and his audience—raising them through the way he has edited the images. This film was shot entirely with a hand-held camera; what makes it superior to the innumerable amateur films shot with hand-held cameras is not only its professionalism but its content.

In the limited space at our command, we have been able to touch only briefly on some of the ways of looking at a movie. It should be clear, however, that watching the screen passively is not at all what we have in mind. "It's more fun when you help—" to quote Bacall to Bogey. For fuller understanding, pleasure, feeling, it's a good idea to open your eyes and make them work vigorously, to bring curiosity and intelligence to your "movie watch." If parents and teachers can give the kids a few of the ground rules, the kids will enjoy the game.

Key to Abbreviations

art	art direction
b&l	book and lyrics
b/w	black and white
c	cast
chor	choreography
col	color
cost	costumes
d	direction
des	design
ed	editing
lyr	lyrics
m	music
narr	narrator
ph	photography
prod	production
sp	screenplay
spec eff	special effects

* An asterisk following a film title above the credits indicates that it is suitable for children under eight. Some annotations contain a recommendation for older children. Naturally, opinions (like children) vary.

For key to abbreviations of film distributors, (noted in parentheses with each entry) see Directory of Film Companies and Distributors, p. 247.

Arrangement of the Book

Each title in the Index to Film Titles is followed by a designating letter or letters:

E = Entertainment feature (minimum length, 50 minutes)
F = Featurette (20 to 49 minutes)
S = Supplement selection, feature length
D = Documentary
CFF = Children's Film Foundation feature
CM = Chaplin Mutual Comedies

The E films (273 in all: 219 fiction, 54 documentary) are arranged alphabetically, with full credits and annotations.

The F films (54 featurettes) are in a separate section, with full credits and annotations.

The S films (103 supplement selections) are also in a separate section, with full credits and capsule annotations. In our judgment, they are choice rather than prime selections, because they are less outstanding than the E films or more specialized in their appeal.

The CFF films and the CM films are grouped in separate sections, with an introduction, full credits, and capsule annotations.

Feature Films

Abe Lincoln in Illinois

*RKO 1940. 110 min., b/w. (d) John Cromwell (sp) Robert E. Sherwood
and Grover Jones, based on the play by Robert E. Sherwood (ph)
James Wong Howe (m) Roy Webb (c) Raymond Massay, Gene Lockhart, Ruth Gordon, Mary Howard, Dorothy Tree, Harvey Stephens,
Minor Watson, Howard da Silva, Alan Baxter, Elizabeth Risdon. (FNC)*

If we wanted to introduce a youngster to the drama of Abe Lincoln's prairie years and Carl Sandburg was a little beyond him,
we wouldn't give him a copy of Robert E. Sherwood's 1938 play
or send him to see it, even though it won a Pulitzer Prize. We'd
show him this fine, dignified, and moving film. Raymond Massey,
the Lincoln in both the stage production and the movie, always
said he thought he was much better in the movie. You can thank
the camera and John Cromwell for that. Sherwood's screenplay
from his original drama is far less episodic, telescoped, wordy.
There are more shades and subtleties, more graphic moments.
(James Wong Howe did the excellent photography.)

ABE LINCOLN IN ILLINOIS is about Lincoln's failures and self-
doubts—as shopkeeper, postmaster, lawyer, reluctant candidate
for the Illinois legislature—and his personal dramas after Ann
Rutledge's death and his marriage to Mary Todd (superbly played
by Ruth Gordon). The film's climax comes when he entrains for
Washington and his destiny as president.

Recommended to the over-tens.

The Absent-Minded Professor*

*Disney 1961. 97 min., b/w. (d) Robert Stevenson (sp) Bill Walsh from
the story by Samuel W. Taylor (c) Fred MacMurray, Nancy Olson,
Keenan Wynn, Tommy Kirk, Ed Wynn. (GEN)*

One of the pleasures of this easy-going screwball comedy produced by Walt Disney is a basketball game in which the short
players soar right over the heads of the tall guys. Another is watching a Model-T Ford fly. The secret in both cases is *flubber*, or
flying rubber, a new substance invented by Professor Fred
MacMurray, which produces remarkable levitation. Though
MacMurray is no Buster Keaton, the movie's gimmick helps him
rise above his limitations, and sight gags and trick photography
are never hard for kids to take. Keenan Wynn plays the heavy,
but watch for Ed Wynn as a fire chief.

The Adventures of Robin Hood*

Warners 1938. 102 min., col. (d) Michael Curtiz, William Keighley (sp) Norman Reilly Raine, Seton I. Miller (c) Errol Flynn, Olivia de Havilland, Basil Rathbone, Claude Rains, Melville Cooper, Eugene Pallette, Alan Hale. (UAS)

There have been many Robin Hoods—Douglas Fairbanks, Cornel Wilde, Jon Hall, Richard Todd, Don Taylor, Richard Greene—but the nonpareil is Errol Flynn, in this Hollywood production as unfaded by time as the legend itself. Though it wasn't shot on location in the original Sherwood Forest, like Disney's 1952 version, it's peopled by the original romantic inhabitants; here are merrie men and double-dyed villains. Academy Awards were presented to Carl Weyl for art direction, Ralph Dawson for editing, and Erich Wolfgang Korngold for the original music score.

The Adventures of Robinson Crusoe

United Artists 1954. 90 min., col. (d) Luis Buñuel (sp) Philip Roll and Luis Buñuel from the novel by Daniel Defoe (c) Dan O'Herlihy, James Fernandez. (MAC)

The distinguished director Luis Buñuel has made a film that will please those who recall the novel and will fascinate those who admire cinematic originality. Buñuel took his company to Manzanillo, a semi-tropical island off the coast of Mexico. Here he shot his story in Pathécolor, with an English soundtrack composed mainly of Defoe's own words. Since Crusoe is alone on the screen for sixty of the film's ninety minutes, Buñuel telescoped many of Crusoe's ingenious adaptations to his environment, retaining only the most dramatic—growing wheat and baking bread, learning to live in a society of insects and small animals, building a canoe for a vain attempt to escape.

Before the appearance of the single footprint in the sand, Crusoe is the man outside society, seeking comfort from within. Some remarkable moments for the imaginative child are Crusoe's fevered dreams of his Puritan father, his symbolic emergence from the sea with a cave-dweller's torch, his awe-inspiring cries to the echoing hills of the island.

The Adventures of Tom Sawyer*

United Artists 1938. 91 min., col. (prod) David O. Selznick (d) Norman Taurog (sp) John Weaver from Mark Twain's novel (ph) James Wong Howe (c) Tommy Kelly, Jackie Moran, May Robson, Walter Brennan, Ann Gillis, Victor Jory. (GEN)

Which one of the movies about Tom Sawyer you prefer will depend on your age and nostalgia quotient. Today's youngsters will probably find the Jackie Coogan version (1930), sometimes on television, the most dated, though its Missouri village is probably the Hannibal that Twain would recognize. All things considered, the best bet before 1973, when the musical version appeared, is this David O. Selznick production of the sure-fire story. It's nowhere near as funny as the book, but Tommy Kelly and Ann Gillis will pass nicely for Tom and Becky, and most of the adventures are here. Children should be encouraged to pick up the book afterward, to discover the difference between Aunt Polly and Injun Joe in print, as alive as a master could make them, and May Robson and Victor Jory in Technicolor.

Tom Sawyer*

United Artists 1973. 99 min., col. (prod) Reader's Digest (d) Don Taylor (sp)(m)(lyr) Richard M. and Robert B. Sherman from Mark Twain's novel (c) Johnny Whitaker, Celeste Holm, Lucille Benson, Henry Jones, Warren Oates, Jeff East, Kunu Hank. (UAS)

For the seventies generation, the musical version. Everything's bigger, brighter, and splashier than life; the school picnic is a lavish production number; Tom is a familiar TV personality, Johnny Whitaker. "Yet with all the worldliness of this TOM SAWYER, there remains the memory of a perfect innocence that is very much the sense of Twain's *The Adventures of Tom Sawyer*" (Vincent Canby, *The New York Times*).

The African Queen

United Artists 1951. 106 min., col. (d) John Huston (sp) James Agee and John Huston from a novel by C. S. Forester (ph) Jack Cardiff (m) Allan Gray (c) Humphrey Bogart, Katharine Hepburn, Robert Morley, Peter Bull, Theodore Bikel. (GEN)

A comic extravaganza, a travesty of adventure yarns, a legend of two ugly ducklings who become swans in each other's eyes, a surprisingly tender love story—THE AFRICAN QUEEN is a whole lush gallery of movies. For the flexible imagination (adult or wise child) it presents an opportunity to "shoot the rapids" and emerge in style. For the style is everything. The plot's not the thing, although there's plenty of it. A prim spinster and a hard-drinking riverboat captain heroically torpedo a German ship in World War I East Africa in a drama of broken rudders, torrential rains, and all sorts of African hazards. The *manner* is everything here. John Huston never directed with more flair; we've never seen Bogart, whose Charlie Allnutt won him his only Oscar, or Hepburn, whose Rosie Sayer is a many-faceted delight, or Robert Morley ("Brother," the Methodist missionary), more to the manner borne by a witty script.

The great inspiration, of course, was to mix the chemistry of Bogart and Hepburn. What a combination, and what a movie!

Alice's Adventures in Wonderland

Britain 1972. 101 min., col. (d)(sp) William Sterling from the book by Lewis Carroll (ph) Geoffrey Unsworth (des) Michael Stringer (m)(lyr) John Barry, Don Black (c) Fiona Fullerton, Michael Crawford, Peter Sellers, Dudley Moore, Flora Robson, Robert Helpmann, Michael Hordern, Dennis Price, Ralph Richardson, Michael Jayston, Spike Milligan. (AIM, BUD, MAC, CWF, UNF)

A new adaptation, with music, of Lewis Carroll's classic. "Ingenious camera work and cleverly designed settings help to translate the charm and mystery of 'Alice' to the screen more successfully than any previous attempt" (Program, Stratford, Ontario, Festival). Production designer Michael Stringer (FIDDLER ON THE ROOF) has adapted the settings from the original Tenniel drawings. Lavish and full of songs (by John Barry and Don Black, who won an Academy Award for their BORN FREE songs), the film attempts to remain as faithful as possible to Carroll's story. What makes it superior to at least three earlier versions is the style of the cast. It is star-studded, and its distinguished British players feel absolutely at home with Carroll.

Amazing Grace

USA 1976. 58 min., col. (prod)(d) Allan Miller (ed) David Hanser. (PYR)

One of the best films to come out of the Bicentennial, AMAZING GRACE was produced by Allan Miller (whose BOLERO won an Academy Award) as a celebration of the vitality of the American experience in song. From gospel hymns to mountain ballads, love songs to logging songs, patriotic songs to protest songs, the film's dimension gives us a dynamic view of the lives and places that have made American history. Each song is filmed in its natural setting, wherever authentic American songs were and are being sung—the hills of North Carolina, the Kansas plains, Chicago streets, or a Los Angeles supper club.

AMAZING GRACE features well-known performers such as Lena Horne and the voice of Woody Guthrie, and it is rich in archival film footage of Billie Holiday and Bessie Smith. In editing and direction, it achieves the goal of the successful documentary: insight and drama. For all young people, a contribution to their knowledge of music and of their country.

And Now Miguel*

Universal 1966. 95 min., col. (d) James B. Clark (sp) Ted Sherdeman and Jane Klove from the book by Joseph Krumgold (ph) Clifford Stine (c) Michael Ansara, Pat Cardi, Guy Stockwell. (COU, ROA, SWA, WHO)

Joseph Krumgold's Newbery Medal book about a family of sheepherders in modern New Mexico, which he later made into a documentary, was filmed in the beautiful high-plateau country near Abiguiu, New Mexico. It is told from the point of view of eleven-year-old Miguel, who is eager to show he is mature enough to assume the responsibilities of the men of the family. "It's so easy to be Gabriel," Miguel tells his older brother, Gabriel, "but it's so hard to be Miguel." The Chavez family has cared for sheep ever since the Spaniards brought in flocks in the sixteenth century. Miguel longs to accompany his father and uncles when they herd the sheep into the Sangre de Cristo mountains, but he is too young and must stay on the ranch to help with the branding and shearing.

One of the many excellent children's movies of producer Robert B. Radnitz (ISLAND OF THE BLUE DOLPHINS, MISTY, MY SIDE OF THE MOUNTAIN), its location scenes have vivid actuality. Sheep-shearing, encounters with coyotes and rattlesnakes, Miguel's rescue of the ewes from wolves, offer a semi-documentary picture of an ancient calling, and the drama of the family gives insight into the relationships between generations.

Around the World in 80 Days

United Artists 1956. 168 min., col. (d) Michael Anderson (sp) S. J. Perelman from the novel by Jules Verne (ph) Lionel Lindon (m) Victor Young for scoring (c) David Niven, Cantinflas, Robert Newton, Shirley MacLaine, Charles Boyer, Joe E. Brown, Martine Carol, John Carradine, Charles Coburn, Ronald Colman, Melville Cooper, Noel Coward, Finlay Currie, Reginald Denny, Andy Devine, Marlene Dietrich, Luis Miguel Dominguin, Fernandel, Sir John Gielgud, Hermione Gingold, José Greco, Sir Cedric Hardwicke, Trevor Howard, Glynis Johns, Buster Keaton, Beatrice Lillie, Peter Lorre, John Mills, Robert Morley, Edward R. Murrow, Jack Oakie, George Raft, Frank Sinatra, Red Skelton, Basil Sydney, Ava Gardner, Victor McLaglen, Colonel Tim McCoy. (UAS)

From its prologue (George Méliès's 1902 film, A TRIP TO THE MOON based on Verne's novel) to the last "cameo" appearance of a member of the all-time, all-star cast, this is really fun. Cantinflas arriving on the back of an ostrich in the Hong Kong ticket office; Fernandel repeating "Cook's?" in rubber-mouthed amazement from the perch of a Paris hansom; David Niven with his top hat tied firmly under his Victorian chin, enjoying *tiffin* during a high gale on a windswept deck; Victor McLaglen and the entire crew tearing apart a schooner to provide fuel for the last lap; Hermione Gingold at a London sidewalk-café table, placing a bet; Dietrich and Sinatra turning up in a frontier saloon; and Col. Tim McCoy rescuing the party from the Indians while Buster Keaton waits, imperturbable as ever, on a fantastic transcontinental train. There are a good many more perfect bits in this delightful spoof, but we shouldn't spoil the surprises.

Shot on location in London, Southern France, the Mediterranean, India, Hong Kong, Pakistan, Siam, Yokohama, Mexico, Spain, Egypt, Colorado, and California, the film won Academy Awards for best picture, color photography, editing, screenplay, and musical scoring.

Arsenic and Old Lace

Warners 1944. 110 min., b/w. (d) Frank Capra (sp) Julius J. and Philip G. Epstein from the play by Joseph Kesselring (c) Cary Grant, Priscilla Lane, Raymond Massey, Jack Carson, Edward Everett Horton, Peter Lorre, James Gleason, Josephine Hull, Jean Adair, John Alexander, Grant Mitchell, Edward McNamara. (UAS)

Black comedy as the subteens like it. Howard Lindsay and Russell Crouse's production of Joseph Kesselring's zany medodrama ran for three and a half years on Broadway, and the movie has been running ever since in school entertainment series—running breathlessly, unsubtly, and hilariously. It seems to be one of the kids' favorite Frank Capra pictures. The idea of those nice little old ladies sweetly dispatching thirteen gentlemen callers with glasses of homemade wine and stashing the corpses in the "Panama Canal" in their cellar, dug by Teddy Roosevelt before he goes charging up the stairs of the family mansion in Brooklyn—well, Brooklyn *is* hilarious, isn't it?—still slays them.

The speed and mugging here remind you that Capra got his training in the old Keystone comedies. Stage favorites Josephine Hull, Jean Adair, and John Alexander are in the movie along with some familiar Hollywood players in unfamiliar roles; Raymond Massey, for instance, acting like Boris Karloff.

The Autobiography of Miss Jane Pittman

CBS-TV 1974. 110 min., col. (prod) Robert Christiansen, Rick Rosenberg (d) John Korty (sp) Tracy Keenan Wynn based on the novel by Ernest J. Gaines (ph) James Crabe (m) Fred Karlin (c) Cicely Tyson, Richard A. Dysart, Katherine Helmond, Michael Murphy, Roy Poole, Josephine Premice, Thalmus Rasulala, Collin Wilcox-Horne, Beatrice Winde. (LCA, MAC, TWY, SWA)

"Quite possibly the finest movie ever made for American television" (Pauline Kael), and winner of nine Emmys, including one each for Cicely Tyson as best actress and John Korty as best director, as well as multiple festival and organization prizes. Nobody seeing this superb portrait of a brave black woman whose life story spans the century between the Civil War and the beginning of the Civil Rights movement in the early '60s can fail to be moved by it. Although novelist Gaines, on whose 1971 book the film is based, disclaims any intention of making it a saga of black Americans (preferring it to be "the story of one woman . . .with no formal education. . .who lived her life with great dignity and strength"), THE AUTOBIOGRAPHY OF MISS JANE PITTMAN achieves the widest possible scope. One woman's life from her days as a slave to the moment when she walks up to the water fountain at the end—it can only be seen as the emergence of a change and a time, a panorama of the experience we call the black experience.

Brilliantly acted and directed, this is a film to see more than once. One waits, with emotion, for Miss Jane, at 110, to take her part in that protest march against the degradation of the human spirit.

The Bad News Bears

Paramount 1976. 102 min., col. (d) Michael Ritchie (sp) Bill Lancaster (ph) John A. Alonzo (m) Jerry Fielding; themes from Bizet's Carmen *(c) Walter Matthau, Tatum O'Neal, Vic Morrow, Joyce Van Patten, Ben Piazza, Jackie Earle Haley, Alfred W. Lutter. (FNC)*

The foul-mouthed smallfry in this highly entertaining film are not for emulation by other kids, we hope; just for a great many laughs. Most children will understand the situation very well: in some Little League games the vanity of adult coaches and parents will drive the young players too far to fulfill their elders' aspirations; in others you can lose but put on a good show, in which even the worst baseball weakling can make the grade.

Walter Matthau, hired to coach a misfit Little League team of boys, acquires two whiz kids, Tatum O'Neal and Jackie Earle Haley. Alfred W. Lutter (ALICE DOESN'T LIVE HERE ANY MORE) is one of many very funny, if often repellent, kids whom director Michael Ritchie (SMILE, DOWNHILL RACER) handles without condescension. What makes the movie are the baseball scenes themselves, for the Bears drop, miss, or fumble every ball.

This first of the BEARS series has a lot of good moments, despite its manipulations; the sequels, THE BAD NEWS BEARS IN BREAKING TRAINING and THE BAD NEWS BEARS IN JAPAN, struck out. Chalk one up for Michael Ritchie: he gave THE BAD NEWS BEARS its pleasant surprises..

Bambi*

RKO 1942. 70 min., col. animation. (prod) Walt Disney (d) David Hand (sp) Larry Morey from the book by Felix Salten (art) Tyrus Wong, Merle Cox (m) Frank Churchill, Edward H. Plumb. (SWA)

As gentle and delicate, for the most part, as Bambi himself, Disney's animated feature is faithful to the spirit of Felix Salten's allegory of the little deer in the forest. It has its serious and dramatic moments. (At least one of them is too much for the very youngest children. When we hear the shot, and Bambi can't find his mother, who can bear it when the Great Prince of the Forest says to the fawn, "Your mother can't be with you any more"?)

BAMBI has less slapstick than the usual Disney. However, Thumper the Rabbit and Flower the Skunk, who are reminiscent of Jiminy Cricket in PINOCCHIO, are amusing as they instruct Bambi in his woodland life. The forest is an important character in the story. Interesting color effects heighten the cycle of the seasons, and the animation technique is naturalistic. (Although the animals were drawn very carefully from nature, this is still Disney, for only in his world do owls fraternize chummily with baby bunnies.)

BAMBI has a lovely quality of its own.

The Bank Dick

Universal 1940. 73 min., b/w. (d) Edward Cline (sp) "Mahatma Kane Jeeves" (W. C. Fields) (c) W. C. Fields, Cora Witherspoon, Jessie Ralph, Evelyn Del Rio, J. Franklin Pangborn, Una Merkel, Grady Sutton, Jack Norton, Pierre Watkin, Jan Duggan. (SWA, TWY, UNI)

"Among the great one-man shows" (Otis Ferguson), THE BANK DICK was written by him, partly directed by him, and then stolen by him in the main role. He is W. C. Fields, alias Mahatma Kane Jeeves and (for this time around) Egbert Souse, habitué of the Black Pussy Cat Cafe, and reluctant family man, in the town of Lompoc, USA. Through a misunderstanding immortalized in the town paper, the *Picayune Intelligentsia*, Souse becomes a hero because he has supposedly foiled two bank robbers, Filthy McNasty and Repulsive Rogan. (With an assegai, by his account.) In the uniform of a detective and all-around doorman for the bank he now protects professionally, Fields becomes a multiple threat. How he repairs a stolen limousine, foils J. Pinkerton Snoopington, the bank examiner, and otherwise scatters a plot in mad disarray, is the substance of THE BANK DICK.

"It is a kind of Fields mosaic, a summing-up of his life's work, favorite gags and pet peeves, but with a new and mellow warmth that is most endearing" (William K. Everson). By any standards, a comedy classic. By Fields's standards, tough, human, and one of his best; with IT'S A GIFT, most people's choice for the undistilled Fields.

Beauty and the Beast

(La Belle et la Bête) France 1946. 90 min., b/w. (d) Jean Cocteau (sp) Jean Cocteau from the fairy tale by Mme. Leprince de Beaumont (ph) Alekan (m) Georges Auric (ed) Claude Ibéria (c) Jean Marais, Josette Day, Marcel André, Mila Parely, Michel Auclair. French dialog with English subtitles. *(JAN)*

"Whenever I am making a film," Jean Cocteau told an interviewer not long after finishing BEAUTY AND THE BEAST, "I find myself in a dream-like trance. The outside world completely disappears and the dream life of the studio fills my whole existence." In this exquisitely beautiful film made from the French fairy tale, his dreamlike trance turns cinema into poetry as image follows image like an enchantment. The technical art of the camera is used to surprise and delight; in one example only, that of *reverse motion*, pearls spill into the hands of the Beast, Beauty's magic glove pulls her through the wall, and at the end the lovers are drawn up into the sky. Cocteau invites us into a world where the language of written lyrics becomes the language of cinema as living hands hold torches to light Beauty on her way.

The lionlike mask of the Beast (Jean Marais, who is also Avenant and Ardent or Prince Charming), the gorgeous costumes and imaginative sets, are the work of Christian Bérard. This lovely tapestry of the supernatural is a designer's masterpiece, but the poignancy of the Beast's love for Beauty is a poet's creation.

The Bellboy*

Paramount 1960. 72 min., b/w. (prod)(d)(sp) Jerry Lewis (ph) Haskell Boggs (m) Walter Scharf. (c) Jerry Lewis, Milton Berle, Walter Winchell, Bill Richmond. (AIM, BUD, TWY, MAC)

As the dimwitted bellhop at Miami Beach's Fontainebleau Hotel, producer-director-writer-star Jerry Lewis is the source of a stream of wild, comic misadventures. Although some of his material is drawn from his personal experience of entertaining at resort hotels, most of it is riotous invention in the Lewis tradition: sheer anarchy sweetened by an amiable disposition. Asked to remove everything from the trunk of a Volkswagen, he brings the engine into the lobby; making a pickup at the airport, he takes off on a solo flight in a jet. Needless to say, there is an audience of youngsters who find all this sidesplitting.

Guest stars help along the Lewis efforts, among them Milton Berle and golfer Cary Middlecoff.

Ben-Hur

MGM 1959. 217 min., col. (d) William Wyler (asst d) Andrew Marton, Yakima Canutt, Mario Soldati (sp) Karl Tunberg based on the novel by Lew Wallace (ph) Robert L. Surtees (m) Miklos Rozsa (c) Charlton Heston, Jack Hawkins, Stephen Boyd, Haya Harareet, Hugh Griffith, Martha Scott, Sam Jaffe, Cathy O'Donnell, Finlay Currie, George Relph. (FNC)

The advance publicity for this blockbuster ("Ten years in preparation, 496 speaking roles, 100,000 extras") was matched by its collection of Academy Awards and its box-office success. Although the biblical drama and the story of a prince of Judea who pits his people's interests against Roman tyranny, with terrible consequences, are both developed with more spectacle than subtlety, the famous chariot race should be part of everyone's screen experience.

Benji*

Mulberry Square 1974. 85 min., col. (prod)(d)(sp) Joe Camp (ph) Don Reddy (m) Euel Box (c) Higgins, Patsy Garrett, Allen Finzat, Cynthia Smith, Peter Breck, Edgar Buchanan, Deborah Walley, Mark Slade. (FNC)

No Oscar nominee of the human species got better notices in the 1974 season than a small dog named Higgins, who played the lead in the enormously popular BENJI. A show-biz veteran of screen and TV, Higgins sustains moods, conveys a wide range of reactions, and responds to supporting players. A heck of an actor—in a movie to delight the youngest audience as well as dog lovers of greater age. Benji—brave, intelligent, tender—saves two kidnapped children. The Nora to Benji's Nick Charles in the case is

Tiffany, a fluffy Pekinese charmer. Happily, neither the direction nor the story goes cute; BENJI is well handled by Joe Camp.

Higgins was awarded a Patsy, the animal Oscar, and the song "I Feel Love" was nominated for a human Oscar.

For the Love of Benji*

Mulberry Square 1977. 90 min., col. (prod)(d)(sp) Joe Camp. (FNC)

The very entertaining sequel to BENJI. Higgins, on vacation in Greece, becomes the hero in a complicated adventure-chase that has something or other to do with international oil. Lively fun.

Bighorn!

Tomorrow Entertainment 1972. 52 min., col. (d)(sp) John Riger (ph) Darcy Marsh, Tommy Tompkins, Joe Longo, Robert Riger (m) John Denver (c) John Denver, Tommy Tompkins (narr) John Denver. (LCA)

Filmed in the Whiskey Basin Winter Range, Wyoming, this interesting documentary is not only good entertainment, with original songs written and performed by singer-composer John Denver, but an effective plea for the survival of the endangered Rocky Mountain bighorn sheep and, in a sense, for the conservation of all aspects of our environment.

"The ram," says Denver (who narrates the film),"will remain the image of survival. . . . Peace, let it be." Denver and his friend and guide, Tommy Tompkins, journey into the beautiful high country of moose, elk, bears, and the unique Rocky Mountain bighorn sheep. With them, we study the bighorn through the seasons and learn about their ritual battles and life-style. (*And one is a teacher and one a beginner/Just wanting to be there, just wanting to know/And together they're trying to tell us the story/ That should've been listened to long, long ago.*)

"Rocky Mountain High" and "Open Up Your Eyes" are two of Denver's songs that children will enjoy. Filmed with the cooperation of several Wyoming and national game and forest preservation agencies, BIGHORN! makes a real contribution to films about nature.

The Big Store*

MGM 1941. 80 min., b/w. (d) Charles Riesner (sp) Sid Kuller, Hal Fimberg, and Ray Golden from the story by Nat Perrin (c) Groucho, Harpo, and Chico Marx, Margaret Dumont, Douglas Dumbrille, Henry Armetta, Tony Martin, Virginia Grey. (FNC)

The very best Marx Brothers film? To most buffs, DUCK SOUP and A NIGHT AT THE OPERA, with THE BIG STORE low on the scales. But British youngsters voted it their favoirte of many movies shown to them, and New York audiences at the Lincoln Center "*Movies for Kids*" programs greeted it with delight. In it Margaret Dumont is defended against the machinations of a department-store manager by a gumshoe named Wolf J. Flywheel. Groucho, for it is none other, is assisted by two store detectives, Wacky (Harpo) and Ravelli (Chico). Funniest sequences: the transformation of Groucho's office when his client arrives, Harpo playing the typewriter, Groucho proposing to Margaret Dumont in verse.

Billy Budd

Britain 1962. 123 min., b/w. (d) Peter Ustinov (sp) Peter Ustinov, Robert Rossen and DeWitt Bodeen from the novel Billy Budd, Foretopman *by Herman Melville, and the play by Louis O. Coxe and Robert H. Chapman (ph) Robert Krasker (c) Terence Stamp, Peter Ustinov, Robert Ryan, Melvyn Douglas, John Neville, Paul Rogers. (CIN)*

A symbol of innocence and natural goodness who turns the surly crew of the *Indomitable* into a cheerful one, Billy Budd (Terence Stamp) incurs the hatred of Claggart, the malignant master-at-arms. When Claggart falsely accuses Billy of inciting the men to mutiny, Billy, speechless, strikes him and accidentally kills him. Under the law of the Mutiny Act, the court-martial condemns Billy to be hanged. His last words are, "God bless Captain Vere!"

Students of Melville interpret the story of Billy Budd in many ways. Is this a parable of absolute goodness and absolute evil destroying each other? An ironic picture of the conflict between man's justice and God's? Or another one of Melville's pessimistic commentaries on man's destiny, like *Moby Dick*? In addition to the intrinsic interest of the story, the film has exellent acting, and stunning photography by Robert Krasker (HENRY V, THE THIRD MAN), whose shots of the sea and of action aboard the eighteenth-century frigate are very exciting. A stimulating experience for older children.

The Biscuit Eater*

Paramount 1940. 83 min., b/w. (d) Stuart Heisler (sp) Stuart Anthony and Lillie Hayward from the short story by James Street (c) Billie Lee, Cordell Hickman, Helene Millard, Richard Lane. (UNI)

When it first came out, the New York Times called it a "fragile, heart-warming pastoral of the Georgia hunting country," but THE BISCUIT EATER is far from fragile, because it has remained one of the most popular boy-and-dog movies to the present day. Lonnie (Billie Lee) takes a runt from a famous litter of thoroughbred Georgia pointers, names him "Promise," and does the very best that a ten-year-old boy can do—despite his father's opposition—to fit him for the field trials. Lonnie has the help of his young black playmate, Text (Cordell Hickman), and of course the boys bring Promise to fulfillment.

The bayous and forests of Albany, Georgia, have been beautifully photographed, and the field trials are interesting. It's unfortunate that the character of Lonnie's black friend, Text, is a 1940 Georgia-model stereotype.

Black Beauty*

Paramount 1971. 106 min., col. (d) James Hill (sp) Wolf Mankowitz based on the novel by Anna Sewell (ph) Chris Menges (m) Lionel Bart, John Cameron (c) Mark Lester, Walter Slezak, Ursula Glas, Peter Lee Lawrence, Maria Rohm, Margaret Lacey, Patrick Mower. (FNC)

An effective filming of Anna Sewell's classic autobiography of a horse, which does not follow the original literally but has virtures of its own. The New York Times said, "An uncommonly interesting, handsome and sometimes quite marvelously inventive movie that might have been called 'The Further Adventures of Black Beauty,' including such episodes as Black Beauty among the Irish gypsies, Black Beauty on the Continent, and Black Beauty preserving the Empire, at battle in India."

There is intensity, dark humor, and pathos in episodes that involve Black Beauty but are not so much about the horse as about the various people who cherish or betray her—the nineteenth-century circus-world figures, squires, coal dealers, thieves, cavalry officers, and romantic lovers. BLACK BEAUTY is concerned, still, with the humane treatment of an animal. At the end, we are introduced to Anna Sewell herself (Margaret Lacey) as the benefactor of Black Beauty's peaceful old age.

The Black Stallion

United Artists 1979. 125 min., col. (exec. prod) Francis Ford Coppola (d) Carroll Ballard (sp) Melissa Mathison, Jeanne Rosenberg, William D. Wittliff, from Walter Farley's novel (ph) Caleb Deschanel (m) Carmine Coppola (c) Kelly Reno, Mickey Rooney, Teri Garr, Clarence Muse, Hoyt Axton, Michael Higgins. (UAS)

A lyrical, beautiful movie, with appeal for both children and adults, which some have hailed as one of the most impressive by a new director in 1979. Carroll Ballard, whose first feature it is, with his gifted cinematographer, Caleb Deschanel, has translated the children's adventure fantasy by Walter Farley about a boy's friendship with a horse into "images charged with a child's sense of wonder . . . THE BLACK STALLION begins, and you know instantly you are in the grip of a cinematic Scheherazade" (*Newsweek*).

Aboard a cruise ship off the northern coast of Africa, eleven-year-old Alex (Kelly Reno) befriends a wild Arabian stallion (Cass Ole, a seven-year-old Arabian show horse from San Antonio). When the ship goes down in flames and Alex's father is lost, the stallion leaps into the dark waters and saves the boy from drowning. They are washed ashore together on a rocky, deserted island. In a wordless, idyllic adventure that is like a courtship, the boy learns to ride the magnificent creature he worships. After the two are rescued and return to a mundane American suburb, they become actors in a more familiar fantasy: Alex and an old horse trainer (Mickey Rooney) turn the stallion into a racing horse—for Alex to ride, of course, despite his mother's skepticism. The Arabian beauty is prepared for the match race that will pit him against the two finest thoroughbreds in the country.

The island sequences were shot in Sardinia. There are breathtaking pictures of child and animal that are legendary in their effect. Before the shipwreck, Alex's father had told him how the young Alexander the Great has ridden his steed Bucephalus, "the biggest, blackest, and strongest horse ever," before his father, King Philip of Macedonia, to show off his skill. Galloping through the surf on his own black stallion, Alex is part of the legend; riding in the match race, he is showing off to his mother. What boy of girl watching this movie will not feel part of the legend? And it is a bonus for child and adult that the legend has been pictured so sensuously by the filmmakers. Walter Farley's original novel and its many sequels are rich in adventure and are faster paced, but this movie is colored by visual, dreamlike imagination that sets it above the usual boy-horse (or girl-horse) story.

Blue Water, White Death

Fox 1971. 99 min., col. (d)(sp) Peter Gimbel and James Lipscomb (ph) Peter Gimbel, James Lipscomb, Stanton Waterman, Ron Taylor (c) Ron Taylor, Rodney Jonklas, Stanton Waterman, Valerie Taylor, and officers and crew of the Terrier VIII. (GEN)

Underwater photographer Peter Gimbel and a small team spent six months combing the Indian Ocean off the coasts of South Africa, Madagascar, and Ceylon and the waters of Dangerous Reef, Australia, in quest of the Great White Shark. *Our purpose was to film a dramatic story about a true and remarkable search. . . .* And a truly dramatic confrontation it is, after a series of exciting incidents, when they meet the world's deadliest cold-blooded predator. Some of the photography is stunning: a night-time attack on a whale by swarms of sharks, divers playing with moray eels and barracuda, and the great white bulk of their star charging straight at their diving-elevator cages.

Without scientific pretensions, the movie is absorbing—it has the visual fascination of sea and sky and creatures above and below the depths.

Born Free*

Columbia 1966. 95 min., col. (d) James Hill (sp) Gerald L. C. Copley from the book by Joy Adamson (ph) Kenneth Talbot (m) John Barry (c) Bill Travers, Virginia McKenna, Geoffrey Keen, Peter Luckoye. (GEN)

The first and best of the three movies made from the books by Joy Adamson, the wife of a Kenya game warden, drawn from her experiences with animal-human friendship. Elsa the lioness was raised by the Adamsons from a cub and then conditioned to return to the life she would face in her natural habitat. A fine re-creation of this process was achieved in a year's shooting on location in East Africa by director James Hill, who has had experience in documentary as well as fiction films, and Peter Whitehead, an animal supervisor. One comes into very moving intimacy with the great lovely cats all through the film, as they stalk wild game, capture a baby elephant, or mate and return with their cubs to their human family for a brief visit.

The score and title song by John Barry won Academy Awards.

A Boy Named Charlie Brown*

CCF 1969. 85 min., col. animation. (d) Bill Melendez (sp)(art) Charles M. Schulz (c)(voices) Peter Robbins, Pamelyn Ferdin, Glenn Gilger, Andy Pforsich, Erin Sullivan, Bill Melendez. (GEN)

Charles M. Schulz's *Peanuts* cartoons are an addiction; kids get hooked on the strips or on the thirty-minute television specials created by Schulz with Bill and Lee Melendez. Now they can take a larger dose with this first theatrical feature and still be into it when SNOOPY COMES HOME plays at their local theater. Though a little padded, the first movie is a good introduction to Charlie, Lucy, Linus, Schroeder, Sally, and Snoopy. Director Melendez, who knows a star part when he sees one, is the voice of Snoopy, dreaming that his doghouse is a Sopwith Camel. Melendez also knows a film trick or two, like the split screen for the spelling bee and the op-art American flag for the baseball sequence.

Brighty of the Grand Canyon*

Feature Film Corp. of America 1967. 89 min., col. (d)(sp) Norman Foster from the novel by Marguerite Henry (c) Joseph Cotton, Dick Foran, Pat Conway. (GEN)

The author of *Misty of Chincoteague* (MISTY), Marguerite Henry, has contributed to this adventure film not only her Newbery Medal book about a burro named Brighty who really lived in the Grand Canyon for thirty years, but her own pet burro to play the title role. Filmed in and around the Grand Canyon in Arizona, the movie follows Brighty from the time his prospector friend, the Old Timer, is killed until Brighty brings the killer to bay. When Brighty escapes to the Kaibab Forest, he makes new friends—the famous woodsman and hunter Jim Owens, young Jim Hobbs, and a visitor named Theodore Roosevelt.

Recommended for suspense without violence and wonderful color shots of the Grand Canyon.

Broken Arrow

Fox 1950. 93 min., col. (d) Delmer Daves (sp) Michael Blankfort from the novel Blood Brother *by Elliott Arnold (c) James Stewart, Jeff Chandler, Debra Paget, Will Geer. (FNC)*

The good guys are the Apache chief Cochise and most of the members of the Chiricahua Apache tribe; the bad guys are the bigoted white citizens of Tucson just after the Civil War. Jimmy Stewart, a Union veteran, tries to make peace between Indians and settlers.

While certainly not the definitive story of injustice done to the Indians, this popular movie is a colorful blend of romance and legend which also has something to say to youngsters as it reverses the conventional stereotypes. It would have been better with an Apache girl instead of Debra Paget as Stewart's lovely bride (and why does she have to be killed off?) but that was in the days before consciousness-raising. Come to think of it, BROKEN ARROW has done its bit to raise questions about the ethnic facts of life.

Broken Treaty at Battle Mountain

CBS-TV, PBS-TV 1974. 60 min., col. (prod)(d) Joel L. Freedman (ph) Chuck Levy. (SOH)

"Better than any other documentary I've seen on the subject, including TV specials. [Freedman] has [let's call it] objective sympathy; he tries to show different sides of the questions, but he got involved initially because of his concern with the Shoshone. It seems to me just the right tone for the film. . .Simple, straightforward, lastingly disturbing" (Stanley Kauffmann, *The New Republic*). This is the dramatic story, filmed as it happened, of the struggle of the traditional Western Shoshone Indians of Nevada to keep twenty-four million acres of Nevada land originally promised them by the federal government. Their rallying cry, "Mother Earth is not for sale," and their way of life—medicine, herb dancing, dance, and prayer—are inspiring. Their confrontation of government officials who are tearing down their sacred piñon trees and allowing deer to be killed for sport raises many questions which must be answered with justice.

For young people, an exciting narrative, honest and important. Winner of awards at the American Film Festival, Nyon, and San Francisco International Film Festival; selected for the Berlin Film Festival.

Bugs Bunny Superstar*

Hare Raising Films/United Artists 1975. 90 min., col. (prod)(d) Larry Jackson (narr) Orson Welles (c) Bob Clampett, Tex Avery, Friz Freleng. (UAS)

An anthology film of ten Warner Brothers animated cartoons produced between 1940 and 1948, seven of them with the superstar of more than thirty-five years, Bugs Bunny himself, the brashest of rabbits with the great voice of Mel Blanc. The cartoons are the work of such animator-directors as Chuck Jones, Robert Mc-Kimson, Bob Clampett, Tex Avery, and Friz Freleng. The last three introduce the cartoons, and Orson Welles bridges them, but none of these gentlemen can hold a candle to the whiz-bang star and his friends—Daffy Duck, Elmer Fudd, Porky Pig, Tweety Bird, Sylvester, Henery Hawk, and Foghorn Leghorn. BUGS BUNNY SUPERSTAR is packed with fun and animation surprises for any young audience. If we had to choose our favorite cartoons, they would include "The Corny Concerto," which is a spoof of Disney's FANTASIA; "Rhapsody Rabbit," in which Bugs and a mouse are in a race to tear a piano, and Liszt's Hungarian Rhapsody, to pieces; and "I Taw a Putty Tat," in which Tweety, the little canary, battles with the raffish cat Sylvester.

The Canterville Ghost

MGM 1944. 95 min., b/w. (d) Jules Dassin (sp) Edwin Harvey Blum from a story by Oscar Wilde (c) Charles Laughton, Margaret O'Brien, Robert Young. (FNC)

An engaging updating of an Oscar Wilde story. When the ghost of Sir Simon de Canterville—a wistful Elizabethan—steals out of the wall of an English castle to startle the G.I.s temporarily billeted there, he steals straight into your affection, because he is Charles Laughton at his best. A coward *par excellence*, Sir Simon was sealed up by his disgusted papa in 1604 and doomed to haunt the castle until freed by the heroism of a Canterville. Unfortunately for Sir Simon, *all* the Cantervilles are cowards *par excellence*. Until, that is, the 1944 scriptwriter introduces the current Lady Jessica de Canterville, six years old (Margaret O'Brien), and a G.I. of the Canterville blood (Robert Young).

In addition to amusing variations on the theme of haunting, the movie offers one of the screen's great stylists in whimsy that never descends into bathos.

Captain Blood

Warners 1935. 99 min., b/w. (d) Michael Curtiz (sp) Casey Robinson from the novel by Rafael Sabatini (ph) Hal Mohr, Ernest Haller (m) Erich Wolfgang Korngold (c) Errol Flynn, Olivia de Havilland, Lionel Atwill, Basil Rathbone, Guy Kibbee, Henry Stephenson, Donald Meek, J. Carrol Naish, Pedro de Cordoba, Jessie Ralph, E. E. Clive. (UAS)

This rousing adventure tale of British physician Peter Blood, who is sentenced to slavery for his part in a rebellion against King James II but escapes to become a famous pirate on the Spanish Main ("We, the hunted, will now hunt") is exciting because of the personal style of Errol Flynn. One of the best inspirations that Jack Warner ever had was that Flynn had the makings of a new Douglas Fairbanks, Sr. In CAPTAIN BLOOD, whose success launched a series of Flynn swashbucklers, there is no doubt that the star has everything to keep romantics of every age on the edge of their seats: good looks, boundless energy, and charm.

Following the underdog crew of pirates and the heroic Doctor-Captain Blood as they do battle with assorted villains is an entertainment in the best vein of the good old days—the days when you could count on somebody like Sabatini, or Fairbanks, or Flynn.

Captains Courageous

MGM 1937. 116 min., b/w. (d) Victor Fleming (sp) John Lee Mahin, Marc Connelly, and Dale Van Every from the novel by Rudyard Kipling (ph) Harold Rosson (c) Freddie Bartholomew, Spencer Tracy, Lionel Barrymore, Melvyn Douglas, Mickey Rooney, John Carradine. (FNC)

The director and the cast are old hands; Kipling sails a smooth course. Twelve-year-old Harvey Cheyne, a rich man's spoiled son, is taken aboard a fishing schooner off the Grand Banks and whipped into shape by Manuel, a stern Portuguese fisherman who loves this "little fish." Though Spencer Tracy won his first Oscar for his Manuel, the real star of the movie is the marine photography of Hal Rosson (THE RED BADGE OF COURAGE, SINGIN' IN THE RAIN), which transforms the life of the old Gloucester fishing fleet into fascinating documentary. To youngsters, the seafaring lore—rowing, fishing, trawling, chopping bait, dressing down herring and cod, steering—is a great adventure. They understand, too, the estrangement between Harvey and his father, and the "sea change" which comes to the boy after his three months on the *We're Here* and the loss of his beloved Manuel.

Casey's Shadow

Columbia 1978. 116 min., col. (prod) Ray Stark (d) Martin Ritt (sp) Carol Sobieski, suggested by John McPhee's story "Ruidoso" (ph) John A. Alonzo (m) Patrick Williams (c) Walter Matthau, Alexis Smith, Robert Webber, Murray Hamilton, Andrew A. Rubin, Stephan Burns. (SWA)

Once a year on Labor Day weekend, the richest horse race in the world takes place in the small village of Ruidoso in the foothills of the Sierra Blanca range, New Mexico. The horses entered for the four events (including the All-American Futurity), which have an aggregate purse of more than a million dollars, are quarter horses, a special breed indigenous to the American Southwest. CASEY'S SHADOW leads up to the big race, which lasts about twenty seconds. The rest of the movie is about the Bourdelle family, unlucky and poor—one acidulous Cajun pop (Walter Matthau), no mom, three appealing young sons—that raises quarter horses in Lousiana. The father falls in love with a promising foal that nobody else has any faith in and has to come up with a stiff entry fee for the big race. He has an obsession with winning and his kids have to ride herd on him. The obstreperous but attractive boys and the training sequences are the best things in the movie. Alexis Smith is around, too, as a rich woman who wants to buy the Bourdelle horse.

"Aimed squarely at eleven-year-old kids," said the reviewer in *Time*, "CASEY'S SHADOW rarely disobeys the time-honored rules of its kid-and-colt genre. Yet the movie proves that these strictures, when applied with a flourish, can still carry an audience across the finish line." Note for younger children: there is some strong language and a strong scene of the star colt's birth and the mare's death.

The Cat From Outer Space*

Disney 1978. 103 min., col. (d) Norman Tokar (sp) Ted Key (ph) Charles F. Wheeler (m) Lalo Schifrin (c) Ken Berry, Sandy Duncan, Harry Morgan, Roddy McDowall, McLean Stevenson, Jesse White, Alan Young, Hans Conried, William Prince. (FNC)

"Jake," a fifteen-month-old Abyssinian cat, is the star of Ted Key's switch on CLOSE ENCOUNTERS OF THE THIRD KIND. A visitor from another galaxy, Jake looks like an ordinary cat, but he wears a crystal collar that enables him to speak English, levitate his friends, "zap" his enemies into a freeze, and alter the future.

When Jake disappears from his space ship, he throws the Pentagon (represented by Harry Morgan) into a panic: will he use his telepathic power to control world events? An adventure-packed plot brings in good guys and bad guys by the score. And all that Jake wants, at first, is to get some metallic ore to repair his ship and go back home. But then Jake meets Lulubelle, the feline *femme fatale* belonging to scientist Sandy Duncan, and Lulubelle and Sandy are kidnapped by spies, and—.

The under-thirteens will be happy to take it from there. This is better-than-average Disney, with special effects, deep-focus photography, and very competent human actors (though nobody steals a scene from Jake).

The Charge of the Light Brigade

Warners 1936. 115 min., b/w. (d) Michael Curtiz (sp) Michael Jacoby, Rowland Leigh (m) Max Steiner (ph) Sol Polito, Fred Jackman (c) Errol Flynn, Olivia de Havilland, Patrick Knowles, Donald Crisp, Henry Stephenson, Nigel Bruce, David Niven. (MAC, UAS)

Why the 1936 film directed by Michael Curtiz, when there's a 1968 film directed by Tony Richardson? The Richardson film, despite its high quality and visual excitement, presents problems for youngsters in its emphasis on the social and political history of Victorian England as the cause of the blunder at Balaclava during the Crimean War. That tragic blunder was not the result of class privilege and injustice so much as the ambiguity of the commands issued by Raglan and Nolan. On the highest level in the '68 film, besides the directing, are the acting (John Gielgud, Vanessa Redgrave, Trevor Howard, David Hemmings); the cinematography (David Watkins); the music (John Addison); and the animated-cartoon sequences of battles and Victorian life (Richard Williams). Yet, on balance, the Richardson film fails in unity and clarity; the Curtiz film is more suited to children. Inspired by the Tennyson poem, the '36 production is action-adventure leading up to the charge of 673 British cavalrymen into the teeth of enemy cannon. For his creation of the charge sequence, assistant director B. Reeves Eason won an Academy Award.

"One of the most dynamic Hollywood films ever made," wrote Ezra Goodman (*The Fifty-Year Decline and Fall of Hollywood*). In its cutting and pace, it is "essentially one elongated spiral of slowly but surely intensifying movement." Children who are swept up in the charge will not need it pointed out to them that the order for the charge, and its execution, represent much, much more than epic thrills.

Cheaper by the Dozen

Fox 1950. 85 min., b/w. (d) Walter Lang (sp) Lamar Trotti from the book by Frank B. Gilbreth, Jr., and Ernestine Gilbreth Carey (c) Clifton Webb, Jeanne Crain, Myrna Loy, Edgar Buchanan, Mildred Natwick, Sara Allgood. (FNC)

The book of family reminiscences on which this film is based is classified by the library as *nonfiction* and by the movie company as a *novel*. It is an understandable slip; the screen household owes much more to Hollywood than to Montclair, New Jersey, in the twenties. But it is a very entertaining household, and its head, as Clifton Webb plays him, is not as outrageously cock-of-the-walk as Father Day in *Life with Father*. Life for Frank B. Gilbreth, Sr., is a "motion study" engineer's dream of domestic efficiency—but life with Father Gilbreth's lively and high-spirited six sons and six daughters refuses to be regimented and often verges on farcical nightmare.

Though very broadly drawn and sometimes sentimental, this picture of a genial disciplinarian and his family is naturally good material for screen comedy. Any way you look at it, the sight of a mass tonsillectomy or twelve kids packing into the family car is funny.

The Children of Theatre Street

USA/USSR 1977. 90 min., col. (prod)(co-d) Earle Mack (assoc. prod) Jean Dalrymple (d) Robert Dornhelm (sp) Beth Gutcheon (ph) Karl Kofler (art) Oleg Briansky (c) Angelina Armeiskaya, Alec Timoushin, Lena Voronzova, Michaela Cerna (of the Vaganova Choreographic Institute); Galens Messenzeva, Konstantine Zaklinsky (of the Kirov Ballet), (narr) Princess Grace of Monaco. (LIB)

On Theatre Street in Leningrad is the great ballet school which produced Pavlova, Nijinsky, Fokine, Balanchine, Karsavina, and Danilova, and whose more recent graduates include Nureyev, Makarova, and Baryshnikov. Informally known as the Kirov School, its formal name is the Vaganova Choreographic Institute. In Earle Mack's charming documentary, narrated by Princess Grace of Monaco, we follow the daily lives of the young students, in their classes and dormitories, as they train to join the company. We see ballets filmed and recorded live at the Kirov, Bolshoi, and Mali Theatres in the USSR. The film begins with the entrance of a new class, children between nine and twelve, survivors of a rigorous screening process, and describes the progress of eleven-year-old Angelina and twelve-year-old Alec. Youngsters enchanted by ballet—will all the children raise their hands?—will not notice the shortcomings of the documentary, which lacks unity and depth of insight into the children's feelings. There are too many lovely moments of dance, and too much to learn about the way one becomes a dancer.

THE CHILDREN OF THEATRE STREET has glimpses with which all children can identify—not only Angelina triumphantly flying across the screen as the nymph in *La Sylphide* but all the sweating trainees earning strict correction and precious applause.

Chitty Chitty Bang Bang*

Britain 1968. 142 min., col. (d) Ken Hughes (sp) Roald Dahl and Ken Hughes from the novel by Ian Fleming (m) Richard M. and Robert B. Sherman (c) Dick Van Dyke, Sally Ann Howes, Lionel Jeffries, Gert Frobe, Anna Quayle, Benny Jill, James Robertson Justice, Robert Helpmann, Heather Ripley, Adrian Hall. (GEN)

Lavish adaptation of Ian Fleming's fairy story about an old car rescued from the rubbish heap and scrap dealer by two children who restore it to magical splendor with the help of their inventor dad. He drives it across the seas and into the air, in his pursuit (and, of course, defeat) of the wicked old baron who hates children. The car is fun, and so are the jokes, puns, patty-cake minuets, puppet dances, Rube Goldberg devices, and all the rest of this lively movie. "A fast, dense, friendly children's musical, with something of the joys of singing together on a team bus on the way to a game," said the *New York Times*.

The largely British cast turns in some nice performances. The choreography (by Marc Breaux and Dee Dee Wood) is often witty. Gert Frobe, who seems to be in everything of Ian Fleming's, plays the balloon-borne Baron Bomburst of Vulgaria almost as if he, too, were choreographed. But then all of CHITTY CHITTY BANG BANG has bounce.

A Christmas Carol

Britain 1951. 86 min., b/w. (prod)(d) Brian Desmond-Hurst (sp) Noel Langley, based on the Charles Dickens story (ph) C. Pennington-Richards (m) Richard Addinsell (c) Alastair Sim, Kathleen Harrison, Mervyn Johns, Hermione Baddeley, Michael Hordern. (MAC)

Dickens's *A Christmas Carol* has been filmed so many times, between the Essanay version in 1908 and the Australian animated version in 1970, that it's easy to become lost among the ghosts of Christmas past and present. Although the CBS version in 1956, with Basil Rathbone and Fredric March, was a creditable one, there's no doubt in our mind that the film that takes top honors, for its cast and its style, is this one. Since it was originally called SCROOGE, and that title now belongs to the 1970 musical version with Albert Finney—a rather weird effort—the wisest course is to think of the 1951 film as "the one with Alastair Sim and Mervyn Johns." (Sim pops up in a guest appearance as Scrooge in another version, but not with Mervyn Johns.) Everything clear?

This definitive version is free from exaggerated sentiment, has perfect Victorian flavor, and captures Dickens's theme. Children who know the characters from the original story will never see them acted with greater shade and depth than here; children who are meeting them for the first time will find them understandable and moving.

The Circus*

United Artists 1928. 72 min., b/w. (d)(sp)(m) Charles Chaplin (ph) Rollie H. Totheroh (c) Charles Chaplin, Merna Kennedy, Allan Garcia, Betty Morrissey, Harry Crocker, George Davis, Henry Bergman, Stanley Sanford, John Rand, Steve Murphy, Doc Stone. Silent, music added in 1970. (PAR)

Shorter, less brilliant and moving than THE GOLD RUSH or CITY LIGHTS, this still breaks up the kids. When it was re-released with music in 1970, Stanley Kauffmann wrote, "The theme of the film is a contrast between life and art. The Tramp is funny as a man. He is unfunny when he tries to amuse in a circus skit. His funniness is in his spontaneous being; consciousness kills it. . . . At the end, in one of the loveliest shots in any Chaplin film, he stands on the circus grounds as the wagons roll away one by one. Finally alone, he sits, and we see he is in the middle of a circle that was marked on the ground by the circus rings. The theater has once again become the world."

Wonderfully structured comedy: the pickpocket mix-up in the carnival crowd, the mirror maze in the fun house, Charlie as the "Vanishing Lady," Charlie and the banana in the "William Tell" act, Charlie as the new prop man chasing a donkey into the ring, Charlie on the high wire. In a word—*Charlie*.

Circus World

Paramount 1964. 145 min., col. (d) Henry Hathaway (sp) Ben Hecht and Julian Halevy from an original story by Philip Yordan (ph) Jack Hildyard, Claude Renoir (m) Dmitri Tiomkin (co-ord) Frank Capra, Jr. (c) John Wayne, Rita Hayworth, Claudia Cardinale, Lloyd Nolan, Richard Conte, Kay Walsh. (BUD, MAC, ROA, WCF)

At the turn of the century, Matt Masters (John Wayne) is a showman who travels around the world with his circus, which includes a Wild West show. Matt rides tall in the saddle, survives a dockside mishap, and sees that all's well under the Big Top. Romance is provided by the lovely Alfredo ladies (Rita Hayworth, Claudia Cardinale); entertainment, by colorful circus acts on a grand scale. The quality of the production owes much to the Henry Hathaway direction, Ben Hecht's hand in the script, the cinematography of Jack Hildyard (THE BRIDGE ON THE RIVER KWAI) and Claude Renoir (THE RIVER), and producer Samuel Bronston's flair for spectacle.

City Lights*

United Artists 1931. 87 min., b/w. (d)(sp)(m) Charles Chaplin (c) Charles Chaplin, Virginia Cherrill, Harry Meyers, Hank Mann. Silent. (PAR)

When we hear that CITY LIGHTS is in release again, we see a figure about whom we made up our minds long ago and whom we love after our own fashion. But what about people born many years after 1931?

We've had a chance to get their reactions, and the verdict's in: Charlie's back and the children love him—as they always did. Today's youngsters are incredulous, startled, delighted. They grow uproarious in the prizefight scene, with the music and Charlie jigging away, and in the restaurant when he is eating confetti like spaghetti. *What a corny gag, but I love to watch him do it,* said one of the children. When the lights go up after that marvelous last moment, some of the audience will be crying. They're not sure what has happened to them: *The first and only comedian who has ever made me feel soft inside while laughing at him. . .* Despite themselves they have fallen in love with *Chaplin's pantomine genious* (sic), with that gallant soul in an ungallant city making a home on a waterfront bench as soon as he dusts it off. Mesmerized by the poet seeking love who gets a pail of water in the face, they have laughed, often, that they might not cry. They have experienced more than a movie.

Close Encounters of the Third Kind

Columbia 1977. 135 min., col. (d)(sp) Steven Spielberg (ph) Vilmos Zsigmond (asst ph) William A. Fraker, Douglas Slocombe, John Alonzo, Laszlo Kovacs (spec eff) Douglas Trumbull (m) John Williams; songs, Johnny Mathis (c) Richard Dreyfuss, François Truffaut, Melinda Dillon, Cary Guffey, Teri Garr. (SWA)

In the American family having the close encounter with the occupants of a huge UFO is a very small boy (Cary Guffey). When he and the French scientist (François Truffaut) meet the visitors, it's clear that there will be no shoot-outs. The extra-terrestrial beings are not hostile. The child and the scientist greet them with wonder and delight, and the child follows them on a journey of sheer exhilaration.

Director-writer Steven Spielberg, whose JAWS appealed to our fears, is saying in CLOSE ENCOUNTERS that there's nothing to fear in the unknown: look *up*; it's warm and kind up there. Unlike STAR WARS' fantasy, in which a whole planet is blown up in the spirit of a Tom and Jerry cartoon, CLOSE ENCOUNTERS is benign. Its hopeful reassurance as well as its dazzling invention made it enormously popular. "The most innocent of all technological marvel movies, and one of the most satisfying. This film has retained some of the wonder and bafflement we feel when we first go into a planetarium: we ooh and ah at the vastness, and at the beauty of the mystery. . .a child's playfulness and love of surprises. . .immense charm" (Pauline Kael, *The New Yorker*). And immensely entertaining for children: the sheer scale, the lights-and-music originality like the "music of the spheres" idea, the comedy of galactic sprites and herald angels for flying saucers. The cinematography and sound-effects editing won Academy Awards.

The Clowns

Italy 1970. 90 min., col. (d) Federico Fellini (sp) Fellini and Bernardino Zapponi (ph) Dario di Palma (m) Nino Rota (c) Pierre Etaix, Annie Fratellini, Anita Ekberg. Italian and French dialog with English subtitles. *(FNC)*

For older children, a frequently fascinating documentary by the great Federico Fellini, "an affectionate memoir" of the lost world that he remembers—the circuses he saw as a boy, especially the clowns. Often on screen as his own ringmaster, Fellini takes us to Paris for interviews with surviving clowns and at the end stages an elaborate, mock "clown funeral" for Auguste, the legendary low clown of clown ritual who is always the butt of White Clown's jokes.

Though it has meaning on a more adult level (Fellini may be viewing himself not only as ringmaster but also as Auguste and White Clown), THE CLOWNS can be a well of great fun for children on the simplest level. There are processions of clowns, fire engines, the front halves of clown horses dancing with the rear halves, explosions of music and confetti. Nino Rota's score alone, which erupts with brilliance, evokes circus excitement.

A Connecticut Yankee in King Arthur's Court

Paramount 1949. 107 min., col. (d) Tay Garnett (sp) Edmund Beloin from the novel by Mark Twain (c) Bing Crosby, Rhonda Fleming, William Bendix, Murvyn Vye, Sir Cedric Hardwicke. (GEN)

Some good things have been mined before from Mark Twain's fantasy—a 1931 movie with Will Rogers and Myrna Loy, *Thou Swell* sung from a Broadway stage—but for today's young audience, Bing Crosby does very nicely as Sir Boss in this musical comedy with some lively tunes by Jimmy Van Heusen and Johnny Burke. Twain himself would probably approve of the mixture of brashness and con-man suavity that Crosby brings to the role of the modern Yankee who is knocked out and comes to in the middle of sixth-century Camelot, where he proceeds to astound the gentry with scientific know-how.

A pleasant romp, and something of a come-on in its own way, for if it cajoles the kids into reading the original, they will get an intellectual shock or two. Twain was not nostalgic about Camelot; he found many of its social and political assumptions lamentable and said so with characteristic force.

The Count of Monte Cristo

United Artists 1934. 119 min., b/w. (d) Rowland V. Lee (sp) Philip Dunne, Dan Totheroh, Rowland V. Lee, based on the novel by Alexandre Dumas (c) Robert Donat, Elissa Landi, Louis Calhern, Sidney Blackmer, Raymond Walburn, O. P. Heggie. (GEN)

In his first American movie, Robert Donat was the definitive Edmond Dantes. His Dumas hero hasn't a trace of ham—a boast that couldn't have been made by the barnstorming James O'Neill, who put his Dantes on the silent screen in 1912, or by John Gilbert, who starred in the 1923 film version.

This adaptation will never be listed among the landmarks of cinema art, but it is a consistently entertaining adventure yarn. The Napoleonic background is well done, the Château d'If and other famous episodes are highly dramatic, and Donat's is one of several good characterizations. Perhaps that's why the story has not been remade in English since 1934, though Louis Jourdan starred in a 1961 French adaptation, directed disappointingly by Claude Autant-Lara. Accept no substitutes—SWORD OF MONTE CRISTO, WIFE OF MONTE CRISTO, MONTE CRISTO'S REVENGE are duds beside the Donat Dantes.

The Court Jester*

Paramount 1956. 101 min., col. (d) Norman Panama and Melvin Frank (sp) Norman Panama and Melvin Frank (m) Sylvia Fine and Sammy Cahn (c) Danny Kaye, Glynis Johns, Basil Rathbone. Angela Lansbury, Mildred Natwick, Cecil Parker, Robert Middleton, John Carradine, Alan Napier. (FNC)

When knighthood was in flower, it *couldn't* have been like this. Never mind Camelot, Ivanhoe, Robin Hood, every story you ever heard about outlaws, knights, missing heirs to the throne, tournaments, and palace intrigues. What they all lacked was Danny Kaye, baby-sitting for a prince, getting an instant induction to chivalry so that he can joust in the lists, and singing wonderful songs by Sylvia Fine. A jester who is nothing but a bundle of nerves, he turns this one over on his tongue: *The pellet with the poison/Is in the vessel with the pestle,/The chalice from the palace/Has the brew that is true.* (To borrow from the movie's dialog: SHE: "Get it?" HE: "Got it!" SHE: "Good!")

Cree Hunters of Mistassini

National Film Board of Canada 1974. 58 min., col. (d) Tony Ianzelo, Boyce Richardson (ph) Colin Low, Len Chatwin. (NFB, CAL)

Informative and richly observed documentary ("Perhaps the best film for conveying the values and way of life of Indians"—*Wilson Library Bulletin*) and winner of the Robert Flaherty Award for best feature-length documentary, 1974, British Society of Film and Television Arts.

The culture and hunting life of the Cree Indians of northern Quebec have been recorded by two National Film Board of Canada filmmakers, who show us three families on a winter hunting trip—their building of a log cabin, canoeing, rituals, teaching of the young, and combination of communal and family living. The way of life that the Crees are afraid of losing, because of the threat of a proposed dam project, reflects not only their approach to nature but profound religious beliefs. For over-twelves interested in ecology and different modes of living.

Cyrano de Bergerac

United Artists 1950. 112 min., b/w. (d) Michael Gordon (sp) Carl Foreman from the play by Edmond Rostand, translated by Brian Hooker (c) José Ferrer, Mala Powers, William Prince, Morris Carnovsky. (IVY)

The play's the thing. Here is José Ferrer's superb Oscar performance as one of the great characters of all time, the seventeenth-century duellist, buffoon, wit, philosopher, and poet who wooed Roxane for another man. No other play in history has ever attained such immediate and enormous popularity; no other play outside the works of Shakespeare has had such an acting history: Coquelin, Richard Mansfield, Walter Hampden, Pasquale Amato, and José Ferrer—on stage, radio, television and screen. Cyrano wins popularity polls. In a university questionnaire, he was the one classic hero nobody was bored by; in a newpaper competition, he was the favorite over Romeo, Don Quixote, Jean Valjean, D'Artagnan, the Count of Monte Cristo, Ruy Blas, and Sherlock Holmes. (On the other hand, the Nazis never cared for him; they closed the play in Prague because of its "libertarian sentiments.")

Older children laugh at the "Nose Speech," enjoy Cyrano's wit, his imagination, his gallant insistence on grace in ugliness—and love the panache of his free spirit.

Darby O'Gill and the Little People*

Disney 1959. 90 min., col. (d) Robert Stevenson (sp) Lawrence E. Watkin, suggested by H. T. Kavanagh's stories (ph) Winton C. Hoch (m) Oliver Wallace (c) Albert Sharpe, Janet Munro, Sean Connery, Jimmy O'Dea, Kieron Moore, Estelle Winwood, Walter Fitzgerald, Denis O'Dea, J. G. Devlin, Jack MacGowran, Farrell Pelly, Nora O'Mahony. (GEN)

This prime Disney, a delightful fantasy and a visual joy, is full of discoveries: performances by a cast picked from the best Dublin stage troupes, wit Albert Sharpe (of the Broadway *Finian's Rainbow* company) turning in "a gem" (*Variety*); a screenplay of genuine wit as well as sentiment; lovely cinematography by Winton C. Hoch (John Ford's photographer), and meticulous detail for its Irish scenes.

The "little people" are treated most convincingly. "My thanks to King Brian of Knocknasheega and his leprechauns," reads a title on the picture, "whose gracious cooperation made this film possible.—Walt Disney." The sequences with the leprechauns, like the scene of Darby standing in the great hall playing the violin as they dance around him, seem perfectly natural; one believes Darby is really talking to a twenty-one inch king. Darby O'Gill is an old storyteller, caretaker on the governor's estate. Lovable yet humanly frail, he is full of deviousness as well as charm—and so are the leprechauns. Their adventures together, told with imagination and taste, make an unusual entertainment.

David Copperfield

MGM 1935. 133 min., b/w. (d) George Cukor (sp) Howard Estabrook from Hugh Walpole's adaptation of the novel by Charles Dickens (c) Freddie Bartholomew, W. C. Fields, Lionel Barrymore, Maureen O'Sullivan, Edna May Oliver, Roland Young, Basil Rathbone, Elsa Lanchester, Lewis Stone, Madge Evans, Jessie Ralph, Hugh Williams. (FNC)

The first of the good Dickens movies, and still one of the best "book films." If you ever had any doubt about its rightness, it was dispelled in 1969, when an "all-star" version of *David Copperfield* was presented on television, a chunk of existentialism that left an unpleasant taste in the mouth, as if someone had doctored a Christmas pudding with absinthe.

The 1935 DAVID COPPERFIELD is the Old Reliable, full of plums: Roland Young's dripping Uriah Heep; W. C. Fields' Micawber, his greatest role (*You perceive before you the shattered fragments of a temple that was once called man*); Maureen O'Sullivan's Dora, a Phiz drawing down to the last curl on her silly little head; Edna May Oliver's Aunt Betsy routing Miss Murdstone. . .A feast, well seasoned by Mr. Cukor.

The Day the Earth Caught Fire

Britain 1961. 99 min., b/w. (prod)(d) Val Guest (sp) Val Guest, Wolf Mankowitz (ph) Harry Waxman (c) Edward Judd, Leo McKern, Janet Munro. (MAC, BUD, TWY, WCF)

In the news room of the London *Daily Express*—so runs the literate script of ex-newsman Val Guest and novelist Wolf Mankowitz—reporters are baffled by unexplained catastrophes throughout the world. They discover that two simultaneous nuclear tests have shifted the earth's orbit, causing it to race toward the sun. Scientists attempt desperately to avert what seems to be inevitable Doomsday.

Reflecting destruction in people rather than in special effects, and relying on such good casting as ex-*Daily Express* editor Arthur Christiansen as the man who holds the paper together during the crisis, this sci-fi movie is still one of the best of its class. "Exciting, brisk and devastating tale," the *New York Herald Tribune* called it. As the world goes wild with earthquakes, tidal waves, and unseasonal blizzards, the young viewer understands that the long fall of the earth into the sun has been caused by a British and a Russian bomb detonating at the same time.

The Day the Earth Stood Still

Fox 1951. 92 min., b/w. (d) Robert Wise (sp) Edmund H. North from the story by Harry Bates (c) Michael Rennie, Patricia Neal, Sam Jaffe, Hugh Marlowe, Billy Gray. (FNC)

"The science fiction films are strongly moralistic," Susan Sontag has pointed out. "The standard message is the one about the proper, or humane, uses of science, versus the mad, obsessional use of science."

Under Robert Wise's practiced direction, the standard message is delivered here with above-standard intelligence. When the rocketship from outer space lands, out steps the immensely suave Michael Rennie, emissary from a distant planet hundreds of years ahead of ours. He is charged with the responsibility of warning us that Earth will be sacrificed to save the rest of the universe unless we stop the atomic testing and warfare which are endangering the balance of the spheres. While heads of state weigh his warning, he cuts off electrical power more effectively than any power company and meets a few of Earth's more civilized and peace-loving citizens, among them Patricia Neal as a young war widow with her eleven-year-old son. Shot partly on location in Washington, D. C., the film combines realistic details with a philosophical fantasy that raises questions rather than goose pimples.

The Defiant Ones

United Artists 1958. 97 min., b/w. (prod)(d) Stanley Kramer (sp) Nathan E. Douglas, Harold Jacob Smith (ph) Sam Leavitt (m) Ernest Gold; song "Long Gone" by W. C. Handy and Chris Smith (c) Tony Curtis, Sidney Poitier, Theodore Bikel, Charles McGraw, Lon Chaney, Jr., Cara Williams, Carl "Alfalfa" Switzer. (UAS, MAC)

Two escaping convicts, one black (Sidney Poitier), and one white (Tony Curtis), are chained together in their flight through the deep South, not only by their shackles but by their consuming mutual race hatred. Eventually they come to understand each other, as they realize their dependency on each other. The ending is one that few thoughtful older children will forget.

What might have been merely an antiracist parable is a strong, warm drama in producer-director Stanley Kramer's hands. Outstanding are Poitier and Curtis as the prisoners, Theodore Bikel as a Georgia sheriff, Cara Williams as a woman encountered on the way, and (in his last screen role) Carl "Alfalfa" Switzer as "The Kid," a coda for his Our Gang career. The screenplay and the photography won Academy Awards.

Don Quixote

USSR 1957. 110 min., col. (d) Grigory Kozintsev (sp) E. Shwartz from the novel by Cervantes (ph) Andrei Moskvin, A. Dudko (c) Nikolai Cherkassov, Yuri Tolubeyev. Available in Russian dialog with English subtitles, or dubbed. (MAC)

If Orson Welles finishes his version of Cervantes's picaresque classic, which he has been filming in sections since 1958, it will make a round dozen movies about the seventeenth-century hidalgo and his squire who set out to defend the poor and oppressed. There have been a Jugoslavic cartoon version and French, American, British, Spanish, and Australian versions. Two of the best were G. W. Pabst's British film (1933) with Chaliapin and George Robey, and Rafael Gil's Spanish film (1948) with Rafael Rivelles and Juan Calvo. Though the latter is lavish and faithful to the original, there has never been any question that the finest cinema DON QUIXOTE is the Russian version made by Grigory Kozintsev—a work of film art made from a great novel. Kozintsev, who directed the 1964 Russian film HAMLET, has somehow managed to make his Russian actors more convincingly Spanish than one could have imagined possible. Don Quixote is played by Nikolai Cherkassov, the distinguished star of S. M. Eisenstein's ALEXANDER NEVSKY and IVAN THE TERRIBLE; Sancho Panza, by Yuri Tolubeyev. They both bring a new dimension to their roles. Cherkassov has a gracious, tragic dignity as he moves against a world of rogues; Tolubeyev does not caricature Sancho Panza but imbues him with a kind of peasant integrity.

The magnificent color and spectacle are no accident; Kozintsev's chief cinematographer here is Andrei Moskvin, who was Edouard Tisse's assistant on IVAN THE TERRIBLE. Not only a superbly beautiful visual achievement but a deeply perceptive interpretation of Cervantes's story, this is an experience to enrich and stimulate young viewers.

Dracula

Universal 1931. 76 min., b/w. (d) Tod Browning (sp) Garrett Fort from the novel by Bram Stoker and the play by Hamilton Deane and John L. Balderston (ph) Karl Freund (c) Bela Lugosi, Helen Chandler, David Manners. (CWF, SWA, TWY)

From the time that Max Schreck played him in F. W. Murnau's silent German film NOSFERATU in 1923, the Transylvanian vampire count created by Bram Stoker in a Victorian novel has been a figure of popular mythology. The child of the eighties knows many of Dracula's brood (the "sons" and "daughters" and "brides" and "blood" of his "returns") as well as many of his interpreters (Lon Chaney, John Carradine, Francis Lederer, Christopher Lee). But the archetype was filmed by Tod Browning in 1931, and Bela Lugosi will always be associated with the definitive role among true cultists. Though DRACULA is not as interesting cinematically as Browning's later FREAKS, it has the right feel, thanks to the photography of Karl Freund, famous for his work in the German silents of the twenties (THE LAST LAUGH, METROP-

OLIS, VARIETY, BERLIN). Atmosphere, makeup, and sets are more effective than the script, which was drawn more from the play than from Stoker's novel.

For the adult who has somehow managed to grow up without an understanding of the Dracula mystique, here is an illuminating explanation by R. H. W. Dillard, who teaches at Hollins College and writes excellent science fiction: "I saw the great horror films in the late 1940's, after the war and the period of their creation, when they were about my age, ten to fifteen years old. . . . We were cast into a world of pure delight, tickled by a fear that we knew was artificial, and at the same time initiated into the mystery of this life and world and into the true wonder of the free imagination."

Duck Soup*

Paramount 1933. 70 min., b/w. (d) Leo McCarey (sp)(m) Bert Kalmar and Harry Ruby (c) The Marx Brothers, Louis Calhern, Margaret Dumont, Edgar Kennedy. (CON, MMA, UNI, SWA, TWY)

The Marx Brothers' style, now more popular than ever, has had a significant influence on today's Theater of the Absurd. At the height of the surrealist movement, Antonin Artaud had praised ANIMAL CRACKERS, calling its comedy "essential liberation. . .a kind of boiling anarchy," and Ionesco said he was trying to imitate the Marx Brothers in *The Bald Soprano*. Their explosive release, annihilation of formal language and logic, and free-spirited attack on all forms of pomposity have many parallels in today's plays and movies. Youngsters make the perfect audience for comedies which set up situations only to reduce them to complete absurdity.

In DUCK SOUP, Rufus T. Firefly (Groucho), President of Fredonia, is waging war on Sylvania, two of whose spies (Chico and Harpo) run a hot dog and peanut stand outside the palace. Though its makers didn't start out to produce a satire, DUCK SOUP was banned by Mussolini. Today's kids consider the sequence at the end, where Firefly goes through a series of costume changes with every cut, a comment on the fact that the dictator didn't know, half the time, what side he was fighting for. Two high spots of the movie are Harpo's assault on Edgar Kennedy's lemonade stand, and the famous mirror sequence with three images of a night-capped Groucho.

Dumbo*

*RKO 1941. 64 min., col. animation. (prod) Walt Disney (d) Ben Sharps-
teen (sp) Joe Grant and Dick Huemer from the story by Helen Aber-
son and Harold Pearl (anim super) Vladimir Tytla, Ward Kimball, Fred
Moore, John Lounsbery, Arthur Babbitt, Wolfgang Reitherman (m)
Oliver Wallace, Frank Churchill (lyr) Ned Washington. (FNC, SWA)*

Mrs. Jumbo's gift from the stork suddenly sneezes—and his ears
become huge. The other lady elephants in the circus are sarcastic:
he ought to be called Dumbo, not Jumbo! When the baby elephant's mama causes a commotion because the circus people are
mistreating her Dumbo, she is locked up. Alone and broken-
hearted, Dumbo finds a friend in Timothy the mouse. To make
a short, simple, sad, funny story end the way it should: Timothy
and some local crows get Dumbo to fly, and overnight he is the
sensation of the circus. Mrs. Jumbo has her own streamlined car
on the circus train, with Dumbo flying alongside.

"The nicest, kindest Disney yet. It has the most heart, taste,
beauty, compassion, skill, restraint. . . .the most enchanting and
endearing of [Disney's] output, maybe because it's the least pretentious" (Cecilia Ager, PM). This innocent and exuberant fable
is still prized as one of the best of Disney. One unfortunate blem-
ish: those helpful hippy crows are, alas, offensive black caricatures.

Elephant Boy

*United Artists 1937. 80 min., b/w. (d) Robert J. Flaherty and Zoltan
Korda (sp) John Collier from Rudyard Kipling's "Toomai of the Ele-
phants" (ph) Osmond H. Borradaile (c) Sabu, Walter Hudd, Allan
Jeyes, Wilfrid Hyde-White. (ROA, ICS)*

There is more than one way of looking at ELEPHANT BOY. To the
knowledgeable admirer of Robert J. Flaherty, one of the unique
masters of film, it is not on a par with his earlier films, NANOOK
OF THE NORTH or MAN OF ARAN. To Arthur Calder-Marshall, for
example, in his Flaherty biography, *The Innocent Eye*, it is "A
Korda picture which contained some Flaherty sequences." Alexander and Zoltan Korda had combined material mocked up in the
London studios with the footage that Flaherty brought back from
the Mysore jungle. Among the authentic Flaherty sequences,
Calder-Marshall lists Toomai's prayer to the Jain statue, the building of the *kheddah* (enclosure to ensnare wild elephants), the
scenes with Toomai and the elephant Kala Nag, the climactic drive

of the elephants into the *kheddah*, and "some magnificent back-lit shots of the massed and massive elephants charging into the river under the dark trees."

Another view of the film has been taken by young audiences since 1937. To them it is a wonderful story of a boy's love for an elephant, and it is a thrilling experience to watch Sabu as he lives with the herd and saves his village from the great stampede. They love the "Elephant Dance." (Frances Flaherty, the director's wife, used this as the title of the book she made of the letters she wrote home to her young daughters during the filming in India.) Flaherty's photographer was Osmond Borradaile, who later shot THE OVERLANDERS with Harry Watt and the impressive SCOTT OF THE ANTARCTIC.

The Emperor's Nightingale*

Czechoslovakia 1951. 60 min., col. (prod)(d) Jiri Trnka (sp)(comm) Phyllis McGinley from the fairy tale by Hans Christian Andersen (m) Vaclav Trajan (narr) spoken in English by Boris Karloff. (MAC, CHA, EMC)

Nobody who's seen this delicate masterpiece forgets it, and it should be a delightful surprise for children who are not put off by the term "fairy tale" and respond to imaginative and original art. Created (over a period of three years) by the world-famous Czech animation artist Jiri Trnka, it is a gem of cinema.

Based on a familiar story by Hans Christian Andersen—the legend of the emperor in the court of Cathay who sought the answer to the question, "What is happiness?"—THE EMPEROR'S NIGHTINGALE is part live action but mostly animation. It is "played" by hundreds of tiny dolls, exquisitely and brilliantly clothed, moving against enchanting backgrounds in spellbinding fashion. The film's live-action frame is about a poor little rich boy who lives alone, surrounded by splendid toys but yearning for the real world outside. He has a dream (told in animation) about the lonely Chinese emperor so hedged in by court artificiality that he can't tell the difference between the whistling of a toy bird and the singing of a live nightingale.

In addition to its lovely visuals, the film has effective music and a fine narration written by the poet Phyllis McGinley and spoken (just right) by Boris Karloff.

Fantasia*

Disney/RKO 1940. 135 min., col. animation. (d) Walt Disney (sp) Joe Grant and Dick Huemer (m) Edward H. Plumb; The Philadelphia Orchestra conducted by Leopold Stokowski. (narr) Deems Taylor. (THEATERS)

Breaking into a new form, Walt Disney attempted in FANTASIA to combine the art of animation with serious music in this full-length film in which several musical works suggest "the mood, the coloring, the design, the speed, the character of motion of what is seen on the screen," as Leopold Stokowski expressed it. In its several revivals since World War II, this holiday treat for children has undoubtedly popularized serious music for many of them. The film includes visual interpretations of Bach's "Toccata and Fugue in D Minor" and of excerpts from Tchaikovsky's "The Nutcracker Suite," Dukas's "The Sorcerer's Apprentice," Stravinsky's "The Rite of Spring," Beethoven's "The Pastoral Symphony," Ponchielli's "The Dance of the Hours," and a sequence that combines Moussorgsky's "Night on Bald Mountain" with Schubert's "Ave Maria."

The most enjoyable cinematic pleasures in FANTASIA are Hop Low and the Mushroom Dancers in "The Nutcracker," Mlle. Upanova and Hyacinth Hippo in the hippo ballet in "Dance of the Hours," and Mickey Mouse in "The Sorcerer's Apprentice" — examples of Disney animation at its very ingenious, broadly funny best. Leopold Stokowski conducts the Philadelphia Orchestra, and Deems Taylor introduces each musical selection. Among the many Disney artists credited for the film, a famous name stands out: John Hubley (THE HOLE, ADVENTURES OF AN *) was one of the art directors for "The Rite of Spring" sequence.

Fantastic Voyage

Fox 1966. 105 min., col. (d) Richard Fleischer (sp) Harry Kleiner from the story by Otto Klement and Jay Lewis Bixby as adapted by David Duncan (spec eff) Art Cruickshank (c) Stephen Boyd, Raquel Welch, William Redfield, Edmond O'Brien, Donald Pleasence. (FNC)

We've always thought that a voyage to *inner* space would make the more spectacular science fiction, so it's satisfying when a first-rate movie comes along to prove it. FANTASTIC VOYAGE, or *Inside Dr. Benes*, as we think of it, starts with an injured Czechoslovakian scientist who has a blood clot on his valuable brain. To remove it, a trip of the CMDF (Combined Miniature Deterrent Forces) is organized. Some fellow-scientists, including technician Raquel Welch in a skin-diving suit, are shrunk to microscopic size, encased in a capsule, and injected into Dr. Benes's bloodstream. Their adventures in his arterial system, lungs, heart, and ear chambers are filmed brilliantly. Academy Awards went to the art directors and to Art Cruickshank for special-effects wizardry.

As beautifully way-out as this exploration of a human body may be, we wouldn't be surprised if it inspired some kids to go beyond Introductory Biology 1.

Fear Strikes out

Paramount 1957. 100 min., b/w. (d) Robert Mulligan (sp) Ted Berkman and Raphael Blau from the autobiography by James A. Piersall and Albert S. Hirshberg (c) Anthony Perkins, Karl Malden, Adam Williams, Norma Moore. (FNC)

One of the few movies which show athletes as people rather than symbols, it is the first screen work of television director Robert Mulligan (TO KILL A MOCKINGBIRD). Based on the book, and the television drama taken from it, it is the true story of the Boston Red Sox's Jim Piersall who was suspended for erratic behavior at Fenway Park and treated for psychological and emotional problems. Anthony Perkins is the son pushed to the breaking point by the loving but impossible demands of a father (Karl Malden) trying to relive his life through his child—a relationship which arouses sympathy in many preadolescents.

Fiddler on the Roof

United Artists 1971. 180 min., col. (d) Norman Jewison (sp) Joseph Stein from his book for the musical play adapted from Sholom Aleichem's "Tevye and His Daughters" (ph) Oswald Morris (m) Jerry Bock (lyr) Sheldon Harnick (chor) Tom Abbott after Jerome Robbins (c) Topol, Leonard Frey, Paul Mann, Michele Marsh, Michael Glaser, Norma Crane, Molly Picon, Rosalind Harris, Neva Small, Raymond Lovelock. (UAS)

The longest-running show in Broadway annals, which has played to more than 35 million people in thirty-two countries, may have generated such emotional impact because, as Tevye says, "Without tradition. . .our lives would be as shaky as a fiddler on the roof." Or maybe people were ready for a show about a man and his children, a man and his God, a show which really is a *show*, full of matchmaking and carousing, persecutions and rescues, joys and fears.

The movie, "opened up" to the exteriors of the Ukrainian village of Anatevka, is on an even bigger scale. To those who first met FIDDLER on the stage, there is a loss in warmth and intimacy. But to those who meet it for the first time on the screen, it is rich in feeling and hugely entertaining. Anatevka is full of dance and song ("Sunrise, Sunset," "Matchmaker, Matchmaker," "If I Were a Rich Man," "Miracle of Miracles"), and interesting to look at, thanks to photographer Oswald Morris (OLIVER!, MOBY DICK). Topol, Rosalind Harris, and Leonard Frey are engaging as Tevye, Tzeitel, and Motel; Isaac Stern plays over the credits. The film won Academy Awards for songs, scoring and sound, and cinematography.

The First Men in the Moon

Columbia 1964. 107 min., col. (d) Nathan Juran (sp) Nigel Kneale and Jan Reed, based on the novel by H. G. Wells (ph) Wilkie Cooper (spec eff) Ray Harryhausen (art) John Blezard (c) Edward Judd, Lionel Jeffries, Martha Hyer. (GEN)

"A delightful slice of tongue-in-cheek science fiction. . . .This version of the famous H. G. Wells novel is ideal for young audiences and as an introduction to SF" (Program, Junior National Film Theatre, London). A trio of modern astronauts who land on the moon discover a tattered Union Jack with a note stating that the first lunar trip took place in 1899. Ray Harryhausen's special effects and the good acting make this an enjoyable adventure among the beetle-eyed moon people, huge caterpillars, and other standbys of Victorian imagination.

Frankenstein

Universal 1931. 71 min., b/w. (d) James Whale (sp) Garrett Fort and Francis Edward Faragoh from John L. Balderston's play based on the novel by Mary Shelley (ph) Arthur Edeson (c) Colin Clive, Boris Karloff, Mae Clarke, John Boles, Dwight Frye. (UNI, SWA, TWY)

Following hot, or rather cold, on the heels of DRACULA, this movie twice-removed from Mary Shelley's classic is itself a classic. James Whale, the director, discovered Boris Karloff; the film showed their combined taste and subtlety and brought them fame.

Makeup man Jack Pierce created the cadaverous face of the Monster Incarnate with its heavy brows and lids, and photographer Arthur Edeson stamped it forever in our memories. Karloff's first appearance and the later scenes of violence are all the more chilling for the absence of gore and the strength of suggestion. The picture is still superior to its numerous progeny.

Disturbing question in the eighties: Will the youngsters find it too tame?

The Freshman*

Harold Lloyd Corp./Pathé 1925. 75 min., b/w. (d) Sam Taylor, Fred Newmeyer (sp) Sam Taylor, John Grey, Ted Wilde, Tim Whelan (ph) Walter Lundin, Henry Kohler (c) Harold Lloyd, Jobyna Ralston, Brooks Benedict, James Anderson, Hazel Keener, Joseph Harrington, Pat Harmon. Silent with music and sound effects. (PAR)

"The last time I saw THE FRESHMAN I saw it in the company of two nine-year-old girls, both experienced moviegoers. Halfway through the film, one of them turned to me in alarm. 'Did this really happen?' she asked, demanding an answer. The structure remains intensely persuasive" (Walter Kerr, *The Silent Clowns*). More of a character comedy than a gag comedy, THE FRESHMAN can still make one sympathize with what is happening to Harold "Lamb," who is determined to be most popular man on campus. Having been to the movies six times to see THE COLLEGE HERO, he believes he knows just how to act as the latest sports-model freshman. Dated as the scene is, the story deals with elements of common experience at any school—the desire to be liked by everybody, the humiliations suffered at the hands of peers, the growth of self-knowledge.

In the climactic football match, Harold is waiting on the bench for his big moment. After all the dreadful things, the dreadfully funny things, that have happened before, we want this Lamb to turn into a lion. And of course he's the real hero of the day, with his nose and the ball just over the goal line. In addition to the football sequences, which are wonderfully ludicrous, there's the party, with Harold in a makeshift disintegrating suit.

The General

MGM 1926. 82 min., b/w. (d) Buster Keaton and Clyde Bruckman (sp) Al Boasberg and Charles Smith (ph) Bert Haines and J. Devereux

Jennings (c) Buster Keaton, Marion Mack, Glen Cavender, Jim Farley, Charles Smith, Frank Barnes, Frederick Vroom. Silent. (GEN)

One of the greatest comedies of all time, and fresher today than ever. This last classic of silent comedy is a revelation for the young. The Great Stone Face plays engineer Johnnie Gray, who is trying to recapture the locomotive *The General* from Union raiders. (The story is a true one, from Pittenger's "The Great Locomotive Chase," which was the title of Disney's movie in 1956.) Shooting the film on the narrow-gauge railways of Oregon, and using only fifty titles, Keaton makes the pursuit of his train and his girl (Marian Mack) one long, side-splitting chase.

"The exploits are preposterously heroic. . . .Confronted with the outlandish or the alarming—the disappearance of his train, the discovery that in setting fire to the railway bridge he has placed himself on the wrong side of the blaze, or that. . .he has directed a cannonball straight into the cab of his own engine—Keaton remains imperturbable," wrote Penelope Houston of his comedy technique. His timing and his marvellous sight gags assure THE GENERAL of its right to the word *masterpiece*. In addition, it is extraordinarily vivid as a Civil War picture; many critics have pointed out that not only does Keaton look like a daguerreotype, but the movie looks like Mathew Brady's photographs.

The Ghost Goes West

Britain 1935. 85 min., b/w. (d) René Clair (sp) Robert E. Sherwood and Geoffrey Kerr from the story "Sir Tristram Goes West" by Eric Keown (ph) Jack Cardiff (m) Misha Spoliansky (art) Vincent Korda (c) Robert Donat, Jean Parker, Eugene Pallette, Elsa Lanchester. (MAC, MOG)

Produced for Alexander Korda's London Films, this first film made outside of France by René Clair (LE MILLION) is a fanciful and amusing tale. Entertaining on any level, it has for older children the bonus of international satire on human foibles.

A ghost (Robert Donat) haunts the castle of an impoverished Scottish laird (Donat). A lovely visitor (Jean Parker), daughter of an American millionaire (Eugene Pallette), meets the ghost on the battlements and persuades her father to buy the castle. Papa proceeds to move it, stone by stone, and complete with ghost, to Florida. At the housewarming there, a black American band dressed in kilts plays jazzed-up Scottish tunes. "A satiric fantasy notable for the qualities of grace, charm, and imaginative wit that have long distinguished its director's work," said *Time* in 1936.

Girl Shy*

Harold Lloyd Corp./Pathé 1924. 65 min., b/w. (d) Fred Newmeyer, Sam Taylor (sp) Sam Taylor, Ted Wilde, Tim Whelan (ph) Walter Lundin (c) Harold Lloyd, Jobyna Ralston, Richard Daniels, Carleton Griffin. Silent with music and sound effects. (PAR)

One of the longest, best constructed, and most sustained chase sequences in the movies—copied in THE BANK DICK, turning up in THE GRADUATE—makes this a wild and delightful comic invention.

Harold is an extremely shy, bashful stutterer from the country who gains courage when his girl (Jobyna Ralston) is about to marry a fortune hunter. He races to save her—on a motorcyle plowing through an open trench full of ditch diggers, in a bootleggers' car, in a truck on a narrow mountain road, on a horse, on a fire engine, in an empty trolley which he drives through teeming streets. Finally, the purloined vehicles get him to the church on time. He is stuttering so badly by now that all he can do to interrupt the minister's "I now pronounce you—" is to run off with the girl over his shoulder, like Dustin Hoffman in THE GRADUATE. Lloyd is said to have had qualms about the stutter of his character. However, audience reactions indicate that most people are not offended; the chase is the thing here.

The Glass Slipper*

MGM 1955. 94 min., col. (d) Charles Walters (sp) Helen Deutsch (m) Bronislau Kaper (chor) Roland Petit (c) Leslie Caron, Michael Wilding, Keenan Wynn, Estelle Winwood, Elsa Lanchester, Barry Jones, Amanda Blake, the Ballet de Paris (voice) Walter Pidgeon. (FNC)

Kids haven't met the real Cinderella until they've seen this pleasant musical, which keeps its tongue in cheek without slighting the fantasy of the popular story. As Walter Pidgeon explains in the narration, Cinderella was suffering from a feeling of rejection until the Prince turned up. (At the beginning he is disguised as the son of the palace cook.) Estelle Winwood, a zany old lady who comes out of the forest, is a more interesting Fairy Godmother than most kids have run across. Leslie Caron *dances* Cinderella, convincing as both a little drudge and a transformed beauty. The fantasy ballets in which she performs with the Ballet de Paris, under the direction of Roland Petit, include the "Son of the Cook Ballet" and "Take My Love."

AROUND THE WORLD IN 80 DAYS (United Artists)

ADVENTURES OF ROBIN HOOD (Warner Bros.)

ARSENIC AND OLD LACE (Warner Bros.)

THE BIG STORE (MGM)

THE BLACK STALLION (United Artists)

THE CHILDREN OF THEATRE STREET (Libra Films)

THE CIRCUS (United Artists)

THE COURT JESTER (Paramount Pictures)

DAVID COPPERFIELD (MGM)

ELEPHANT BOY (United Artists)

FANTASTIC VOYAGE (20th Century-Fox)

FEAR STRIKES OUT (Paramount Pictures)

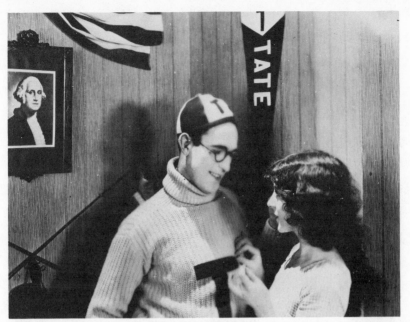

THE FRESHMAN (Pathe-Harold Lloyd Corporation)

THE GENERAL (MGM)

The Gold Rush*

United Artists 1925. 81 min., b/w. (d)(sp) Charles Chaplin (ph) Rollie Totheroh and Jack Wilson (c) Charles Chaplin, Mack Swain, Tom Murray, Georgia Hale, Henry Bergman. Silent. Rereleased with music and effects added in 1942. (GEN)

"Of all comedians [Chaplin] worked most deeply and most shrewdly within a realization of what a human being is, and is up against," James Agee wrote. "The finest pantomime, the deepest emotion, the richest and most poignant poetry were in Chaplin's work." For many people, THE GOLD RUSH is their favorite Chaplin, and he himself said this was the film he wanted to be remembered by. Here he is the Lone Prospector in the Klondike, sharing a shack and hard times with Big Jim McKay (Mark Swain) and falling in love with Georgia, the dancehall queen.

Many moments in the fim, drawn out of Alaskan privations or the disappointments of a lover, are glorious humor and inspired fantasy. The classic New Year's Eve dinner sequence with the dance of the rolls, the scene of the prospector's shack teetering on the edge of the cliff, the pantomime of starving Charlie salting and eating a candle or making a Thanksgiving Day feast of a boiled shoe (twirling the laces as if they were spaghetti), the moment in hunger-crazed Jim's delirium when he mistakes Charlie for a tasty fowl—well, George Bernard Shaw *did* call Charlie the only genius the movies had developed.

Gone With the Wind

MGM 1939. 219 min., col. (prod) David O. Selznick (d) Victor Fleming (sp) Sidney Howard from Margaret Mitchell's novel (ph) Ernest Haller, Ray Rennahan (m) Max Steiner (des) William Cameron Menzies (art) Lyle Wheeler (c) Clark Gable, Vivien Leigh, Leslie Howard, Olivia de Havilland, Hattie McDaniel, Thomas Mitchell, Barbara O'Neill, Victor Jory, Evelyn Keyes, Ann Rutherford, Butterfly McQueen, Carroll Nye, Laura Hope Crews, Harry Davenport, Jane Darwell, Ona Munson, Isabel Jewell. (FNC)

Our favorite young history teacher takes his seventh and eighth graders to see GWTW every time it comes around in term time. He reports that they continue to find it one of the movies of their lifetime. The strong narrative of war and love, the romance and nostalgia—men in uniform dancing with belles in hoopskirts in square-pillared mansions—the shattering scenes of the burning of Atlanta and the postwar debacle attract the young as much as they have attracted millions of adults all over the world since its release.

At Tara we meet the legends and the characters of Margaret Mitchell's novel. At Twelve Oaks, at Atlanta, in Georgia after Sherman and during the Reconstruction, the canvas is vast but the figures are well drawn. The real director of GWTW was its producer, David O. Selznick, who not only supervised Victor Fleming, after firing George Cukor and Sam Wood, but rewrote several versions of the dialog. It is still Margaret Mitchell's story. Despite the nine Academy Awards (out of a total of twenty-one possibles), it's the original story that counts for most. After one has taken the youngsters to enjoy GWTW as a story, time enough for flack and feedback. For of course it is not all history, children.

Grandma's Boy*

Hal Roach/Pathé 1922. 83 min., b/w. (d) Fred Newmeyer (sp) Hal Roach, Harold Lloyd, Sam Taylor, Jean Havez, Thomas J. Crizer (ph) Walter Lundin (c) Harold Lloyd, Mildred Davis, Anna Townsend, Charles Stevenson, Noah Young, Dick Sutherland. Silent with music and sound effects. (PAR)

Lloyd's favorite film, about which he said to Hal Roach, "This has got heart"; it helped make him the leading male box-office star of the 1920s.

He is a young man who thinks of himself as a coward. His grandmother tells him a story of his grandfather, a coward who was inspired to heroic deeds in the Civil War by carrying a witch's lucky charm. When grandma gives him the charm, he leads a posse to capture the town bully. Then he learns that the charm is only an old umbrella handle; it was not the talisman but his own courage that worked. The flashback in which we find Lloyd playing grandpa (in square horn-rims to suggest the Civil War period) contains a series of amusing gags that rise logically out of the story and the character. (With GRANDMA'S BOY is Lloyd's first feature film, the four-reel A SAILOR-MADE MAN, 1921, rich in outrageous comic adventure.)

The Great Dictator

United Artists 1940. 128 min., b/w. (prod)(d)(sp) Charles Chaplin (ph) Karl Struss, Roland Totheroh (m) Meredith Willson (c) Charles Chap-

lin, Jack Oakie, Paulette Goddard, Reginald Gardiner, Henry Daniell,
Billy Gilbert, Chester Conklin, Hank Mann, Bernard Gorcey. (PAR)

Chaplin's devastating caricature of Hitler created a sensation with
audiences in 1940, when it was one of the few pre–Pearl Harbor
American films to attack German fascism. It is still one of his most
popular films, chiefly because of Chaplin's performances in the
double role of a Jewish barber and Adenoid Hynkel, dictator of
Tomania. Hynkel is "a combination of Napoleon and Nijinsky.
Playing the dictator and myself, one a tragic figure the other a
comic, I can no longer distinguish one from the other," Chaplin
said. His first all-dialog film, THE GREAT DICTATOR has a wonderful
cast, with Jack Oakie outstanding as Benzini Napaloni, dictator
of Bacteria, and Billy Gilbert as Herring, one of Hynkel's lieutenants.

Among the most famous scenes: Hynkel's speech in guttural
German-English doubletalk with the microphones bending under
the onslaught; Hynkel's ballet with the globe of the world; the
barber shaving a man to the tune of a Brahms Hungarian Dance;
the cream-cake battle between Hynkel and Napaloni. The barber's
six-minute speech at the end ("You the people have the power
to make this life free and beautiful. . . .Let us fight for a new
world. . .that will give youth a future and old age a security.")
expresses Chaplin's own deep feelings. Critics felt the speech was
banal, but young audiences have always responded to its sincerity.

Great Expectations

Britain 1946. 118 min., b/w. (d) David Lean (sp) David Lean and Ronald
Neame from the novel by Charles Dickens (c) John Mills, Alec Guin-
ness, Valerie Hobson, Jean Simmons, Martita Hunt, Francis L. Sul-
livan, Finlay Currie, Torin Thatcher, Bernard Miles, Freda Jackson,
Anthony Wager. (GEN)

Not to be confused with the 1934 Hollywood version starring
Henry Hull and Jane Wyatt, David Lean's film is technically brilliant. The opening sequence, with young Pip and Magwitch in the
graveyard on the marshes, is required viewing in cinema courses
for its editing, composition of framing shots, and symbolism. Lean
has said that he tried to make everything larger than life, as it was
in the boy's imagination and as it always is in Dickens. In such
scenes as Pip's meeting the child Estella at Miss Havisham's, he
certainly has succeeded.

All of the first part, Pip's childhood, takes us inside the time,
the place, and the character, but the second part of the film does

not satisfy those who know the original. The key character of Orlick is missing, the major themes of self-deception and self-discovery are displaced by the love story, and the ending is more sentimental than either of the two provided by Dickens. Yet in the world of Pip's childhood, Lean can do no wrong, and few films can match the first half hour of this one. It is not difficult, either, to see why the cinematographer, Guy Green, and the production designer, John Bryan, won Academy Awards.

The Great Race

Warners 1965. 158 min., col. (d) Blake Edwards (sp) Arthur Ross from a story by Blake Edwards and Arthur Ross (ph) Russell Harlan (m) Henry Mancini (c) Jack Lemmon, Tony Curtis, Natalie Wood, Peter Falk, Keenan Wynn, Arthur O'Connell, Vivian Vance, Dorothy Provine, Larry Storch, Ross Martin. (GEN)

"To Mr. Laurel and Mr. Hardy," runs the dedication by Blake Edwards, creator of THE PINK PANTHER series. "RACE," said Mr. Edwards, "is an accumulation of dozens of the great comedy clichés." But Mr. Laurel and Mr. Hardy never saw anything like the two thousand custard pies in this reenactment of their pie-throwing "Battle of the Century." On the same giant-size scale are the death-defying acts of Tony Curtis as The Great Leslie (in white); the dastardly deeds of Jack Lemmon as Professor Fate (in black); the distress of Natalie Wood as the damsel (in pink); the sequences in the barroom of the Old West, on the ice-floe in the Bering Strait, in the mythical kingdom of Carpania; the long parody of the novel *The Prisoner of Zenda.*

This is a Hall of Fame for every time-honored gag in the history of slapstick, with a few modish touches, for Mr. Edwards is also taking off on AROUND THE WORK IN 80 DAYS and THOSE MAGNIFICENT MEN IN THEIR FLYING MACHINES. The story is loosely hung around a mythical auto race in 1908 from New York to Paris, with two delightful turn-of-the-century automobiles, and enhanced by special sound effects by Tregoweth Brown, which won an Oscar. There are songs by Johnny Mercer and Henry Mancini—"The Sweetheart Tree," and "He Shouldn't-a, Hadn't-a, Oughtn't-a Swang on Me!" Very big, very broad, very entertaining for practically any kid.

The Greatest Show on Earth

Paramount 1952. 153 min., col. (prod)(d) Cecil B. DeMille (sp) Frederick M. Frank, Barre Lyndon, Theodore St. John (ph) George Barnes, J. Peverell Marley, Wallace Kelley (m) Victor Young (cost) Edith Head, Dorothy Jeakins (chor) Richard Barstow (c) Betty Hutton, Cornel Wilde, Charlton Heston, Dorothy Lamour, Gloria Grahame, James Stewart, Emmett Kelly. (FNC)

The only DeMille to win an Academy Award as best picture, this mammoth tribute to the Big Top owes more to the magic of circus showmanship than to Hollywood. But That's Entertainment. An overloaded smorgasbord table of a movie, it has enough circus flavors to satisfy one's taste.

Filmed at Ringling Brothers–Barnum & Bailey headquarters at Sarasota, Florida, it profits from documentarylike details. It's absorbing to watch the circus settling into winter quarters. And who will cavil at watching Betty Hutton emote, when there's Emmett Kelly to come? The clown incarnate is worth the price of admission. There's even a train wreck for youngsters who like disaster movies. John Ringling North, playing himself, wrote one of the songs, along with Ned Washington, John Murray Anderson, and Ray Goetz.

Gunga Din

RKO 1939. 129 min., b/w. (prod) (d) George Stevens (sp) Joel Sayre and Fred Guiol from a story by Ben Hecht and Charles MacArthur based on a poem by Rudyard Kipling (ph) Joseph H. August (m) Alfred Newman (c) Cary Grant, Victor McLaglen, Douglas Fairbanks, Jr., Sam Jaffe, Eduardo Ciannelli, Joan Fontaine, Montagu Love, Robert Coote, Cecil Kellaway. (FNC)

Indian curry hash, with ingredients not to be believed, but an extremely satisfying dish. "One of the most enjoyable nonsense-adventure movies of all time," said Pauline Kael, "full of hokum and heroism and high spirits." Presumably "inspired" by Rudyard Kipling's barrackroom ballad, it owes its charm more to its scriptwriters—Hecht and MacArthur and even (we're told) William Faulkner, an uncredited aide.

The characters are played absolutely straight: Douglas Fairbanks, Jr., as the essence of gentlemanly dash; Cary Grant as the essence of tongue-in-cheek heroism; Victor MacLaglen as the essence of Kipling's MacChesney; Eduardo Ciannelli as the essence of something quite mad named Gura; and Sam Jaffe as the essence of native loyalty, Gunga Din. Mix together with thug

chieftains, a lady named Emmy, and the Charge of the Sepoy
Lancers and you have this wonderful concoction. The *New York
Times* observed thoughtfully that GUNGA DIN is not really an adult
film. Take it away, kids.

Gus*

*Disney 1976. 96 min., col. (d) Vincent McEveety (sp) Arthur Alsberg
and Don Nelson from a story by Ted Key (ph) Frank Phillips (c) Ed
Asner, Don Knotts, Gary Grimes, Tom Bosley, Tim Conway, Liberty
Williams. (GEN)*

The California Atoms are the kind of football team whose pass
receiver looks the other way when the ball finally arrives. It's all
too much for Coach Don Knotts. Then apoplectic owner Ed Asner
hires a Yugoslav mule named Gus and his handler. Gus unerringly
kicks 100-yard field goals that take the Atoms to the Superbowl.
When an attempt is made, by a disgruntled bettor against the
Atoms, to subvert and kidnap Gus, it comes to nothing. (The con
men are Tim Conway and Tom Bosley.) "A far better than average
Disney comedy. . . .Lively, fast-moving, and highly recommended for children" (*Film & Broadcasting Review*).

The Happiest Days of Your Life

*Britain 1950. 81 min., b/w. (d) Frank Launder (sp) John Dighton and
Frank Launder from John Dighton's play (c) Alastair Sim, Margaret
Rutherford, Joyce Grenfell. (MAC)*

School, as every schoolboy knows, is a farce. But real school days
were never like this. They weren't written by John Dighton (KIND
HEARTS AND CORONETS), produced by Frank Launder and Sidney
Gilliat (the three "St. Trinian's" films), or supervised by Headmaster Alastair Sim, Headmistress Margaret Rutherford, and
Games Mistress Joyce Grenfell. Their planned pandemonium is
hilarious. The situation is one of those possible in any educational
bureaucracy. In England during World War II, a period when most
adults took a very dim view of coeducation, the Ministry of Education, in error, assigns a girls' school, St. Swithin's, to share
accommodations with a boys' school, Nutbourne. The facts of
coeducation have to be hidden when both sets of parents and
trustees descend together on Nutbourne. Since the two student
bodies do not share the faculties' fears, the stratagems are joyous
as well as frenzied and full of surprise.

This is a very British movie, but its broad caricatures of teachers and school programs are universal. A civilized farce with some very witty lines, for older children.

A Hard Day's Night

Britain 1964. 85 min., b/w. (d) Richard Lester (sp) Alun Owen (ph) Gilbert Taylor (m) John Lennon and Paul McCartney (c) The Beatles, Wilfrid Brambell, Victor Spinetti, Kenneth Haigh, Anna Quayle. (UAS)

"They have made a film, not an illustrated juke box," said Arthur Knight about the Beatles' first movie. "They" are director Richard Lester (HELP!, THE KNACK); scriptwriter Alun Owen, television's gift to the British theater; and John, Paul, George, and Ringo at the height of Beatlemania.

The film is a semi-documentary of a day in the life of the Beatles when they were trying to duck the result of being a social phenomenon, but it's not all that serious. A knockabout comedy of great charm and lighthearted improvisation, it is served up with fast cutting, visual gags, absurdist dialog. ("What do you call that hairdo?"——"Arthur.") and a decided Marx Brothers flavor. A lot of it is highly imaginative, like their dance on a heliport square, and a lot of it is good moviemaking, like their game in the field outside the television studio and Ringo's walk around London, shot with a hand-held camera. "It was of its period, of the pop explosion," Lester says, and certainly nothing that's come out of the pop explosion has more charisma.

Not only for young Beatle-maniacs but for everyone who enjoys free-association camera style.

The Harlem Globetrotters*

Columbia 1951. 80 min., b/w. (d) Phil Brown (c) Thomas Gomez, Dorothy Dandridge, and the Original Harlem Globetrotters. (GEN)

Here are the famous black basketball players who have won fans all over the world for their fancy ball-handling and razzle-dazzle clowning on the court. "Sweetwater" Clifton, "Goose" Tatum, Marques Haynes, and the other members of the Original Harlem Globetrotters team are great performers, in sports and in high jinks. The games are connected by an unobtrusive, well-handled story about a college student who leaves chemistry research to make money in pro basketball and learns sportsmanship from the Trotters.

Heidi*

NBC-TV 1968. 120 min., col. (d) Delbert Mann (sp) Earl Hamner from Johanna Spyri's novel (c) Maximilian Schell, Jean Simmons, Michael Redgrave, Walter Slezak, Jennifer Edwards, Peter Van Eyck, John Moulder Brown, Zuleika Robson. (TV)

If your TV set was tuned to the football game that Sunday in November 1968 when HEIDI preempted it, you may have been one of the thousands who gave NBC a hard time. But in the audience of 70 million, lovers of the story knew that this was the HEIDI of a lifetime, the best film adaptation ever made. Klaus Von Rautenfeld's location shots of the Swiss Alps and Germany, Delbert Mann's directing, Jennifer Edwards's Heidi, are tops. This little girl doesn't melt into fudge, and her bedroom fight with Klara (Zuleika Robson) has more spark than Shirley Temple's in 1936. No other Heidi, of course, has had Maximilian Schell for her uncle or Sir Michael Redgrave for her grandfather.

Heidi*

Warners/7 Arts 1968. 95 min., col. (d) Werner Jacobs (sp) Richard Schweizer from Johanna Spyri's novel (c) Eva Maria Singhammer, Gustav Knuth, Ernst Schroder, Margaret Trooger. Dubbed version. (BUD, MAC, SWA, WCF)

Another good adaptation, also filmed in color in the Swiss Alps. The cinematography is excellent, and the demure if not pretty little Heidi (Eva Maria Singhammer) is just as forlorn and homesick as ever when she is transported to Frankfort, although the city has been updated. This is the only change; the story is still nineteenth century.

Heidi and Peter*

Switzerland 1955. 89 min., col. (prod) Lazar Wechsler (d) Franz Schnyder (sp) Richard Schweizer from the novel Heidi Makes Use of What She Has Learned (ph) Emil Berna (c) Elsbeth Sigmund, Heinrich Gretler, Thomas Klamath. Dubbed version. (MAC)

A sequel to HEIDI, with new adventures, when Klara comes from Frankfort to visit Heidi and Peter in their mountain home.

Help!

United Artists 1965. 90 min., col. (d) Richard Lester (sp) Marc Behm and Charles Wood from a story by Marc Behm (ph) David Watkins (m) John Lennon and Paul McCartney (c) The Beatles, Victor Spinetti, Leo McKern, Bruce Lacey, Eleanor Bron. (UAS)

The characters are the same, and there are a few slanting references to the first Beatles movie, but this sequel to A HARD DAY'S NIGHT is mostly new. The title song, "When I was young, oh so much younger than today," suggests the mood for a story of the "Oriental menace," of a Caliph and his henchmen trying to steal Ringo's sacrificial Indian ring—a story for a simpler day, but told with some fine new tricks of our time.

Director Richard Lester (THE RUNNING, JUMPING AND STANDING STILL FILM; THE KNACK) is famous for film virtuosity. This high-caloric feast for Beatles fans is served up with visual spice, with color and op-art techniques (particularly the cartoon strip). From the first titles to the sequences in the Alps and the Bahamas, it teases and pleases the eye. One of the best descriptions of HELP!—its combination of derivative adventure cartoon-strip material and innovative film style—comes from Richard Lester himself: "It's Wilkie Collins' *The Moonstone* drawn by Jasper Johns."

Henry V

Britain 1944. 137 min., col. (prod)(d) Laurence Olivier (sp) Edited by Alan Dent from the text of Shakespeare's play (ph) Robert Krasker (m) William Walton (art) Paul Sheriff (cost) Roger Furse (ed) Reginald Beck (c) Laurence Olivier, Robert Newton, Leslie Banks, Renée Asherson, Leo Genn, Max Adrian, Felix Aylmer, Esmond Knight. (GEN)

Shakespeare's historical drama of Henry Plantagenet's bid for the throne of France, with its famous patriotic affirmation of the spirit of "This England," is "a stunningly brilliant and intriguing screen spectacle" (*The New York Times*), full of imagination and excitement, whether you care about Plantagenets or not.

(HENRY V, in addition to being the first Shakespeare film in color, and the first to treat the soliloquy as thought, heard but not visibly spoken, was also the first to win box-office popularity to match the critical acclaim.)

It opens with an aerial shot which carries us into sixteenth-century London, where we see the play performed in the Globe Theatre. Then the Chorus leads us away into another imaginative flight; we are in the modern color film. Paul Sheriff's sets, with their color, "flat" quality, and perspective, might be medieval paintings, but such scenes as the Battle of Agincourt and the wooing in the French court come vibrantly to life. The editing and rhythms of the film are superb.

As Henry, Olivier is simply the best in a very fine cast. (He won the award of the New York Film Critics as best actor of the year.)

High Noon

United Artists 1952. 85 min., b/w (d) Fred Zinnemann (sp) Carl Fore-man from the story "The Tin Star" by John W. Cunningham (m) Dmitri Tiomkin (ed) Elmo Williams and Harry Gerstad (c) Gary Cooper, Grace Kelly, Lloyd Bridges, Katy Jurado, Thomas Mitchell. (GEN)

Many Westerns have tried to copy the moral and the formula of this classic, but they haven't been directed by Fred Zinnemann or written by Carl Foreman.

In a small town in 1870, the ex-marshal, just married, learns that an outlaw whom he had sent to prison is now free and returning on the noon train for revenge. Will the marshal take on a one-sided duel when no one in town will lend him a hand? The theme song says: *I do not know what fate awaits me./I only know I must be brave./And I must face a man who hates me/Or lie a coward in my grave.*

The song (sung by Tex Ritter) is one of many things in the movie which work. Most effective is the editing of Elmo Williams and Harry Gerstad. The camera builds toward the climax at noon—to the clock, down the train tracks, back to the man making a coffin.

The editors and Gary Cooper won Oscars, as did Dmitri Tiomkin for the score and for the song "High Noon" (lyrics by Ned Washington). Zinnemann was voted best director of the year by the New York Film Critics, who also named HIGH NOON the best picture. Kids not only enjoy humming "Do not forsake me" and feeling the suspense mount, but they also understand the theme as a challenge to individual conscience.

A Hole in the Head

United Artists 1959. 120 min., col. (d) Frank Capra (sp) Arnold Schul-man from his TV play adapted from his story "The Heart Is a Forgotten Hotel" (ph) William H. Daniels (m) Nelson Riddle; songs by Sammy Cahn and James Van Heusen (c) Frank Sinatra, Eddie Hodges, Edward

G. *Robinson, Eleanor Parker, Carolyn Jones, Thelma Ritter, Keenan Wynn, Joi Lansing, George De Witt. (UAS)*

Who could love Tony Manetta (Frank Sinatra), the grandstanding, irresponsible owner of a third-rate Miami Beach hotel who has pipe dreams of being a big-time promoter? Only his ten-year-old son, Ally (Eddie Hodges), who plays gin rummy with him at 4:00 A.M. and gives him unswerving devotion. "Chiseler, cheap conniver—but that's pop," says Ally, and when his good uncle and aunt (Edward G. Robinson and Thelma Ritter) urge him to go back to New York with them and be properly cared for, you know Ally will never go, even though his father tells him he doesn't want him hanging around anymore.

Frank Capra has made a believable, moving love story about Tony and his son. The cast is excellent; one of the songs, "High Hopes," won an Oscar; and there's even a reassuring ending. Tony is on the verge of matrimony with a most attractive widow (Eleanor Parker), who has appeal not only for father and son but for everyone worried about Ally's future; you just know she will do right by the growing boy.

The movie will please youngsters not only because of its quality as entertainment but because of its confirmation of one of their secret beliefs—that living with a nonconformist adult beats ordinary family living every time.

Hot Lead and Cold Feet

Disney 1978. 90 min., col. (d) Robert Butler (sp) Joe McEveety, Arthur Alsberg, Don Nelson, based on a story by Rad Piffath (ph) Frank Phillips (m) Buddy Baker (c) Jim Dale, Karen Valentine, Don Knotts, Jack Elam, Darren McGavin, Debbie Lytton, Michael Sharrett. (FNC)

Former child actor Kevin Corcoran, associate producer of this slapstick saga of the sagebrush, must have felt right at home. Despite its parody of spaghetti westerns, it's really a Disney family entertainment.

British stage comic Jim Dale is the prime mover in the spoof. All Dale is divided into three parts. He plays not only old Jasper Bloodshy, founder of the town named in his honor, but Jasper's twin sons: outlaw Wild Billy, terror of Bloodshy, and long-lost brother Eli. Reared in England, Eli is a Salvation Army preacher who arrives with two young orphan wards under his gentle wing to collect his share of the family inheritance. Old Jasper, who fell off a cliff, is thought to be dead; actually he's sitting back and watching the twins race to carry out the last will and testament.

And race they do—in steam engines, wagons, and canoes, over mountains and across gorges. Somewhere along the crowded story line are Karen Valentine as the schoolmarm and Don Knotts and Jack Elam, as the gunshy sheriff and the gun-weary outlaw whose shootouts always backfire.

All this is played against some nice scenery near Bend, Oregon, and in Deschutes National Forest.

Houdini

Paramount 1953. 106 min., col. (prod) George Pal (d) George Marshall (sp) Philip Yordan from a book by Harold Kellock (c) Tony Curtis, Janet Leigh, Torin Thatcher, Angela Clarke, Sig Ruman. (FNC)

"Magic is all I know," said its most legendary practitioner. All that youngsters need to know about this film of Houdini's life is that it re-creates his feats of escape and legerdemain; his personal dramas and obsessive personality are not its strong point.

From his beginning as Bruto the Wild Man in a carnival to his death, here is the Houdini saga. He escapes from a straitjacket while suspended head down from a Manhattan rooftop; he breaks out of a presumably secure London jail. The most remarkable sequence is the one of his immersion in the freezing waters of the Detroit River while incarcerated in a steel casket. Before director George Marshall cuts to the frame showing us that Houdini has located the hole in the ice that leads to the surface, we are as breathless as the original audience.

Houdini's belief in the supernatural and his hope that he might communicate with his mother after her death are part of the story, which (fortunately for the child audience) omits some of the more lurid details of his life featured in a 1978 television film about him.

How Green Was My Valley

Fox 1941. 118 min., b/w (d) John Ford (sp) Philip Dunne from the novel by Richard Llewellyn (ph) Arthur Miller (c) Walter Pidgeon, Maureen O'Hara, Donald Crisp, Anna Lee, Roddy McDowall, John Loder, Sara Allgood, Barry Fitzgerald, Patrick Knowles, The Welsh Singers, Arthur Shields, Rhys Williams, Ethel Griffies. (FNC)

"I'm the youngest of thirteen—I was a fresh young kid at the table," John Ford told an interviewer. Perhaps that is why he shows so much loving comprehension of the young boy (Roddy McDowall) growing up in a large family in a Welsh mining town.

Boyhood, unrequited love, social change, and conflict between generations are beautifully realized in this moving film. It won Ford his fourth award from the New York Film Critics. "You don't compose a film on the set," Ford has said. "You put a predesigned composition on film. It is wrong to liken a director to an author. He is more like an architect." In this film, which has a special place for many Ford admirers, every detail is integrated into the whole to make a harmony of style and feeling.

Academy Awards went to Arthur Miller for his nostalgic, romantic photography, to Richard Day and Nathan Juran for art direction, to Ford for direction, to the film as best picture of the year, and to Donald Crisp for a memorable performance as the Welsh father of another day.

I Will Fight No More Forever

ABC-TV 1974. 106 min., col. (prod) Stan Margulies for David Wolper/ Xerox (d) Richard T. Effron (sp) Jeb Rosebrook, Theodore Strauss (ph) Jorge Stahl (m) Gerald Fried (c) James Whitmore, Sam Elliott, Ned Pomeray. (BUD, FNC, MAC)

Winner of the 1977 American Film Festival Blue Ribbon, this edited version of the original television production is a dramatization of an important event in our history, the 1877 war of General Oliver Otis Howard against a band of Nez Perce Indians led by Chief Joseph.

"The Story of Chief Joseph," the film's subtitle, indicates its focus. He refused to give up his people's tribal lands in Oregon's Wallawalla Valley, as provided for by a treaty with the U.S. Government.

As General Howard, James Whitmore reflects the inner conflicts of the man whose respect for Chief Joseph is in conflict with his army command. The anguish of two combatants, each acting in good faith, in a situation of cultural clashes and opposed necessities, suggests modern parallels.

With the final surrender of the Nez Perces, the military conquest of the native Americans was practically complete. The postscript to I WILL FIGHT NO MORE FOREVER, taken from one of Chief Joseph's speeches, should leave something with young people: "Treat all men alike. Give them all the same law. Give them all an even chance to live and grow. All men were made by the Great Spirit Chief. They are all brothers."

Ichabod and Mr. Toad*

RKO 1949. 68 min., col. animation (d) Jack Kinney, James Algar, Clyde Geronimi, based on The Wind in the Willows by Kenneth Grahame and "The Legend of Sleepy Hollow" by Washington Irving (m) Al Teeter (narr) Bing Crosby, Basil Rathbone (voices) Eric Blore, Pat O'Malley, Claud Allister, John Ployardt, Collin Campbell, Campbell Grant, Ollie Wallace. (GEN)

In its two sequences, Kenneth Grahame's The Wind in the Willows (narrated by Basil Rathbone) and "The Legend of Sleepy Hollow" (narrated by Bing Crosby), this animated feature has some of the finest work the Disney studio has ever done. *Time* called it a "lighthearted, fast-moving romp" that "inspired some of Disney's most inventive draftsmanship and satire."

In the sequence based on *The Wind in the Willows*, each animal has delightful individual traits, with the voice of Eric Blore a standout as J. Thaddeus Toad, Toad of Toad's Hall. In one of the cartoon's chase sequences, there is more than a suggestion of Keystone Kops. In the second section of the film, about Ichabod and the Headless Horseman, Ub Iwerks's multiplane camera is used to good effect in the ride through Sleepy Hollow; the details of animation create depth and lighting similar to those in live-action films.

There is music, like Brom Bones's song, "Don't try to figure out a plan: You can't reason with a Headless Man," an exciting trial scene (with the prosecuting attorney often seen as just a flowing cape, and Mr. Toad as his own counsel striking poses as a parody British barrister), and lots more fun. In reissue and in non-theatrical release, a great favorite, especially with the under-tens.

The Incredible Shrinking Man

Universal 1957. 94 min., b/w. (d) Jack Arnold (sp) Richard Matheson from his novel The Shrinking Man (c) Grant Williams, Randy Stuart, April Kent. (UNI, SWA, TWY)

At one point in his gradual disintegration, the "shrinking man" (Scott Carey) says, "Easy enough to talk of soul and spirit and essential worth, but not when you're three feet tall." Eventually, he is only six inches tall, reduced to living in a doll's house, and afraid his cat will break in.

Kids are fascinated by the entire process. Technically and imaginatively, this is one of the most effective science-fiction mov-

ies. Its skillful direction by Jack Arnold, who had previously made
IT CAME FROM OUTER SPACE and CREATURE FROM THE BLACK LAGOON,
and the suspenseful screenplay by Richard Matheson, who went
on to write some of Roger Corman's best Poe-derived thrillers,
are superior in the field. There are many ingenious special effects
and well-visualized battles between Scott and creatures of his
once-familiar environment.

Indian Paint*

*Eagle/American 1966. 91 min., col. (prod) Gene Goree (d)(sp) Norman
Foster from the story by Glenn Balchi (c) Johnny Crawford, Jay Sil-
verheels, Robert Crawford, Jr. (GEN)*

It is long before the coming of the white man, in a small Indian
tribe of the far West. The fifteen-year-old son of the chief falls in
love with a "painted" colt, the skittish offspring of the tribe's
finest mare, sired by the leader of a herd of wild horses, a proud
white stallion. The story centers around the boy's struggle to raise
the pony. When they become separated from the tribe for a long
time in the course of their adventures, they mature together; the
boy who returns to the tribe is a man and a warrior.

The difference between INDIAN PAINT and other boy-horse films
is that it is a fine picture of Indian life. Its feeling of authenticity
is the achievement of Norman Foster, who also directed the excellent NAVAJO (1952), and Glenn Balchi, who wrote the story.

Intruder in the Dust

*MGM 1949. 87 min., b/w. (d) Clarence Brown (sp) Ben Maddow from
the novel by William Faulkner (ph) Robert Surtees (c) David Brian,
Claude Jarman, Jr., Juano Hernandez, Porter Hall, Elizabeth Patterson, Will Geer. (FNC)*

Ralph Ellison, the distinguished black novelist, said of this movie,
"Not only have we been watching the consciousness of a young
Southerner grow through the stages of a superb mystery drama,
we have participated in a process by which the role of Negroes
in American life has been given what, for the movies, is a startling
new definition."

Blacks could identify, Ellison believed, with the character Lucas
Beauchamp (magnificently played by Juano Hernandez, who won
two European festival awards); he refused to act the way Southern
blacks were expected to. Many white adolescents can identify

with Chick Mallison, a twelve-year-old who has been indroctri-
nated in a community code governing race relations but rejects
it and saves an innocent black man from being lynched.

Faulkner liked Ben Maddow's screenplay and Clarence Brown's
direction; this is the best movie from his work. It is full of suspense and excitement; the men and the milieu are alive. The very
able photographer Robert Surtees (THE GRADUATE) shot the film
in Oxford, Mississippi, with the inhabitants playing in bit parts
and crowd scenes.

"If it had been produced in Europe," said critic Pauline Kael,
"it would probably be widely acclaimed among American students of the film as a subtle, sensitive neo-realistic work. . . .Melo-
drama, yes, but melodrama that serves as a framework for an
ironic study of the dignity of man."

The Invisible Man

*Universal 1933. 72 min., b/w. (d) James Whale (sp) R. C. Sherriff and
Philip Wylie from the novel by H. G. Wells (ph) Arthur Edeson and
John Mescal (c) Claude Rains, Gloria Stuart, William Harrigan, Henry
Travers. (UNI, SWA)*

Boris Karloff must have regretted turning down this part. In his
screen debut, Claude Rains is swathed in bandages or invisible,
except for half a minute near the end, but he scores on his voice
alone. He gets a lot of help, of course.

The H. G. Wells story is an invitation to cinema magic, and
special-effects director John P. Fulton realizes every possibility.
When the megalomaniac chemist begins to terrorize an English
village by his ghastly appearance, or rather nonappearance, the
fantasy piles up entertainingly. The invisible man is a bubble in
the fog, his headless and footless pajamas crawl into bed by themselves, books leap off tables as he passes, and a policeman's pants
skip down a country road sans policeman. Still a lot of fun, and
a tribute to the durability of talent—Wells, Fulton, writers R. C.
Sherriff and Philip Wylie, and director James Whale of FRANKEN-
STEIN fame.

The Island at the Top of the World

*Disney 1973. 96 min., col. (d) Robert Stevenson (sp) John Whedon,
based on Ian Cameron's The Lost Ones (ph) Frank Phillips (m) Maurice Jarre (c) David Hartman, Donald Sinden, Jacques Marin, Mako,*

David Gwillim, Agneta Eckemyr, Gunnar Ohlund. (SWA, TWY, MAC, CWF)

Ian Cameron, author of *The Lost Ones*, on which this topnotch fantasy adventure is based, learned from Defoe, Swift, and Verne that the best fantasy is fact, or a tale plausibly related as fact. His manner and style have been well served by the Disney production, one of their best in years.

In 1907, Donald Ross, son of the explorer Sir Anthony Ross, disappears in the Arctic while searching for an island known in Norse myth as the graveyard of whales. Sir Anthony, with an archaeologist and the designer of the experimental airship *Hyperion*, sets out for the North Pole on a rescue mission. They have Donald's map, and his Eskimo guide. But they lose their ship and find themselves in a terrifying lost world of Vikings who have lived undisturbed for a thousand years. Before father and son are reunited and their party manages to escape from their captors (headed by the bloodthirsty Viking high priest, Godi), excitement builds on excitement.

Researchers and special-effects men have created a most realistic fantasy: the Vikings are exact to the last detail. Excellent casting, a well-paced script, and lovely photography of the Arctic scene make this good entertainment for children who like their spines tingled in style.

Island of the Blue Dolphins*

Universal 1964. 101 min., col. (d) James B. Clark (sp) Ted Sherdeman and Jane Klove from the novel by Scott O'Dell (ph) Leo Tover (c) Celia Kaye, Carlos Romero, George Kennedy, the Manchester and Kashai Tribes of the Poma Nation, and Junior. (GEN)

Scott O'Dell's Newbery Medal book tells of an Indian girl's adventure in solitude. Karana, a survivor of her tribe, lives on an island off California with her six-year-old brother and the dog Rontu which they have tamed. Junior, who plays the mongrel Rontu, has two distinctions: he is the son of the dog who played Old Yeller for Disney, and he was awarded a "Patsy," a Picture Animal Top Star of the Year award, for his performance as Rontu.

The primary stimulus to imagination here is visual; Leo Tover has captured with his color camera all the beauty of a remote sector of the California coast, the Anchor Bay country in the North. Against the background of rocks and surf, the young girl's Robinson Crusoe story is simple yet appealing.

It's a Gift

Paramount 1934. 71 min., b/w. (d) Norman McCleod (sp) Jack Cunningham from a story by W. C. Fields, based on J. P. McEvoy (c) W. C. Fields, Jean Rouverol, Julian Madison, Baby LeRoy, Charles Sellon, T. Roy Barnes, Kathleen Howard. (UNI)

When Junior wants another tomato sandwich at the picnic, "No!" says his mother, "Take one of your father's."

Father is Harold Bissonette (W. C. Fields), a grocer, who leads a "rabbity white-collar life," says James Agee. IT'S A GIFT might be a realistic family comedy of the thirties, except that it's pure Fields surrealism: Selling kumquats in the store to Jasper Fitchmueller; wrapping a steak, and a stick of chewing gum; store closed on account of molasses (due to Baby LeRoy); sleeping on the porch in a squeaky hammock to escape a wifely tirade; shaving. . . .Has anyone ever shaved as Fields shaves here?

This good-natured, long-suffering man sells the store and moves out to California, where he has bought an orange grove. He wins through to riches and a happy ending. Of course, there is that shower of tomatoes at the picnic. . . .And enough other gags, enough dialog crossfire, to make this "not only his best comedy. . .but surely among the finest comedy work from any period and any country" (William K. Everson), if you're a Fields fan.

It's A Wonderful Life

RKO 1946. 130 min., b/w. (prod)(d) Frank Capra (sp) Frances Goodrich, Albert Hackett, Frank Capra, Jo Swerling, based on the story "The Greatest Gift" by Philip Van Doren Stern. (ph) Joseph Walker, Joseph Biroc (m) Dmitri Tiomkin (c) James Stewart, Donna Reed, Lionel Barrymore, Thomas Mitchell, Henry Travers, Beulah Bondi, Ward Bond, Gloria Grahame, H.B. Warner, Samuel S. Hinds. (GEN)

From Philip Van Doren Stern's Christmas story for his friends, to Capra's favorite among his works, to its current status as one of the best-loved classics of American cinema, it's been a wonderful life for this warm movie.

"I thought it was the greatest film I'd ever made," says Capra in his autobiography, *The Name Above the Title.* Into the tale of a man who thought he was a failure, and who was given a chance to come back and see the world as it would have been had he not been born, Capra poured the essence of his style and his spirit. Here is his strongest affirmation of the power of the common man, of his conviction that love, goodness, and the need for others can be their own reward.

If youngsters had but one Capra to see, this is it—for its delightful angel winning his wings (Henry Travers), for its wealth of good performances of people in an American town in microcosm, for its turns of plot surprise. And at the end, if they are not cynics, they will share the jubilation felt by George Bailey (James Stewart) after his journey of self-discovery.

François Truffaut has said that Capra "was a navigator who knew how to steer his characters into the deepest dimensions of desperate human situations. . .before he reestablished a balance and brought off the miracle that let us leave the theater with a renewed confidence in life. . . .Capra was a kind of healer, that is, the enemy of 'official' medicine. This good doctor was also a great director" (The Films in My Life).

Ivanhoe

MGM 1952. 106 min., col. (d) Richard Thorpe (sp) Noel Langley and Aeneas MacKenzie from the novel by Sir Walter Scott (c) Robert Taylor, Elizabeth Taylor, Joan Fontaine, George Sanders, Finlay Currie, Emlyn Williams, Felix Aylmer, Norman Wooland, Guy Rolfe, Basil Sydney. (FNC)

In a compliment to Jane Austen, Sir Walter Scott once disparaged his own "big bow-wow style." Anyone could do it, he said. Not so—not in the movies, at any rate.

Few pictures have been so successful as this one in filling a large canvas with the excitement of pageantry, of sieges and the schemes of kings, while accurately presenting a social era and complex characters. Richard Thorpe did so well that he was immediately assigned to direct THE PRISONER OF ZENDA, KNIGHTS OF THE ROUND TABLE, THE STUDENT PRINCE, and QUENTIN DURWARD—none of which matched his "big bow-wow." The all-star cast (even a small role like Wamba is played by Emlyn Williams) satisfies every romantic expectation. The scenes, which were shot in England, are a series of twelfth-century illuminated manuscripts.

Since the movie has not only adventure but a glimpse of such medieval customs as beating a Jew and putting a Jewess on trial for witchcraft, it is a vivid introduction to the historical period.

"J.T."

CBS-TV 1969. 51 min., col. (prod) Barbara Schultz, Jackie Babbin (d) Robert M. Young (sp) Jane Wagner (m) Frank Lewin (c) Kevin Hooks, Jeanette Dubois, Theresa Merritt. (BUD, PYR, ROA, TWY)

Produced for a CBS-TV children's program, "J.T." continues to interest children of minority groups who empathize with the drama of the small black boy in Harlem. The feedback about the ending—is it too rosy and simple?—is illuminating.

Kevin Hooks is excellent as the boy, alone in his ghetto apartment while his mother is at work. He loudly plays his radio, stolen from a parked car under the noses of big boys. He plays it in bed, in the bathroom, in school, to drown out his troubles.

Then J.T. picks up a stray cat, starved and torn from the fray of the streets, and shelters it in his hideaway in an abandoned refrigerator. He feeds it by charging tuna to his mother's account at the grocery. The cat is killed; the radio is stolen. But in his grief, J.T. learns that some people really care—for instance, the Jewish grocer and his family. We're led to hope that J.T. will be less lonely soon: there's a warm grandma, an understanding teacher, and a new kitten.

Johnny Tremain

Disney 1957. 80 min., col. (d) Robert Stevenson (sp) Tom Blackburn from the novel by Esther Forbes (ph) Charles P. Boyle (m) George Bruns (c) Hal Stalmaster, Luana Patten, Jeff York, Sebastian Cabot, Dick Beymer, Walter Sande, Rusty Lane, Ralph Clanton. (FNC, TWY, MAC, SWA)

If you are not a stickler for absolute historical accuracy or flawless cinema style, JOHNNY TREMAIN is a good adaptation of a fine novel by Esther Forbes about a young boy caught up in the American Revolution. It re-creates authentically enough, and with more drama than the textbook pages, Paul Revere's ride, the Boston Tea Party, and decisive engagements at Concord and Lexington. Moreover, it's a lesson about involvement—it shows how young people were fired to take part in the fight for freedom.

In 1773, Johnny Tremain, who has ambitions to become a silversmith, suffers an injury which makes him unemployable. But he is welcomed as one of the Sons of Liberty. The young apprentice is one of the "Indians" at the Boston Tea Party who "seem to prefer principle to profit," as the British admiral in charge of the harbor comments.

Hal Stalmaster is a sympathetic figure as Johnny, in his personal as well as his patriotic trials. Many of the British and Tory "villains," as well as the colonists with mixed emotions about the revolution, are treated like people instead of stereotypes—perhaps because the director, Robert Stevenson, is British. There's a nice theme song, "The Liberty Tree."

Journey to the Center of the Earth

Fox 1959. 123 min., col. (d) Henry Levin (sp) Walter Reisch and Charles Brackett from the novel by Jules Verne (ph) Leo Tover (m) Bernard Herrmann (c) James Mason, Pat Boone, Arlene Dahl, Diane Baker, Thayer David. (FNC)

For Jules Verne fans who don't get claustrophobic while spelunking. The cave exploration here is undertaken by a Scottish geologist (James Mason), who leads an expedition through an Icelandic passageway in search of the center of the earth.

While Verne didn't have Pat Boone or Arlene Dahl in mind for this trip, the movie doesn't take them too seriously. The man who did such beautiful color photography for ISLAND OF THE BLUE DOLPHINS, Leo Tover, does some fascinating color photography for this cave of giant mushrooms, prehistoric lizards, floods, and tumbling rocks. There is a trip on a raft in an intraglobal sea, a victory over a mad Count, and the discovery of the lost city of Atlantis—a lot of what they like for kids who like this kind of thing.

Julius Caesar

MGM 1953. 121 min., b/w. (d) Joseph L. Mankiewicz, based on the play by William Shakespeare (c) Louis Calhern, Marlon Brando, James Mason, John Gielgud, Edmond O'Brien, Greer Garson, Deborah Kerr. (FNC)

There are Shakespeare movies for every taste. For pedants, there are those with the fewest missing lines. For *auteur* admirers, there are such *outré* samples of directorial whim as Orson Welles's CHIMES OF MIDNIGHT and Roman Polanski's MACBETH. Existentialists have Peter Brook's KING LEAR. People with cinematic as well as literary taste (our bias is showing) enjoy Laurence Olivier's HENRY V and RICHARD III and will give you an argument about his HAMLET.

For the kids there has never been any question; the only stills that are stolen from school bulletin boards are those from Franco Zeffirelli's ROMEO AND JULIET and JULIUS CAESAR with Marlon Brando. This is a sure bet; if they have never seen a Shakespeare movie before, start them with JULIUS CAESAR. The play is one they know well; Brando is a splendid as well as handsome Antony; the assassination is excitingly filmed; Gielgud is there to give them an idea of Shakespearean acting at its subtlest. (In addition to playing Cassius, he is rumored to have taken a hand in guiding some of the other actors.)

Altogether good entertainment and effective Shakespeare in the traditional style. An Oscar for black-and-white art direction was awarded to Cedric Gibbons and Edward Carfagno.

The Jungle Book*

United Artists 1942. 115 min., col. (prod) Alexander Korda (d) Zoltan Korda (art) Vincent Korda (sp) Lawrence Stallings from the stories by Rudyard Kipling (ph) Lee Garmes, W.H. Greene (m) Miklos Rozsa (c) Sabu, Joseph Calleia, John Qualen, Patricia O'Rourke, Rosemary De Camp, Frank Puglia. (GEN)

"Critics and children never seem to get enough of Kipling. Psychologists are forever picking at the locks of his personality, while kids pass effortlessly through to enter the artist's realm of enchantment and adventure" (*Time*, 1978).

In the dark-green, fierce jungle of this lush fantasy-adventure film created by the three Korda brothers, Sabu, as Mowgli, swings joyously from tree to tree. Few children will fail to envy him. To be a wild child raised by wolves, to have as friends Shere Khan the man-eating tiger, Bagheera the black panther, and Baloo the bear!

Stallings's screenplay has too many human beings in it, but the bizarre adventures are not missing: Mowgli protecting the vast treasure from the villagers; the python; the ruined city. The Technicolor is glamorous, the special effects still special, the final scene terrific. But Kipling and Mowgli-Sabu take the honors.

Kes

Britain 1970. 109 min., col. (d) Ken Loach (sp) Barry Hines, Ken Loach, and Tony Garnett from the novel A Kestrel for a Knave by Barry Hines (c) David Bradley, Colin Welland, Lynne Petrie, Freddie Fletcher. (UAS)

Many youngsters unhappy at home and at school turn to a pet for consolation, but few have the experience of the fifteen-year-old Yorkshire schoolboy in this British movie who captures and trains a kestrel (small hawk). With the encouragement of one of his more sympathetic teachers, he takes up the ancient sport of falconry. When his own brother kills the kestrel, his grief is reminiscent of the boy's in THE YEARLING.

Filmed in the Northern British mining town of Barnsley, home of many of its actors, KES is an absorbing combination of documentary and drama. Winner of the Grand Prize at Karlovy-Vary and a selection for The New York Film Festival in 1971, it is the second film of British television director Ken Loach (POOR COW), whose documentary dealing with the treatment of mental illness, WEDNESDAY'S CHILD, was selected for the 1972 New York Film Festival.

The Kid*

First National 1921. 60 min., b/w. (d)(sp)(m) Charles Chaplin (assoc d) Chuck Riesner (ph) Rollie Totheroh (c) Charles Chaplin, Jackie Coogan, Edna Purviance, Henry Bergman, Lita Grey. Silent; score added by Chaplin in 1971. (PAR)

More than fifty years later, the five-year-old gamin (Jackie Coogan) is still unique. In this silent classic, "his eyes speak," said Francis Hackett. "No child that I have ever seen on a stage created so full a part before." And, we can now add, very few have created one since that can match the Kid.

The child with a natural gift was tutored by a genius, and between them they made a wonderfully funny, wonderfully moving film. The love between the kid and the tramp, who is both foster father and foster mother, holds all the gags firmly in place.

The story is almost a chapter out of Chaplin's boyhood in the London slums; even the garret room is said to be a copy of the one in which he had lived with his mother. But it is also inspired invention. The Tramp is on promenade, selecting a butt from his sardine-can cigarette case, when he's stuck with a bundle, the baby of unmarried Edna Purviance. He cares for it in his garret: Charlie makes a cradle from a hammock, a nursing bottle from a suspended coffeepot, a commode from a spittoon under a chair. He gives him lessons in manners (examining his hands and ears before setting out to break windows with his apprentice to the profession). There is a plotful of drama with the police, the now-rich mother, a flophouse owner. It all ends well, of course; first in a dream "Heaven," then in reality.

The gamin miming the tramp he adores is every small boy walking like his father. Exquisite, coarse, natural, fantastic—the pair lift up one's heart. Prime Chaplin for children.

The Kid From Brooklyn

RKO 1946. 113 min., col. (prod) Samuel Goldwyn (d) Norman Z. McLeod (sp) Grover Jones, Frank Butler, and Richard Connell from the play The Milky Way *by Lynn Root and Harry Clark; adapted by Dan Hartman and Melville Shavelson (m)(lyr) Jule Styne, Sammy Kahn; words and music of "Pavlova" by Sylvia Fine, Max Liebman (c) Danny Kaye, Virginia Mayo, Vera-Ellen, Steve Cochran, Eve Arden, Walter Abel, Lionel Stander, Fay Bainter. (MAC, AIM, WIL)*

Harold Lloyd's THE MILKY WAY, retailored by Danny Kaye, is now a comedy with songs about a milkman from Brooklyn who becomes a one-punch ring champion. Funnier than in many more recent films, Kaye gives hilarious demonstrations of how not to box and in "Pavlova," he performs a musical travesty of ballet. Harold Lloyd didn't have the advantage of being married to song writer Sylvia Fine.

Though it lags here and there, THE KID FROM BROOKLYN is such good Kaye, especially when he's in the ring, that it holds up as entertainment.

Kim

MGM 1950. 113 min., col. (d) Victor Saville (sp) Leon Gordon, Helen Deutsch, Richard Schayer from the novel by Rudyard Kipling (c) Errol Flynn, Dean Stockwell, Paul Lukas, Robert Douglas, Cecil Kellaway, Arnold Moss, Reginald Owen. (FNC)

You remember Kim, the young orphan son of Kimball O'Hara, trooper of the Queen, who becomes a courier and spy on the Indian frontier, working to forestall the Russian infiltration of the Khyber Pass. Kipling's adventure story is very faithfully followed, perhaps too faithfully for the movie's pace. But the eye is filled with the color of nineteenth-century India's bazaars and caravans, and there are lots of elephants. Errol Flynn is a red-bearded horse thief and British agent, and Paul Lukas is a Buddhist lama. Most kids will envy Dean Stockwell. He is much smarter than the grown-ups, and they all depend on him.

The King and I

Fox 1956. 133 min., col. (d) Walter Lang (sp) Ernest Lehman from the book Anna and the King of Siam *by Margaret Landon (m) Richard Rodgers (b&l) Oscar Hammerstein II (chor) Jerome Robbins (cost) Irene Sharaff (c) Yul Brynner, Deborah Kerr, Rita Moreno, Terry Saunders, Yuriko, Marni Nixon (voice). (FNC)*

There are those who will tell you that the best King of Siam on the screen is Rex Harrison, who played in the 1946 Fox film made from Margaret Landon's book, with Irene Dunne as the governess, Mrs. Anna Leonowens. But Yul Brynner's king won the Oscar. Whichever movie adults prefer, kids vote enthusiastically for this musical version, rich in color, beautifully choreographed by Jerome Robbins, and joyous with the music of Rodgers and Hammerstein. Some of the song-and-dance moments linger in any moviegoer's memory: "Getting to Know You," "Shall We Dance?," "Is a Puzzlement," and "The Small House of Uncle Thomas." Oscars were awarded for art direction, set direction, costume design, and scoring.

King Kong

RKO 1933. 105 min., b/w. (d) Merian C. Cooper and Ernest B. Schoedsack (sp) James Creelman and Ruth Rose from a story by Edgar Wallace and Merian C. Cooper (ph) Edward Lindon (spec eff) Willis O'Brien (m) Max Steiner (c) Fay Wray, Robert Armstrong, Bruce Cabot, Noble Johnson. (JAN, FNC)

Who has ever forgotten the sight of the fifty-foot ape climbing up the Empire State Building with Fay Wray in his paw, setting her gently down on a ledge, and snarling in fury at the airplanes that eventually blast him to the ground? Like Frankenstein and Dracula, Kong is part of our folklore. Much has been written about the movie's symbolism. To Bosley Crowther, for instance, it is an allegory of the gap between the primate and the urban cliff dweller, with "several ironies of social imbalance remarkably and morbidly symbolized." To many people, the monster is more appealing than terrifying: the gigantic ruler of a prehistoric kingdom, lost, bewildered, and doomed in the city.

Many of the violent details are still strong stuff for the youngest kids. What every one agrees on is the movie's technical brilliance. Willis O'Brien is still unsurpassed in the creation of special effects such as animated scale models, multiple exposures, and process shots. With clever editing and Max Steiner's musical score, the suspense and excitement build powerfully. Recommended for older children with a taste for the best of the genre. There have been many imitations, but there is only one KING KONG.

King of the Hill

National Film Board of Canada 1974. 56 min., col. (d) William Canning, Donald Brittain (sp) William Canning, Colin Low (m) Scott Joplin. (NFB)

Big-league baseball from the inside, in a fine National Film Board of Canada documentary based on the experiences of Ferguson Jenkins, Canadian-born black superstar, who was pitcher for the Chicago Cubs before being traded to the Texas Rangers. Jenkins and the Cubs were filmed in the 1972-73 season, which was full of suspense and failure, satisfactions and frustrations.

Winner of the Main Prize in the Oberhausen Sport Film Festival, 1975, KING OF THE HILL is a crisply edited blend of narration, human interest shots, and backstage as well as ballpark humor and drama. Baseball fans will enjoy the mini close-ups of Wild Joe Pepitone, Leo Durocher, Ernie Banks, and Pistol Pete Reiser. An exciting as well as revealing picture of what really happens in a ball game and what lies behind the rise of a star like Jenkins, who was winner of the 1971 Cy Young Award as the National League's best pitcher.

King Solomon's Mines

MGM 1950. 102 min., col. (d) Compton Bennett and Andrew Marton (sp) Helen Deutsch from the novel by H. Rider Haggard (ph) Robert Surtees (c) Deborah Kerr, Stewart Granger, Richard Carlson, Siriaque. (FNC)

Remember the duel between two seven-foot Watusi nobles, the tribal dances, the stampede of thousands of animals, the prodigality of nature "red in tooth and claw"? Chances are you've seen them not only in KING SOLOMON'S MINES but in several later African movies. MGM liked the 1950 footage so well that they used a lot of it in 1959 in WATUSI. This 1950 movie from H. Rider Haggard's novel is better than the Gaumont-British version in 1937 with Sir Cedric Hardwicke and Paul Robeson. The reason is the color cinematography of Robert Surtees (THE GRADUATE, OKLAHOMA!), which won an Oscar, as did the editing of Ralph Winters and Conrad Nervig.

The movie was shot on location in the former Belgian Congo, Tanganyika, Uganda, and Kenya and has many native players in the cast. Allan Quartermain's long safari into the wilds in search of a missing explorer, accompanied by the explorer's wife (Deborah Kerr), sometimes bogs down into conventional romance. In the main, however, the film offers high adventure and an exciting view of a continent.

Knock on Wood

Paramount 1954. 103 min., col. (d)(sp) Norman Panama and Melvin Frank (m) Sylvia Fine (chor) Michael Kidd (c) Danny Kaye, Mai Zetterling, Diana Adams, Torin Thatcher, Leon Askin, Abner Biberman. (FNC)

All the things Danny Kaye does best, he does better than ever in this very amusing farce. A ventriloquist whose dummies have started to talk back to him, Danny goes to Zurich for psychiatric help. There he becomes entangled with some international spies who are fooling around with the dummies' heads (something to do with atomic secrets). To escape from the spies, he assumes a number of disguises. Imagine Danny as an Irish tenor in a pub singing a song by Sylvia Fine to end all Irish songs, "Monahan O'Han," or a British car salesman trying to demonstrate a low-slung model, or a Russian ballet dancer performing with ballerina Diana Adams and the *corps de ballet* (choreography by Michael Kidd). One of our greatest mimics at work.

The Lady Vanishes

Britain 1938. 101 min., b/w. (d) Alfred Hitchcock (sp) Frank Launder and Sidney Gilliat from Ethel Lina White's story "The Wheel Spins" (c) Margaret Lockwood, Michael Redgrave, Paul Lukas, Dame May Whitty, Basil Radford, Cecil Parker, Naunton Wayne. (JAN, BUD, IMA, KPF)

Even those who know every turn of plot can watch this classic thriller again and again with undiminished pleasure, for it is a joy to see how the master illusionist pulls his rabbits out of hats. Hitchcock and Launder and Gilliat have given us a gallery of characters we are delighted to meet again. From Miss Froy, the governess whose train journey leads to great adventure, to the inimitable British travelers who care only about the cricket scores at home, these are fully rounded people, not sticks in a melodrama.

What Hitchcock called his "oblique approach" to melodrama is completely successful here. "The really frightening thing about villains," he once observed, "is their surface likableness." Likable villains and extremely funny dialog, clues that mesh like magic, and a camera that always catches us by surprise—in a word, Hitchcock at his best.

Lassie Come Home*

MGM 1943. 90 min., col. (d) Fred M. Wilcox (sp) Hugo Butler from the novel by Eric Knight (c) Roddy McDowall, Donald Crisp, Dame May Whitty, Ben Webster, Edmund Gwenn, Nigel Bruce, Elsa Lanchester, Elizabeth Taylor, Arthur Shields. (FNC)

The first and best of the movies about the kids' favorite collie. Loving hands transform Eric Knight's novel, which is an account of the long trek of an English boy's dog, sold and transported to Scotland, that finally returns to its owner. There is plenty of adventure, photographed against attractive natural backgrounds. In the excellent cast is eleven-year-old Elizabeth Taylor in her first major role as a child star.

The Lavender Hill Mob

Britain 1951. 80 min., b/w. (d) Charles Crichton (sp) T.E.B. Clarke (c) Alec Guinness, Stanley Holloway, Alfie Bass, Sidney James, Marjorie Fielding. (GEN)

An absurdity of the most consummate skill written by T.E.B. Clarke. Alec Guinness is a trusted employee of the Bank of England who, with three accomplices, steals a shipment of gold bullion, exports it to Paris as miniature Eiffel towers, and *almost* fools half the police in England.

If you haven't seen Mr. Guinness's left shoulder in this spoof, you haven't seen the best supporting player of the year. Runners-up are Mr. Guinness's steel spectacles, bowler, umbrella, bland smile, lisp, giggle, Policy Athletic League sweater, and South American suntan. In addition to Mr. Clarke's wit and Mr. Guinness's art, the film has a lot of London in it, many freshly viewed ordinary people, and several extraordinary characters of great charm: Alfie Bass, one of the mob who presents references in the form of press clippings about his former arrests; Stanley Holloway, the "artistic gentleman" with the plummy voice; and the gentlewoman in the Queen Mary hat who reads American crime fiction.

A comic masterpiece, with a lot of camera fun such as the descent from the Eiffel Tower and the Keystone Kops chase at the police exhibition.

Life with Father

Warners 1947. 118 min., col. (d) Michael Curtiz (sp) Donald Ogden Stewart from the play by Howard Lindsay and Russel Crouse (ph) Peverell Marley, William V. Skall (m) Leo F. Forbstein (c) William Powell, Irene Dunne, Elizabeth Taylor, Moroni Olsen, Monte Blue, Elizabeth Risdon, Edmund Gwenn, Zasu Pitts, Jimmy Lydon. (MAC, CON, TWY)

The movie from the Lindsay-Crouse play from the Clarence Day stories has seen a lot of mileage. While the Victorian paterfamilias who rules his beloved brood with an iron hand is dated, the comedy is enduring. Moonstruck young sons who suffer from papa's temper are still with us, they still fall in love with beautiful visitors (the girl here is Elizabeth Taylor in bud), and wives like Vinnie still have to plot to win their way against macho husbands.

The New York Film Critics circle gave William Powell its best actor award, and his Father Day is a delightful characterization. Donald Ogden Stewart's script includes every possible nuance of comedy.

Lili

MGM 1953. 81 min., col. (d) Charles Walters (sp) Helen Deutsch from the story by Paul Gallico (c) Leslie Caron, Mel Ferrer, Jean-Pierre Aumont, Zsa Zsa Gabor, Kurt Kasznar. (FNC)

Bronislau Kaper's prizewinning score, with its accordion music and the song "Hi-Lili, Hi-Lo," sets the tone for this warm, light, and ingratiating film, at the opposite end of the spectrum from Hollywood's more pretentious musicals.

Leslie Caron is perfectly cast as a sixteen-year-old French orphan who joins a carnival. There is a youthful infatuation with the carnival magician, not to be taken too seriously, and a delightful series of dances, puppet shows, and backstage carnival preparations. About as real as pink cotton candy—but not without nourishment for the imagination, especially when the puppets are around.

Lilies of the Field

United Artists 1963. 97 min., b/w. (d) Ralph Nelson (sp) James Poe, based on the novel by William E. Barrett (ph) Ernest Haller (m) Jerry Goldsmith (c) Sidney Poitier, Lilia Skala, Lisa Mann, Isa Crino, Francesca Jarvis, Pamela Branch, Stanley Adams, Dan Frazer, Ralph Nelson. (UAS, MAC)

A cheerful traveler on his way through Arizona, the black veteran Homer Smith (Sidney Poitier) is gently but firmly conned by Mother Maria (Lilia Skala) into staying with her and her group of refugee East German nuns and building a chapel on their barren land. The building of the chapel leads to a building of love and charity between them.

The "odd couple," Homer and Mother Maria, are warmly and believably presented, with every quirk in place. The German sisters in the Southwest, sustained by more faith than solid food, are both comic and poignant. LILIES OF THE FIELD works because the sentiment and the characters are true. By affirming our faith in a common humanity, the film says a great deal to young people.

Credit for the quality of the production goes to the director, Ralph Nelson (SOLDIER BLUE), and to the fine cast. For his Homer Smith, Poitier won an Oscar. Lilia Skala should have won another for her tart, wise, unrelenting Mother Superior, who is quite as much the soldier as Homer.

The Little Ark*

Radnitz 1972. 101 min., col. (d) James B. Clark (sp) Joanna Crawford from the novel by Jan De Hartog (ph) Austin Dempster, Denys Coop (m) Fred Carlin (c) Theodore Bikel, Genevieve Ambas, Philip Frame. (MAC, TWY, ROA, CWF)

Adapted from Jan De Hartog's novel about the disastrous 1953 floods in Holland, THE LITTLE ARK shows how two young children caught in the deluge and its aftermath are matured by their experience. "Radnitz has learned how to make children stay believably childlike" (Arthur Knight, *Saturday Review*). In this film, not so well known as other productions of award-winning Robert B. Radnitz (SOUNDER), both children and adults can identify with his characters.

A Dutch boy of ten (Philip Frame) and an Indonesian girl of eleven (Genevieve Ambas), who are orphans, have many adventures after the flood as they search for their foster father, a minister who had provided a home for them. They find a brief refuge in an abandoned houseboat; then they are rescued by the captain of a trawler (Theodore Bikel), who teaches them to care for a menagerie of pets, and for other human victims of the flood. Eventually picked up by a hospital ship, they escape from the threat of a transfer to an orphanage. There is a happy ending, with the children safe in the arms of the captain again. Bikel is a warm, wise father figure; he doesn't sing, but the bedtime story he tells, with the help of an animation sequence, is one of the pleasures of this charming movie.

Little Women

RKO 1933. 107 min., b/w. (d) George Cukor (sp) Sarah Y. Mason and Victor Heerman from the novel by Louisa May Alcott (c) Katharine Hepburn, Joan Bennett, Frances Dee, Jean Parker, Paul Lukas, Douglass Montgomery, Edna May Oliver, Henry Stephenson, Spring Byington, Samuel Hinds. (FNC)

Little girls still love Meg, Jo, Beth, and Amy, though they discover them years earlier than little girls used to. And as television sophisticates, they will tell you that "the Katharine Hepburn movie" is much better than the 1949 remake and the seventies TV series. They are perfectly right. When Katharine Hepburn cries, "Look at me, World, I'm Jo March, and I'm so happy!" she is just the girl Miss Alcott had in mind. The joys and sorrows of the Marches have been beautifully orchestrated by director George Cukor. For their adaptation of a literary classic, Sarah Y. Mason and Victor Heerman won an Academy Award.

The Littlest Horse Thieves*

Disney 1976. 104 min., col. (d) Charles Jarrott (sp) Rosemary Anne Sisson (ph) Paul Beeson (m) Ron Goodwin (c) Alastair Sim, Peter Barkworth, Maurice Colbourne, Susan Tebbs, Andrew Harrison, Chloe Franks, Benjie Bolgar, Prunella Scales, Geraldine McEwan. (GEN)

Ten minutes into THE LITTLEST HORSE THIEVES and you know it is topnotch, many cuts above the usual Disneys. British made and British played, its three child "thieves" are natural and charming, and the late Alastair Sim heads an impeccable cast. The script by Rosemary Anne Sisson ("Elizabeth R" and "Upstairs, Downstairs" on television) and the direction by Charles Jarrott (ANNE OF THE THOUSAND DAYS) are superior.

The endangered species in the story is the pit ponies that haul coal to the surface and live underground in a coal mining town in Yorkshire in 1909. When a new mine manager plans to make a profit by replacing the ponies with machinery, the children come to the rescue of the beloved animals. The manager's eleven-year-old daughter and a miner's two small stepsons match wits with the adults and save the ponies from the slaughterhouse.

The characterizations of the children, the aristocratic mine owner blinded by class prejudice, the boys' stepfather, and the icy manager who is a loving father, lift the film above others of its type.

The Living Desert

Disney 1953. 75 min., col. (d) James Algar. (GEN)

What fiction could possibly match the life and adventures of the gila monster, the gekko lizard, the spotted skunk, the pepsis wasp, the vulture, the tarantula, the sidewinder, the peccary, the bobcat, the desert toad, the kangaroo rat, the red-tailed hawk, the burrowing snake, the scorpion, the elf owl, the bat, the sand lizard, the long-horned bettle, the chuckawalla, or the coati-mundi? This Walt Disney "True-Life Adventure" was photographed in Death Valley, the Yuma sand dunes, and the Salton Sea mud pots. Its incredible setting gives the film a nightmare brilliance. There are many heroic things—evidences of escape and survival, glimpses of murder and arrest at split-second intervals—but humor alternates with excitement throughout.

People have different opinions about Disney's taste in music, his color, the length of the film and the commentary, but the subject of the film is spellbinding. It won an Academy Award as best documentary feature.

Lost Horizon

Columbia 1937. 118 min., b/w. (d) Frank Capra (sp) Robert Riskin from the novel by James Hilton (ph) Joseph Walker (m) Dmitri Tiomkin (c) Ronald Colman, Jane Wyatt, Margo, Isabel Jewell, Thomas Mitchell, Edward Everett Horton, Sam Jaffe, H.B. Warner. (GEN)

Today it is difficult to admire the art direction and sets which won Academy Awards, along with the editing, in 1937, or to find anything out of the ordinary in the photography of Joseph Walker, a pioneer of the zoom lens. But the romance of Shangri-La is still intriguing to the youthful imagination. In Capra's terms, it is often more vivid than in Hilton's. Who with a spark of fantasy has seen the hidden paradise in Tibet where the High Lama is building his rampart against barbarism, or Margo's metamorphosis in the final sequence, can drop them from his movie memory?

The original film is something for older children to enjoy; the 1973 remake with music, whose first half hour copies the 1937 film scene for scene, is a sad failure of taste and imagination once it gets to Shangri-La.

Louisiana Story

Lopert 1948. 77 min., b/w. (prod)(d) Robert J. Flaherty (sp) Frances and Robert J. Flaherty (assoc prod) Richard Leacock, Helen Van Dongen (ph) Richard Leacock (ed) Helen Van Dongen (m) Virgil Thomson, played by the Philadelphia Symphony Orchestra, Eugene Ormandy, conductor. (CAL, FNC, PYR, KPF)

Flaherty's classic documentary about a Cajun boy's life in the bayou country and the changes brought about when a monster oil derrick invades it. The machine is transmuted into poetry as it moves into the wilderness and then moves on, leaving the land still untouched.

Eleven-year-old Joseph Boudreaux (called in the film Alexander Napoleon Ulysses Latour) is strong, curious, and fearless. He triumphs over the alligator and over the new beast, the invading derrick. Acting with him are two other nonprofessionals, Frank Hardy and Lionel Le Blanc, as the adults in the story.

There is no comment and little dialog. Flaherty called the film a fantasy, suggesting that it takes place within the consciousness of a boy who is not only Cajun but universal, a symbol of the childhood of the human race; his enemies in the swamp, and the imagined monsters in his mind, are part of the life of primitive man.

Children will enjoy the world of nature that the boy inhabits—friendly raccoons, catfish to catch and alligators to kill, spiders' webs and Spanish moss dripping from the cypress trees. They will also identify with the boy's triumph over the invader. At first he fears the oil men who mock his "magic" (his spit, his bag of salt inside his shirt, his frog). Later, when the blowout comes, he tries to help them, and there's a smile on his face as he sails out to the pipe spouting oil: his magic, not theirs, brought in the treasure! The last symbol in the film is not the machine.

Macbeth

Britain 1961. 107 min., col. (prod) Sidney Kaufman (d) George Schaefer (sp) George Schaefer and Anthony Squire from Shakespeare's play (ph) Frederick A. Young (m) Richard Addinsell (c) Maurice Evans, Judith Anderson, Michael Hordern, Ian Bannen, Felix Aylmer. (MAC, CCC)

Shakespeare's drama of ambition and retribution has fascinated filmmakers; there have been treatments for many tastes. The subject was just right for Orson Welles, whose 1948 black-and-white MACBETH (filmed in twenty-one days), despite its burr-laden and frequently unintelligible soundtrack, has some interesting effects. Polanski's 1972 MACBETH with Jon Finch and the BBC film in 1976 with Eric Porter and Janet Suzman have their adherents, as do such offshoots as Kurosawa's THRONE OF BLOOD (1957) and Ken Hughes's JOE MACBETH (1956). But the most generally satisfactory version for young people is this British film made by George Schaefer, starring two of the most famous players of our time in the leading roles.

Schaefer had first cast Maurice Evans as Macbeth and Judith Anderson as Lady Macbeth in a Hallmark Hall of Fame television program in the fifties. He reunited them for this screen version, which was filmed by Frederick A. Young (LAWRENCE OF ARABIA) in Scotland and at Elstree Studios in Britain.

The force of Evans's playing and the clarity of his and Judith Anderson's interpretation of their roles should bring the poetry as well as the bloody events of MACBETH to life for older children.

The Magic Horse*

USSR 1941. 57 min., col. animation (d) I. Vano (sp) E. Pomeschikov and P. Pozhkov from the story "The Little Humpbacked Horse" (ph) N. Voinov (m) V. Oransky (art) L. Milchik. English dialog. (MAC)

Novel and charming for young children, this Russian color cartoon feature is based on a favorite folktale, one of the *skazki*, generations old. Verses and authentic background material (ancient miniatures, icons, and sixteenth-century ornaments) enrich the excellent drawing.

The simple story tells of a small boy, his tiny humpbacked horse, and its magical powers. "Imaginative and cheerful entertainment," said the *New York Times*. "Its visual attributes are universal and can be appreciated by youngsters and oldsters alike."

The Man in the White Suit

Britain 1952. 85 min., b/w. (d) Alexander Mackendrick (sp) Alexander Mackendrick, Roger Macdougall, and John Dighton from the play by Roger Macdougall (m) Benjamin Frankel (c) Alec Guinness, Joan Greenwood, Cecil Parker, Ernest Thesiger, Vida Hope, Michael Gough, Miles Malleson. (BUD, LCA, ROA, TWY)

One of the funniest of the Ealing Studios comedies, this satire on what a new invention does to vested interests has more point than ever today, when even children know the meaning of planned obsolescence, biodegradable, and recycling. A textile chemist (Alec Guinness) has perfected a formula for a fabric that is ever-wearable, indestructible, and stain-proof. Manufacturers, unionists, tailors, and laundresses go into shock over his lovely white suit.

Director Mackendrick (TIGHT LITTLE ISLAND, THE LADY KILLERS) works with an ingenious and witty screenplay which he wrote with Roger Macdougall (THE MOUSE THAT ROARED) and John Dighton (THE HAPPIEST DAYS OF YOUR LIFE, KIND HEARTS AND CORONETS). A moment of high comedy is the arrival of the tottering textile tycoons in a fleet of funereal limousines at the parley where the new invention is killed. Another is the sight and sound of the invention itself at the instant of birth as a Rube Goldberg creation gurgling portentously in its glass viscera. The cast is perfect, especially Mr. Guinness; oleo wouldn't melt in his mouth. If your kids are planning a party for Ralph Nader, this is the movie to screen for him.

Man of Aran

Britain 1934. 77 min., b/w. (d)(ph)(sp) Robert J. Flaherty (assoc) Frances Flaherty (asst) David Flaherty (ed) John Goldman (m) John Greenwood (c) Tiger King, Maggie Dirrance, Mikeleen Dillane. (BUD, EMG, KPF, PYR)

In one scene of this classic documentary, the man of Aran is thirteen-year-old Mikeleen (an unprofessional, like the others in the cast). Within the ancient fortress of Dun Aengus, he is fishing from the treacherous cliff edge high above the sea—for food, not for fun.

Here is the life of a family on one of the Aran Islands thirty miles off the west coast of Ireland, not far from Galway: the great storms, the arduous fishing in the little boats called curraghs, the dangerous harpooning of the basking shark. To plant potatoes for her family's subsistence, a mother makes a plot of soil in barren rock by filling the cracks laboriously with stones for a base, then with seaweed, sand, and loam.

The visual imagery and natural sounds have great force. To Pauline Kael, MAN OF ARAN is "undoubtedly the greatest film tribute to man's struggle against hostile nature" (*Kiss Kiss Bang Bang*). To the over-twelves, it should be a glimpse of the existence not only of the Aran Islanders in 1934 but of many people in the world today who must survive in similar circumstances.

The Man Who Could Work Miracles

Britain 1937. 82 min., b/w. (prod) Alexander Korda (d) Lothar Mendes (sp) H.G. Wells (ph) Harold Rosson (spec eff) Ned Mann (c) Roland Young, Joan Gardner, Ralph Richardson, Ernest Thesiger, Wallace Lupino. (BUD, CHA, MOG)

Written for the screen by H.G. Wells himself, this classic sci-fi fantasy is balanced between fun and profundity. With almost as many visual tricks as THINGS TO COME, it raises the question of whether human nature can really be changed for instant Utopia. When its rabbity protagonist is incapable of making good use of his power to work miracles, and almost destroys the world, the spirits conclude, "Once an ape, always an ape."

George McWhirter Fotheringay (Roland Young), a clerk in a small English town, is a very ordinary sort of man. He is short on imagination and long on frailty. He can make so little of his gift— to work magic on those around him, and finally the world—that in the end he can only return to the taproom of the Long Dragon Inn, scratch his head, and wonder what on earth happened.

Among the funniest things that happen in this entertaining film is that Colonel Winstanely (Ralph Richardson), when Fotheringay tells him of his intention to launch the Golden Age immediately, takes down an elephant rifle and goes gunning for him as a dangerous lunatic.

Provocative and original for older children.

THE INCREDIBLE SHRINKING MAN
(Universal-International)

HOW GREEN WAS MY VALLEY (20th Century-Fox)

MAN WITH A MILLION (United Artists and J. Arthur Rank)

MR. SMITH GOES TO WASHINGTON (Columbia Pictures)

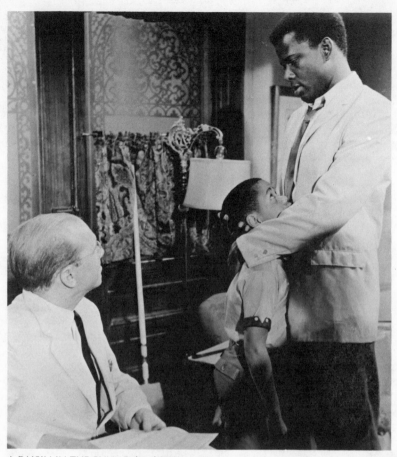

A RAISIN IN THE SUN (Columbia Pictures)

THE RED SHOES (Eagle Lion-J. Arthur Rank)

RUGGLES OF RED GAP (Paramount Pictures)

STAR WARS (20th Century-Fox)

THIRD MAN ON THE MOUNTAIN (Walt Disney)

THE THIRTY-NINE STEPS (Gaumont British)

A TREE GROWS IN BROOKLYN (20th Century-Fox)

WHERE'S CHARLEY? (Warner Bros.)

THE YEARLING (MGM)

WUTHERING HEIGHTS (Samuel Goldwyn)

YELLOW SUBMARINE (Subafilms)

Man with a Million

J. Arthur Rank (Britain) 1954. 90 min., col. (d) Ronald Neame (sp) Jill Craigie from Mark Twain's story "The Million Pound Bank Note" (c) Gregory Peck, Jane Griffiths, Ronald Squire, Joyce Grenfell, A.E. Mathews, Wilfrid Hyde-White, Reginald Beckwith. (UAS, MAC, BUD, ROA)

Among the movies which have improved on their source, count Ronald Neame's happy adaptation of Mark Twain's story about the magnetism of money. Gregory Peck, a penniless American in London, agrees to hold a million-pound bank note for two old gentlemen, to settle a bet. Of course, he finds he can't spend it, but he doesn't need to, since most people treat a reputed millionaire like the real thing. The situation takes amusing turns, and the tone is gently satirical until the romantic ending. The cast is the very best: British, but not *too* British.

Mary Poppins*

Disney 1964. 140 min., col. (d) Robert Stevenson (sp) Bill Walsh and Don DaGradi from the Mary Poppins books by P.L. Travers (m) Richard M. Sherman and Robert B. Sherman (cost) Tony Walton (c) Julie Andrews, Dick Van Dyke, David Tomlinson, Glynis Johns, Ed Wynn, Hermione Baddeley, Elsa Lanchester, Arthur Treacher, Reginald Owen, Jane Darwell. (THEATERS)

Just as Dickens must have known that W.C. Fields would be born to play Mr. Micawber, P.L. Travers surely knew that Julie Andrews would come along to be Mary Poppins, the governess who would take no nonsense from anyone from the moment she flew in on her umbrella.

Disney's production creates a world of cartooned and live characters in Edwardian London who walk through chalk drawings on the sidewalk, drink tea on the ceiling, sweep in and around chimneys and rooftops, slide upstairs on the bannisters, and sing and dance in a cartoon wonderland. If flying nannies and whirling chimney sweeps don't grab your kids now, they will when they see MARY POPPINS. The special effects and the music and dance sequences are highly entertaining. Oscars were awarded to the music and lyrics, the film editing, the special effects, and of course, the special nanny of Miss Andrews.

Masters of the Congo Jungle

Belgium 1959. 88 min., col (d) Heinz Sielmann and Henry Brandt.
Commentary by Max-Pol Fouchet, narrated by Orson Welles and
William Warfield. (m) Richard Cornu. (BUD, PNX, SEL, WIL)

Pauline Kael wondered how we could take pleasure in artificial
movies about animal life after seeing the grandeur of a movie like
this one, "a vast and visually elegant record of the interrelations
of men, animals and birds in Africa, with young Watusi girls performing a ritual dance in imitation of the crowned cranes." There
is little of the artificial about this superb documentary; it contains
some of the best footage ever photographed of African flora and
fauna and native life. It was produced by the Belgian International
Scientific Foundation and by Henri Storck, the distinguished Belgian artist and filmmaker (RUBENS), to provide a record of the
former Belgian Congo before civilization should change it.

Filmed entirely in Ruanda-Urundi during a two-year expedition,
it is a visually exciting experience, with a sense of the poetry in
the parallel life cycles of man and animal in nature. "There is a
communion between the man of the forest and his natural sur-
roundings which inspires in us a sense of respect, a recognition
of spiritual heritage," said King Leopold III of Belgium about the
film. The narration is spoken by Orson Welles and William Warfield; the effective music was composed by Richard Cornu.

Meet Me in St. Louis

MGM 1944. 113 min., col. (d) Vincente Minnelli (sp) Irving Brecher
and Fred F. Finkelhoffe from Sally Benson's New Yorker stories and
novel (c) Judy Garland, Margaret O'Brien, Leon Ames, Mary Astor,
Lucille Bremer, Harry Davenport, Marjorie Main, June Lockhart, Tom
Drake. (FNC)

When Judy Garland is singing "Skip to My Lou" or "The Trolley
Song," when a romantic camera picks up the girls in their long
white dresses on the lawn in spring or behind a horse and buggy
on a clear autumn night, and when Vincente Minnelli is coloring
St. Louis at the turn of the century and Sally Benson's nice people
are clinging to the ways and the places they love, this is a very
entertaining, quite unremarkable musical. But when little Margaret O'Brien takes a walk on Hallowe'en—when she does almost
anything—the picture springs into vivid life. She got a special
Academy Award as the best child actress of 1944.

The Member of the Wedding

*Columbia 1952. 91 min., b/w. (d) Fred Zinnemann (sp) Edna and Ed-
ward Anhalt from the play by Carson McCullers (c) Julie Harris, Ethel
Waters, Brandon de Wilde, Arthur Franz, James Edwards. (MAC)*

Frankie, for Frances, Addams, the scrawny twelve-year-old as awk-
ward as a boy—she's cut her hair so short she even looks like
one—is the prototype of isolated girlhood; her need to identify
with something is as lyrical and powerful today as it ever was.
Because Fred Zinnemann's direction and Carson McCullers's play
are so good, it doesn't matter much that Julie Harris doesn't look
like a twelve-year-old, as she managed to do for the sixty-two
weeks of the play's run. The character transcends all problems
of adaptation.

The summer of the story is very lonely for Frankie; she's ignored
by the slightly older neighborhood girls and her widower father.
She sits around in the kitchen with her two friends, Berenice Sadie
Brown (Ethel Waters), the cook, and John Henry (Brandon de
Wilde), her old little seven-year-old cousin. Frankie's needs and
fantasies culminate in her decision to become a member of the
wedding of her brother and his sweetheart: then she will belong;
she will be a part of the "we" of a group. In the end, of course,
she cannot go with the couple. Reality crowds in, through John
Henry's death, Berenice's troubles. When we take leave of Frankie, she has made a new friend. Life takes a different turn. She's
growing up.

For the over-twelves, an experience of depth and insight. The
characterization of Berenice by Ethel Waters is one of the rewards
of the film, as it was of the play.

Men of Bronze

*PBS-TV 1977. 58 min., col. (prod)(d)(sp) William Miles (exec prod)
Paul Killiam (ph)(ed)co-d) Richard M. Adams (narr) Melville T. Miller.
(FNC)*

"This is a highly entertaining and historically instructive documentary of a black regiment in World War I. Thanks in considerable measure to the presence, humor and humanity of a survivor, Melville T. Miller, now 75, there is an engaging perspective"
(*Variety*).

Because AEF Headquarters had decreed that black men could
not fight beside white men and could only be used as stevedores
"in this war," black volunteers of the 369th Regiment served

under the Fourth French Army. The "Harlem Hellfighters" were elevator boys, porters, waiters, society jazz musicians; their officers, both black and white, came from Harvard and the elite middle class. The 369th spent 191 days under fire in the front-line trenches and lost half their men. Eleven times cited for bravery, they were the first Allied regiment to reach the Rhine and were awarded 171 French Croix de Guerre.

Through rare photographs, archive film footage, and on-camera comments from surviving veterans, we see the "Men of Bronze" serving with pride in the midst of racist prejudice. Both on and off camera, the charming Private Melville T. ("Doc") Miller tells his part in the remarkable story.

MEN OF BRONZE, winner of the Red Ribbon Award of the American Film Festival, is an excellent documentary, highly recommended for its picture of social history, World War I, and men of extraordinary valor. Lively and gripping, it should hold young people.

Miguelin

Spain 1964. 63 min., b/w with col. (d) Horatio Varcarcel (sp) Horacio Varcarcel, Joaquin Aguirre Bellver (ph) Francisco Fraile (c) Luis-Maria Hidalgo, Luis Domingo Luna. Spanish dialog with English subtitles. (TWF)

"Perhaps the most delightful film about children to come out of Spain since MARCELINO PAN Y VINO," said *Variety* about this 1965 Cannes Festival prizewinner. Marcelino, in the 1956 film (no longer in release here), gives his bread and wine to a figure of Christ that he imagines is real. Miguelin, raised not in a monastery but in the streets of a poor village, is a very different small boy. Alive with mischief, older and more sensitive than his years, he makes a bold stab at changing the misery of the life he sees around him.

By conning the sacristan of the village cathedral into teaching him the Latin responses, Miguelin has become an altar boy. He declares a personal war against poverty and steals the church poor box. With his beloved burro, he tries to solicit contributions from the villagers. No luck. Still in his garb as altar boy, he stops motorists on the highway. Still no luck. Then, in a dream, Miguelin receives the revelation that charity begins at home. He sells his burro and gives the money to the poor. In remorse, the villagers get it back for him in time for the annual blessing of the animals.

Dark-eyed Miguelin appeals to children as well as adults, and the discovery he makes, as well as the details of his village life, can be believed; MIGUELIN has authenticity.

The Million Dollar Duck*

Disney 1971. 92 min., col. (prod) Bill Anderson (d) Vincent McEveety (sp) Roswell Rogers (c) Dean Jones, Sandy Duncan, Joe Flynn, Tony Roberts, James Gregory, Arthur Hunnicutt. (GEN)

Charley (really a she), a behavioral-test duck, is a dropout from Prof. Jones's lab, where she was accidentally exposed to radiation. Jones's neighbor, Treasury man Joe Flynn, discovers that Charley lays eggs with a solid-gold yolk, evidently the result of the radiation plus some of the professor's wife's homemade applesauce.

From this beginning, you can imagine what develops. On second thought, you can't. Enough to say that there are Keystone car chases, Pearl White serial thrills, and a trial of the professor on the charge of violating federal gold regulations. Forced to lay an egg to have its gold content tested, Charley saves the day. According to critic Judith Crist and many audiences, the movie is "full of nice wholesome family fun."

Million Dollar Legs

Paramount 1932. 65 min., b/w. (d) Edward Cline (sp) Henry Myers and Nick Barrows from the story by Joseph L. Mankiewicz (c) W.C. Fields, Jack Oakie, Billy Gilbert, Andy Clyde, F. Hugh Herbert, Lyda Roberti, Susan Fleming. (MMA, SWA, UNI)

How W.C. Fields governs as president of Klopstokia, a bankrupt country on the verge of revolution where every citizen is an athletic superman. How he and Secretary of the Treasury F. Hugh Herbert leave off Indian wrestling at the conference table and decide to win all the events in the Olympics held in the United States. How Lyda Roberti is a sexy spy named Mata Machree and Susan Fleming is a girl named Angela (all girls in Klopstokia are named Angela) who falls in love with an American, Jack Oakie. How W.C. Fields wins the weight-lifting contest and the shotput, too. . . .How have we lived without MILLION DOLLAR LEGS since 1932?

To critic Pauline Kael, this is *the* screwball comedy. Fans have their favorite sight gags. For example, the black-cloaked Klopstokian spies rising on hydraulic elevators from woodland hideouts. "Although slapstick seemed to have died in the early days of the talkie, this picture—a combination of the spleen of Fields with the irrationality of the Sennett tradition—reaffirmed all of the near-surrealistic values of the genre, using gymnastic events at the Olympic Games as the finale" (Museum of Modern Art).

Miracle on 34th Street

Fox 1947. 96 min., b/w. (prod) William Perlberg (d) George Seaton (sp) George Seaton from the story by Valentine Davies (ph) Charles Clarke, Lloyd Ahern (m) Cyril Mockridge (c) Maureen O'Hara, John Payne, Edmund Gwenn, Gene Lockhart, Natalie Wood, Porter Hall, William Frawley, Thelma Ritter. (FNC)

"Will the real Santa Claus please stand up?"

In this sparkling seasonal fable about Macy's and the Christmas spirit, the question is whether Kris Kringle, the kindly old gentleman hired for the role by Macy's, really is Santa, as he confidently claims. Overflowing with warmth of heart and real cheer, the bogus—or the genuine?—exemplar of the Christmas ideal touches the lives of those around him. Some of the effects (on Macy's and Gimbel's, for example, and on a psychiatrist and a judge) are very funny. Others are romantic.

The effect on almost all audiences has always been salutary. The delightful character of Kris Kringle created by Edmund Gwenn, who won an Academy Award for the role, would be welcomed by every youngster during the holiday season.

The Miracle Worker

United Artists 1962. 107 min., b/w. (d) Arthur Penn (sp) William Gibson from his play based on Helen Keller's The Story of My Life (ph) Ernest Caparros (m) Laurence Rosenthal (c) Anne Bancroft, Patty Duke, Victor Jory, Inga Swenson, Andrew Prine. (UAS)

Anne Sullivan (Anne Bancroft) and Helen Keller (Patty Duke) were matched in profound understanding of what they wanted. The "miracle" in their story—superbly directed by Arthur Penn—is the miracle of the meeting of two minds of equal temper. The life principle was so strong in Anne Sullivan that she had never given up, not even in her own blind childhood, prisoned in an orphanage with her crippled little brother. In seven-year-old Helen Keller, blind, speechless, and deaf, the will to possess her own life raged so savagely that it almost tore her apart; unable to escape from her inner darkness, the child clawed and gasped like an animal.

But as we all know, when these two extraordinary human beings came to grips with each other (literally) in a battle royal, the teacher was able "to disinter the soul" of her pupil. The moment when Helen realizes the connection between the finger-spelled word "water" and the reality it stands for is one of the great moments in the history of impaired children (Mrs. Keller's term). And it is one of the great moments in cinema, as the Oscar-winning portrayals of Anne Bancroft and Patty Duke are among the great roles.

Exciting, moving, humorous, and deeply inspiring for older children, THE MIRACLE WORKER is a film they will never forget.

Miss Goodall and the Wild Chimpanzees

National Geographic Society and Wolper Productions 1966. 52 min., col. documentary. (d)(ph) Baron Hugo van Lawick (c) Jane Goodall van Lawick (narr) Orson Welles. (NGE, FNC, WHO)

The world of animals brought to us in a series of documentaries by famous British zoologist Jane Goodall and her husband, the noted animal photographer Baron Hugo van Lawick, is fascinating every time we enter it.

MISS GOODALL AND THE WILD CHIMPANZEES is an in-depth picture of the behavior of wild chimpanzees in Africa, documenting a five-year study in Tanzania's Gombe Stream Preserve. Miss Goodall discovered that primates other than man make and use primitive tools and hunt big game for meat. We see the wild chimpanzees eating, sleeping, working, and living in social groups. Their observed behavior is interpreted in terms of its significance to the study of man.

"Possibly the best film on the natural behavior of any species of apes," (EFLA Evaluation) and an entertaining and informative prizewinner. The narrator's voice emerging from the Tanzanian rain forest is Orson Welles's.

Mr. Hulot's Holiday   *(Les vacances de M. Hulot)*

France 1954. 90 min., b/w. (d) Jacques Tati (sp) Jacques Tati and Henri Marquet (c) Jacques Tati, Nathalie Pascaud, Louis Perrault, Michèle Rolla. French dialog with English subtitles. (BUD, EMG, KPF)

"I don't like the way they do comedy today. They talk too much," Jacques Tati says. "For me comedy is observation. I am a visual person." Tati, the actor, is one of our greatest mimes and has much in common with the silent comedians, particularly Keaton. Tati, the writer-director, has a kind but accurate eye for people at their innocently bumbling funniest. Children enjoy his sight gags, which build slowly but are irrepressible.

In this very funny view of M. Hulot, a bachelor on vacation at the seashore, Tati is at his best. Though the movie is in French with English subtitles, the comedy is so largely visual that little language is needed. Two typical Tati sequences: the vacation-bound crowds driven like ants by the railroad's incomprehensible public-address sytem; the boy trying to carry two ice cream cones at once. This little classic of humor was a *Grand Prix* winner at Cannes.

Mr. Smith Goes to Washington

Columbia 1939. 130 min., b/w. (d) Frank Capra (sp) Sidney Buchman from a story by Lewis R. Foster (m) Dmitri Tiomkin (c) James Stewart, Jean Arthur, Claude Rains, Edward Arnold, Guy Kibbee, Thomas Mitchell, Eugene Pallette, Beulah Bondi, H.B. Warner, Harry Carey, Ruth Donnelly, Grant Mitchell, Porter Hall, William Demarest, H.V. Kaltenborn, Jack Carson. (GEN)

In 1939 black-and-white, this has the color of Frank Capra's humor and style, the camera following a man's words as if the man and the words really mattered. In Lewis R. Foster's Academy Award original story, scripted by Sidney Buchman, they still do.

Jefferson Smith, short-term junior senator from his state, goes to Washington with the blessing of his Boy Rangers back home and falls for a frame-up engineered by the senior senator and the political machine. His filibuster on the floor of the Senate is typical Capra, with Jimmy Stewart whistling to make the Senators turn around and listen to him.

Youngsters in the eighties could teach Capra a thing or two about corruption in politics. What Capra has to teach them, perhaps, is that some of the good guys are not only honest but occasionally foolish, and some of the bad guys are not only dishonest but occasionally likeable. Though it makes for good discussion, the movie is not preachy but warm and funny romantic comedy, with several very moving reminders of Lincolnian democracy, and a score of good characterizations.

Misty*

Fox 1961. 92 min., col. (d) James B. Clark (sp) Ted Sherdeman from Marguerite Henry's novel Misty of Chincoteague (c) David Ladd, Pam Smith, Anne Seymour, Arthur O'Connell, Duke Farley, and the people of Chincoteague. (FNC)

It's a wonder that any child audience, once having seen Chincoteague, will want to go home. Chincoteague and Assateague are islands off the coast of Virginia, a preserve for wild horses and game. Every year, the yearlings and the foals of the herd of Shetland ponies on Assateague are rounded up and sent across the water to Chincoteague where they are auctioned off for the benefit of the local fire department. An orphaned brother and sister, Maureen and Paul, whose grandparents take care of the ponies, fall in love with a beautiful brown mare, Phantom, and her foal, Misty, and enter their favorite in the annual race at the Chincoteague fair.

The natives of Chincoteague and their customs supply charming local color. It's a very nice place to visit, if only for ninety-two minutes. The movie was made by the producer-director-screenwriter trio, Robert B. Radnitz, James B. Clark, and Ted Sherdeman, responsible for ISLAND OF THE BLUE DOLPHINS and MY SIDE OF THE MOUNTAIN. All three of these films for children have won prizes in international festivals.

Moby Dick

Warners 1956. 116 min. col. (d) John Huston (sp) Ray Bradbury and John Huston from the novel by Herman Melville (ph) Oswald Morris (c) Gregory Peck, Richard Basehart, Leo Genn, Orson Welles, James Robertson Justice, Harry Andrews, Bernard Miles, Mervyn Johns, Joseph Tomelty, Royal Dano. (UAS)

What strikes you first is the *color* of the movie. Cinematographer Oswald Morris and John Huston made two sets of negatives, one in color and one in black and white, and printed them together on the final print. The result is full of mood, of antique gray and taupe, water-whitened wood and smoky timber; as full of tints as an aquarelle, as strong as a man's sooty skin, as bright as gold on a black and white sea. You never forget you're in Peter Coffin's Spouter Inn in 1841 or on a whaleboat, but you are ready to believe, too, that you're in the world of Ahab's fantasy.

Moby Dick is not just a yarn about a whaling voyage, though it is the best yarn that will come bursting from the screen for a long time. Huston has made a social microcosm of the *Pequod*, as Melville did. The types of men emerge: Orson Welles's Father Mapple, Leo Genn's Starbuck, Richard Basehart's Ishmael, all have the stamp of the director in command of his theme and style. Gregory Peck is sometimes wooden in the role of Ahab, but we see him struggling with the paradoxes of the human spirit. A superb film, with the meaning as well as the sight and sound of a great novel; recommended for older children.

Modern Times

United Artists 1936. 85 min., b/w. (d)(sp)(m) Charles Chaplin (ph) Rollie Totheroh and Ira Morgan (c) Charles Chaplin, Paulette Goddard, Henry Bergman, Chester Conklin, Stanley Sanford, Hank Mann, Louis Natheaux, Allan Garcia. (PAR)

Chaplin's foreword characterizes MODERN TIMES as "the story of industry, of individual enterprise—humanity crusading in the pursuit of happiness." The pursuit includes factory workers flocking like sheep into the subway, Charlie going berserk on the assembly line from tightening nuts and bolts, whirling in the cogs of a dynamo, being attacked by a feeding machine, being followed by the boss even into the washroom, going on strike, being unemployed, and spending time in jail on a false charge.

When the picture was re-released in 1972, Vincent Canby commented in the *New York Times*: "Quite as astonishing to me as the toughness and precision of the movie itself was the reaction of children in the audience. I don't know how long it's been since I've heard children explode with the kind of helpless laughter that, if left unchecked, turns into the sort of hysteria that leads to exhausted tears. Well, things never got quite that far out of hand. . .but it was only because the Tramp's encounter with the Bellows Automatic Feeding Machine is of limited duration."

The concession Chaplin made to sound in this film—his own musical accompaniment, sound effects, and a few sentences from loudspeakers or television—is interesting, but his song to the tune of "Titina," mixing gibberish and the tongues of Babel and accompanied by hilarious pantomime, is inimitable Chaplin.

Moonwalk

Francis Thompson, Inc./NASA 1976. 94 min., col. (prod) Peretz W. Johnnes (d) Theo Kamecke (sp) Peretz W. Johnnes (ph) James Allen,

Urs Furrer, Alexander Hammid, Adam Holender, Robert Ipcar, Victor Johnnes, Theo Kamecke, Hideaki Kobayashi, Edwin Lynch, Zie-mowit-Maria Kozbial, James Signorelli, Jeri Sopanen (m) Charles Morrow (comm) E.G. Valens (narr) Lawrence Luckinbill. (LCA)

The 1969 flight to the moon, from the tension of the lift-off to the astronauts' jubilant return and the New York City parade.

The commentary puts the flight in the perspective of history and science and raises a philosophical question or two. Shots of people around the world on the morning of July 17 are accom-panied by reflections on what that day meant to the 3 billion in-habitants of the globe. The fascinating mini-planet of the Com-mand module, Columbia; the mystery and beauty of the trip through space; the organization of the launch control center at Cape Kennedy—all are captured in this documentary by extraor-dinary photographers.

An experience no youngster should miss. "We had walked on the moon. . . . We opened our minds to the universe."

The Most Dangerous Game

RKO 1932. 65 min., b/w. (prod) David O. Selznick, Merian C. Cooper (d) Ernest B. Schoedsack, Irving Pichel (sp) James Ashmore Creelman from the short story by Richard Connell (ph) Henry Gerrard (m) Max Steiner (c) Joel McCrea, Leslie Banks, Fay Wray, Robert Armstrong. (AIM, BUD, JAN, MAC)

This taut melodrama, one of the best of its genre, was shot on the same set as KING KONG. Made by the same director and pro-ducer, it also was marked by a relentless buildup and a release of physical shocks maintained with grim (but not gory) details to the end. Like KONG, it was achieved with masterful technical ingenuity.

Leslie Banks, as the mad Count Zaroff, is chillingly restrained; his performance distinguishes the film. A once-famous explorer now isolated on a remote tropical island, Zaroff can recapture the thrill of the hunt only by going after the biggest game of all—man. To provide himself with victims, he causes shipwrecks and then pursues the survivors with a bow and arrow. Robert Rains-ford, another explorer (Joel McCrea), and Eve (Fay Wray) fall into his trap. But Rainsford is also a big-game hunter, a thinking animal who proves more than a match for Zaroff.

The chase is the thing and a dynamic camera involves us in it, and in the fantastic jungle backdrop. The same basic plot (from Richard Connell's short story) has been used over and over again—A GAME OF DEATH, RUN FOR THE SUN, JOHNNY ALLEGRO, KILL OR BE KILLED, THE NAKED PREY, BLOOD FEAST, etc.—but never with as much cinematic effect as in THE MOST DANGEROUS GAME.

The Mouse and His Child

(a.k.a *The Extraordinary Adventures of the Mouse and His Child*)

DeFaria-Lockhart-Sanrio/Murakami Wolf 1976. 83 min., col. animation (d) Fred Wolf, Charles Swenson (sp) Carol Mon Pere from Russell Hoban's novel (ph) Wally Bullock (m) Roger Kellaway (lyr) Gene Lees (c) (voices) Peter Ustinov, Cloris Leachman, Sally Kellerman, Andy Devine, Neville Brand, Bob Holt, Marcy Swenson, Alan Barzman, Joan Gerber. (SAN)

A good animation feature from Russell Hoban's charming novel (1967 American Library Association Notable Book Award), THE MOUSE AND HIS CHILD won the Ruby Slipper Award for best picture, Seventh International Children's Film Festival, Los Angeles, and the "Annie" (animation) Award. "Certainly the story, the characters, the incidents, the humour, the art work, and the animation should please" (Program, 1976 London Film Festival).

A windup mouse and his child long to be self-winding. But before their dream is realized, they experience many trials. Cast out of the toy shop into the world of Manny the Rat (voice of Peter Ustinov), who uses windup toys to build his empire on a city dump, they live through a war between shrews and wood-mice; a bank robbery; a stay with a forest theater group, and a descent into a pond. Their friends are a tin seal (Sally Kellerman), a fortune-telling frog (Andy Devine), an actress parrot (Cloris Leachman), and the mechanical-genius muskrat (Bob Holt) who finally makes them self-winding, free individuals.

Operating on several levels, from exciting adventure to allegory and philosophical quest, THE MOUSE AND HIS CHILD is a fantasy of true originality which should appeal to imaginative children.

The Mouse That Roared

Columbia 1959. 83 min., col. (d) Jack Arnold (sp) Roger MacDougall and Stanley Mann from the novel by Leonard Wibberley (c) Peter Sellers, Jean Seberg, David Kossoff. (GEN)

International relations reduced to absurdity, with moments of pure Mack Sennett. The tiny duchy of Grand Fenwick, of which Peter Sellers is the Grand Duchess, the Prime Minister, and the hereditary Field Marshal, has just sent its army of twenty bowmen in chain mail to invade the United States. Landing in New York during an air raid drill, the Fenwickians are mistaken for men from Mars. Things take a surprising turn; they win the war, and acquire the bomb, the inventor of the bomb, and the inventor's daughter. But Fenwick still has Peter Sellers, and he is more than enough. Cheerful nonsense, with class.

The Music Man

Warners 1962. 151 min., col. (d) Morton Da Costa (sp) Marion Hargrove from the Broadway musical by Meredith Willson and Franklin Lacey (m) Meredith Willson (chor) Onna White (c) Robert Preston, Shirley Jones, Buddy Hackett, Hermione Gingold, Paul Ford, Pert Kelton, Timmy Everett. (GEN)

In 1912, "Professor" Harold Hill (Robert Preston) arrives in the small town of River City, Iowa, and cons the townspeople into subsidizing a boys' band. When the boys finally play, the sound only remotely resembles music, but the folks of River City are delighted. They pour joyously into the the street right behind high-stepping Robert Preston as he leads the kids to the rousing tune of "Seventy-Six Trombones." The ebullience and charm of Robert Preston's performance and the oomp-ah of the movie that Morton Da Costa has made from the Broadway muscial may make it hard for kids in the audience to keep their seats at this point. All three of the big song-and-dance numbers, choreographed by Onna White with effective use of the wide screen, are infectious.

The picture is full of show-biz Americana—fireworks on the Fourth, barbershop quartets, Wells Fargo wagons—photographed with little subtlety but great zing. Really funny is Hermione Gingold in one of her best zany characterizations. But THE MUSIC MAN, in the last analysis, is Robert Preston, and he is something to see and to listen to. Meredith Willson's sure-fire music has been well-scored by Ray Heindorf, who was awarded an Oscar.

Mutiny on the Bounty

MGM 1935. 132 min., b/w. (d) Frank Lloyd (sp) Talbot Jennings, Jules Furthman and Carey Wilson from the novel by Charles Nordhoff and James Hall (ph) Arthur Edeson (m) Herbert Stothart (c) Charles Laughton, Clark Gable, Franchot Tone, Herbert Mundin, Dudley Digges, Donald Crisp, Eddie Quillan, Spring Byington, Movita. (FNC)

Lewis Milestone's 1962 remake of this story, with Marlon Brando, Trevor Howard, and some psychosociological overtones, has its partisans, but we prefer the classic 1935 version produced by Irving Thalberg and Albert Lewin. Nobody who has heard Charles Laughton's *"Mis-ter Chr-r-rist-i-an"* ringing down the years can imagine a better Captain Bligh. The rest of the cast is also legendary. Perhaps we have a special affection for this movie because we remember coming out of a revival of it at the Museum of Modern Art with some teenagers and hearing a cherubic honor student say, with a sigh of delight, "Now I'm going home and give my little brother twenty lashes."

My Childhood

Metromedia 1967. 51 min., b/w. (prod) Arthur Barron (d) Don Horan (ph) Ross Lowell (c) Hubert Humphrey, James Baldwin. (BEN)

A powerful and poignant documentary which will spark the older child's desire to understand the contrasts in the childhoods that shaped the lives and visions of two famous men in "the two Americas." Told in the first person by Hubert Humphrey and James Baldwin, the two parts re-create Hubert Humphrey's childhood in South Dakota—white, small town, loved—and James Baldwin's in Harlem—black, urban ghetto, rejected.

"My childhood was as American as apple pie—really as the Fourth of July. It was a wonderful time of life and I loved it," Humphrey reminisces appreciatively about what home and the influence of his father meant to him.

"My life had begun. . .in the invincible and indescribable squalor of Harlem. . .here in the ghetto I was born," Baldwin says, describing the harsh poverty, despair, and his father's hatred, which led the boy to despise both white and black people.

A multiple award-winner, MY CHILDHOOD is the kind of film that stretches a youngster's knowledge and insight while it absorbs him.

My Fair Lady

Warners 1964. 170 min., col. (d) George Cukor (sp) Alan Jay Lerner from his stage musical from the play Pygmalion by George Bernard Shaw (ph) Harry Stradling (m) Frederick Loewe, scored by André Previn (sets) Cecil Beaton (cost) Cecil Beaton (chor) Hermes Pan (c) Rex Harrison, Audrey Hepburn, Stanley Holloway, Wilfrid Hyde-

White, Gladys Cooper, Jeremy Britt, Theodore Bikel, Mona Washbourne, Isobel Elsom, Henry Daniell (voice) Marni Nixon. (SWA)

Kids don't know about all the awards—Oscars for best picture, Rex Harrison's performance, George Cukor's direction, Cecil Beaton's production design and costumes, and André Previn's scoring; New York Film Critics' awards for best picture and for Harrison's performance. And those who haven't read *Pygmalion* may have no idea of the story. But there's hardly anyone around who hasn't grown up with "Wouldn't It Be Loverly?," "With a Little Bit of Luck," "I'm an Ordinary Man," "Just You Wait," "Why Can't the English?" "I Could Have Danced All Night," "The Rain in Spain," "You Did It," "Show Me," "On the Street Where You Live," "Get Me to the Church on Time," and "I've Grown Accustomed to Her Face."

With a little bit of luck and a tremendous amount of expertise, the musical has been made into a movie that's as much fun to look at as to listen to. Cecil Beaton's decor and costumes are stunning, and Rex Harrison's Professor Higgins, of course, is every intelligent boy's and girl's guide to great acting. As Judith Crist said, they ought to call this My Fair Harrison.

My Friend Flicka

Fox 1943. 90 min., col. (d) Harold Schuster (sp) Lillie Hayward and Francis Edwards Faragoh from the novel by Mary O'Hara (c) Roddy McDowall, Preston Foster, Rita Johnson, Jeff Corey. (FNC)

You're ten years old, and your poor school marks and daydreaming both puzzle and disturb your father, a West Pointer who has a beautiful ranch in Wyoming. When he offers you a colt of your own and you choose an outcast filly bred of a troublesome mare, he is even more disappointed. But you understand your friend Flicka, and after weeks of loving training, she redeems your faith in her, as you redeem your father's faith in you. You, by the way, are Ken, or Roddy McDowall, or any kid dreaming about growing up and *showing them.*

My Side of the Mountain

Paramount 1969. 100 min., col. (d) James B. Clark (sp) Ted Sherdeman, Jane Klove, and Joanna Crawford from the novel by Jean George (ph) Denys Coop (c) Ted Eccles, Theodore Bikel, Tudi Wiggins, Frank Perry, Peggi Loder. (FNC)

This attractively photographed movie about a thirteen-year-old boy who decides rebelliously to go off on his own, packs gear and camping equipment, and sets out with his pet raccoon for the Laurentian Mountains, has a theme to which youngsters respond. They know how disappointed the boy is when his father reneges on a promised camping trip, and they sympathize with his desire to be totally self-sufficient in the woods like his idol Thoreau. They share his friendship with the itinerant folksinger (Theodore Bikel) and the librarian (Tudi Wiggins), but they know what makes Sam leave camp and return to his parents and civilization.

There are absorbing bits of natural history—conducting algae experiments, capturing and training a baby falcon, living in a hollow tree trunk, foraging for food in the wilds—and lovely color photography by Denys Coop. The picture was shot in Toronto, Ontario, and Knowlton, Quebec.

Nanook of the North

Pathé 1922. Original silent version, 60 min., b/w. (d)(sp)(ph) Robert J. Flaherty (asst ed) Charles Gelb (titles) Carl Stearns Clancy and Robert J. Flaherty. (MMA)
United Artists 1947. Reissue, sound and music added, 55 min., b/w. (d)(sp)(ph) Robert J. Flaherty (narr) Ralph Schoolman, spoken by Berry Kroger (m) Rudolph Schramm. (CAL, KPF, PYR, WIL)

"I wanted to show the *Innuit* (the Eskimos). And I wanted to show them not from the civilized point of view but as they saw themselves. . . .I realized then that I must go to work in an entirely different way" (Flaherty). By living and working closely for a year and a half with the great hunter Nanook and his family in the far north of sub-Arctic Canada, Flaherty made a picture (his first) which is not only a remarkable, creative treatment of the actuality of Eskimo life but a classic that established a new approach to the documentary film.

Survival against the elements and the struggle for food—basic in the sub-Arctic—are the core of a vivid true story. Nanook's hunting of the walrus, fishing, building an igloo, teaching his son, relating to his family: here is a great deal for our ecology-minded younger set, which is into wilderness pictures these days.

NANOOK OF THE NORTH received worldwide attention, new for the documentary. Two years after it appeared, when Nanook the great hunter died of starvation deer hunting in the interior of Ungava, the news was reported as far away as Japan. Frances Flaherty tells of buying an Eskimo Pie in the Berliner Tiergarten in the thirties that was called "Nanuk," with Nanook's face on the paper wrapper.

National Velvet

MGM 1944. 123 min., col. (d) Clarence Brown (sp) Theodore Reeves and Helen Deutsch from the novel by Enid Bagnold (c) Elizabeth Taylor, Mickey Rooney, Donald Crisp, Anne Revere, Angela Lansbury. (FNC)

When Elizabeth Taylor was twelve, the most enchanting twelve the screen has seen, she turned a pleasant little story about racing into something special. The butcher's little girl and the sorrel gelding she loves are not just any girl and gelding; they are both stars of myth-making loveliness. Enid Bagnold's story tells how the girl and her rascally friend (Mickey Rooney) turn a hunter into the winner of the Grand National Steeplechase. Clarence Brown gives us some fine views of Aintree and of the English downs near the sea.

Navajo

Lippert 1952. 71 min., b/w. (prod) Hall Bartlett (d) (sp) Norman Foster (ph) Virgil E. Miller (c) Francis Kee Teller, Mrs. Teller, John Mitchell, Linda and Eloise Teller, Hall Bartlett, Billy Draper. (narr) Sammy Ogg. (BUD)

A feature-length dramatization which might deserve the term *documentary*, this compassionate study of the Navajo people through the eyes of a seven-year-old Navajo boy "captures without histrionics the historic background, the ancient folkways and the vast and majestic habitat of the tribe" (*The New York Times*).

Hall Bartlett is the only professional actor in the cast; the others are Indians, with Francis Kee Teller playing the boy, Son of the Hunter. The people of the Arizona reservation bring alive (with the help of Virgil E. Miller's camera) the mesas, the Canyon of Death, the hogans trading post, Navajo cliff dwellings and the sheepherding life of Son of the Hunter's family.

The story tells how the boy learns of his traditions from his beloved foster grandfather, and how he rebels against the threat of the white man's school by running away. Eventually, with the old man's help, Son of the Hunter becomes reconciled to the white man, realizing that the promise of friendship is genuine.

For its information and understanding, presented simply and without didacticism, NAVAJO is excellent fare for children.

The Navigator

*Metro 1924. 62 min., b/w. (d) Buster Keaton, Donald Crisp (sp) Jean
Havez, J. A. Mitchell, Clyde Bruckman (ph) Elgin Lessley, Byron
Houck (c) Buster Keaton, Kathryn McGuire. Silent; music on sound-
track. (MAC)*

Buster Keaton, always fascinated by machinery, based THE NAVI-
GATOR on the delightful notion of a young millionaire couple
adrift on an ocean liner, with Buster's ingenuity applied to adapt-
ing resources intended for a thousand people to the necessities
of two.

"One of Keaton's two perfect films" (Walter Kerr, *The Silent
Clowns*)—the other being THE GENERAL—it is full of inspired silent
comedy: The cooking problems (boiling six coffee beans in six
gallons of water, etc.); the problems of the vicious deck chair and
the wet cards in the ship's saloon; the problem of signaling for
help to a Coast Guard ship by raising the yellow quarantine flag;
the problem of floating near an island inhabited by cannibals. . . ."Buster in a tiny rowboat trying to pull the great liner
after him in hot pursuit of their vanishing visitor. . .is one of
the most sublimely impractical shots in all of Keaton, the image
of minnow tugging whale, and its balance of miniature and mass
is exquisitely characteristic of the man" (Walter Kerr).

THE NAVIGATOR explains why Keaton's reputation grows with the
years. It is a marvelous voyage for children, on the ship with no
crew and no passengers, with only one of the world's masters of
comedy, playing Man against Machine.

A Night at the Opera

*MGM 1935. 90 min., b/w. (d) Sam Wood (sp) George S. Kaufman and
Morrie Ryskind from a story by James Kevin McGuinness with ad-
ditional material by Al Boasberg (c) Groucho, Harpo, and Chico Marx;
Margaret Dumont, Siegfried Rumann, Kitty Carlisle, Allan Jones.
(FNC)*

To the manic mixture as before, new elements have been added—
fine sets and costumes, romance, music, and a plot. Generally
considered the Marx Brothers masterpiece, it is inspired insanity.

Otis B. Driftwood (Groucho) plans to invest the fortune of Mrs.
Claypool (Margaret Dumont) in the New York Opera. On board
ship en route to New York, there are two stowaways, Tomasso
(Harpo) and Fiorello (Chico). The opening night of the opera arrives. The rest is history. Among the many famous sequences:

contract negotiations between Chico and Groucho (*The first part of the party of the first part.* . . .); the order to the steward (*eggs, and roast beef rare, medium, well done, and overdone*); the mass of bodies crowding into Groucho's tiny stateroom; "Cosi-Cosa" played by Harpo on the kazoo; Harpo and Chico slipping "Take Me Out to the Ball Game" into the overture to *Il Trovatore*—but how does one choose? Maybe the best of all is Harpo scampering up the scenery and swinging from the ropes.

A Night to Remember

Britain 1958. 123 min., b/w. (d) Roy Baker (sp) Eric Ambler, based on the book by Walter Lord (c) Kenneth More, Honor Blackman, David McCallum, John Merivale, Laurence Naismith. (BUD, KPF, LCA, MAC)

A forerunner of current disaster epics, A NIGHT TO REMEMBER outclasses them all, not only because it is based on tragic history—the sinking of the *Titanic* on April 14, 1912—but because it offers insight rather than contrived mechanical sensation. Here to the life are the officers, crew, and passengers in the moment of truth.

On the terrible night when the magnificent, doomed ship was ripped by a giant iceberg and sank within two and a half hours with 1,500 of the 2,200 aboard, the staterooms were filled with the elite and the steerage with emigrants. We see heroism as well as naked selfishness, philosophical stoicism as well as moral collapse, efficiency and dedication as well as bumbling error.

In Eric Ambler's script there are many fine cameo portraits of the famous and the obscure. As Officer Lightollel, Kenneth More provides the eyes through which we interpret events.

"A drama of monumental unity and scope," said the *New York Times*. Young people should be fascinated and moved.

Of Stars and Men

John and Faith Hubley 1964. 55 min., col. animation. (prod) John and Faith Hubley (d) John Hubley (sp)(narr) Dr. Harlow Shapley (m/dir) Walter Trampler (m) Petzel, Gabrielli, Bach, Handel, Vivaldi, Mozart. (FIR)

Based on the book by noted astronomer Dr. Harlow Shapley, which he says "was written to tell in simple language what man is and where he is in the universe of atoms, protoplasms, stars and galaxies," this delightful and vivid color animation by John and Faith Hubley makes the scientific concepts not only clear but entertaining.

In a style which the gifted Hubleys called "animage," OF STARS AND MEN is informative about "A Journey through Space," "A Journey through Time," "Matter and Energy," and "Life on Other Planets." Amusing animals, forms, and configurations abound. The lion wears a crown; as man assumes preeminence in the animal kingdom, the crown is passed to a small boy, who (in his moods of boldness and timidity) is Man. And Man is somewhat shaken to discover that he is *not* the center of the universe. He finally comes around to some deep thinking about the meaning of life on earth and the possibility of life on other planets.

It's difficult to imagine anyone, from nine years up, who would not enjoy learning from OF STARS AND MEN. In the prologue and in several key segments, Dr. Shapley is a most lucid narrator, but the real teacher is the cinematic imagination of the creators.

Oklahoma!

Magna 1955. 140 min., col. (d) Fred Zinnemann (sp) Sonya Levien and William Ludwig from the play Green Grow the Lilacs *by Lynn Riggs (m) Richard Rodgers (b&l) Oscar Hammerstein II (chor) Agnes de Mille (c) Gordon MacRae, Shirley Jones, Gloria Grahame, Rod Steiger, Charlotte Greenwood, James Whitmore, Eddie Albert, James Mitchell, Bambi Linn, Marc Platt. (GEN)*

When the governor of Oklahoma attended the New York premiere of the movie made from Rogers and Hammerstein's trailblazing musical, he raised the flag of his state atop the Rivoli Theatre and annexed it into Oklahoma Territory. As well he might—for the wide-angled cameras look right down into the rows of corn, and "Oh, What a Beautiful Mornin'" is everything a morning in the Southwest should be, all sun and sky and vast expanse of color. The historical gesture was right, too; this musical was the first to break ground that was well furrowed after it. Above everything it was a *play*, with all the songs and dances beautifully integrated.

"They sat right back and opened their hearts," Agnes de Mille has written of the audience on opening night. "The show rolled." And the movie rolls. The de Mille ballets seem more enchanting than ever. James Mitchell and Bambi Linn are Curley and Laurey in "Out of My Dreams," and Marc Platt is around, too. Rogers and Hammerstein are said to have kept a sharp eye on the making of the movie, and the scoring won an Oscar.

Old Yeller

Disney 1957. 83 min., col. (d) Robert Stevenson (sp) Fred Gipson and William Tunberg from Gipson's novel (ph) Charles P. Boyle (m) Oliver Wallace (c) Dorothy McGuire, Fess Parker, Tommy Kirk, Kevin Corcoran, Jeff York, Chuck Connors, Beverly Washburn, Spike. (GEN)

Low-key, tasteful direction, good playing, and Fred Gipson's script from his novel save this story of a boy and his dog from being caramel custard. It's popular not only for its child-animal story but for its pleasant frontier flavor. In it young Tommy Kirk has his one good role before he was typecast in a string of Disney formula comedies.

The pioneer Coates family in Texas in 1869 temporarily loses father Jim (Fess Parker) when he goes off on a cattle drive, and fifteen-year-old Travis (Tommy Kirk) becomes the head of the house. His lonely little brother, Arliss (Kevin Corcoran), adopts a big stray dog, "Old Yeller" (Spike), who has wandered into the farm and become part of their lives, a faithful friend and protector. When Old Yeller, on a trapping expedition, catches rabies from some some wild pigs, he must be shot. Travis does it and is devastated. But later he makes friends with one of Old Yeller's pups. His father, home after three months, has helped him to understand that we can't always control things and we must make the best of them.

Oliver!

Britain 1968. 146 min., col. (d) Carol Reed (sp) Vernon Harris from the musical play by Lionel Bart as adapted from Oliver Twist *by Charles Dickens (ph) Oswald Morris (m) Lionel Bart (sets) John Box (chor) Onna White (c) Ron Moody, Oliver Reed, Mark Lester, Hugh Griffith, Shani Wallis, Jack Wild, Harry Secombe, James Hayter. (CCC, CWF, MAC, ROA, SWA)*

What the Dickens—this is Ron Moody's show. The title FAGIN! would be justified, for there's no better music-hall fun on the screen than his miming of "You've Got to Pick a Pocket or Two" and "Reviewing the Situation." When Carol Reed opens up Lionel Bart's stage hit to show the thieves' alleys of the London underworld of the 1830's, the mood is Dickensian, but John Box's sets of the West End and Bloomsbury are more in the musical-comedy style. A typical production number is "Who Will Buy?"—the Georgian facade of a smart London square overrun with singing and dancing nursemaids, soldiers, bobbies, children, window cleaners, and street vendors.

It's all very lively and entertaining; Mark Lester is an appealing Oliver Twist and Jack Wild is a wonderful Artful Dodger, but it is Ron Moody, as a non-Semitic and almost nonvillainous Fagin, who earns the exclamation point. Oscars were awarded for best picture, direction, sets, sound, score, and choreography.

Oliver Twist

Britain 1947. 116 min., b/w. (d) David Lean (sp) David Lean and Stanley Haynes from the novel by Charles Dickens (ph) Guy Green (art) John Bryan (ed) Jack Harris (c) John Howard Davies, Robert Newton, Alec Guinness, Kay Walsh, Francis L. Sullivan, Henry Stephenson, Mary Clare, Kathleen Harrison, Anthony Newley. (JAN)

One of the most realistic representations of mid-Victorian London ever screened, and a filming of Dickens that ranks with David Lean's earlier GREAT EXPECTATIONS, this extraordinary blend of cinematic brilliance and literary richness ran into trouble in some quarters because of Alec Guinness's Streicher-like Fagin, but it endures for its perfect young Oliver—the delicate-featured John Howard Davies—who remains the image of Dickens's workhouse child.

"Oliver Twist's ninth birthday found him a pale, thin child, somewhat diminutive in stature, and decidedly small in circumference"—that is the orphan parish drudge in his Poor Law clothes of the 1830s. Farmed out to a coffin-maker, he runs away and is engulfed by the harsh London of poverty and crime, where he is the natural prey of Fagin and the Artful Dodger (Anthony Newley). As he cries to Mr. Bumble on his way to the Sowerberry establishment, "I am a very little boy, sir; and it is so lonely, sir! So very lonely!"

From the evil company of Bill Sikes (Robert Newton) to the kind protection of Mr. Brownlow (Henry Stephenson), everything has Dickens's heightened dimension of reality. The world of Oliver Twist is magnificently, and often brutally, drawn, as in the novel itself—prime Dickens, prime cinema, and strong stuff for over-tens.

One of Our Dinosaurs is Missing

Disney 1975. 97 min., col. (d) Robert Stevenson (sp) Bill Walsh from the novel The Great Dinosaur Robbery by David Forrest (ph) Paul Beeson (art) Michael Stringer (c) Peter Ustinov, Helen Hayes, Clive Revill, Joan Sims. (GEN)

In London in the 1920s—a deliberately unreal London of fantasy settings—a nicely weird collection of characters becomes strenuously entangled in a plot. Lord Southmere has smuggled out of China a secret formula, "Lotus X," on microfilm. Pursued by Quon (Clive Revill), the right-hand man of Hnup Wan (Peter Ustinov), head of Chinese Intelligence, Southmere hides the microfilm in a skeleton of a dinosaur in the Natural History Museum. Naturally, the dinosaur is stolen. A nannie named Hettie (Helen Hayes), flanked by two children, rallies all the nannies of London in a hunt. After adventures too sinister to get straight, they defeat a War Lord and his minions in Intelligence and recover the missing dinosaur. Quon flees to Outer Mongolia. When "Lotus X" turns out to be a recipe for a product (which we shall not identify for you), Hnup Wan becomes an enthusiastic salesman for it.

The verdict on DINOSAURS has been unanimously thumbs up. "Very pleasing entertainment, wittily played and written and efficiently directed by Disney's old faithful, Robert Stevenson," according to the Monthly Film Bulletin of the British Film Institute.

Peter Rabbit and Tales of Beatrix Potter*

Britain 1971. 90 min., col. (d) Reginald Mills (sp) Richard Goodwin and Christine Edzard from stories and characters created by Beatrix Potter (ph) Austin Dempster (m) John Lanchbery and the orchestra of Covent Garden Opera House (chor) Frederick Ashton (cost) Christine Edzard (art) John Howell (c) Frederick Ashton and members of the Royal Ballet: Alexander Grant, Michael Coleman, Brenda Last, Ann Howard, Robert Mead, Lesley Collier, Sally Ashby, Carole Ainsworth, Avril Bergen. (FNC)

Entirely through the medium of ballet, without one word of dialog, episodes from five of Beatrix Potter's stories are performed by members of the Royal Ballet, wearing animal masks and costumes. In imaginative dances by choreographer Frederick Ashton, to music arranged by John Lanchbery and played by the orchestra of the Covent Garden Opera House, we follow the adventures of Mrs. Tittlemouse and Johnny Townhouse, Jemima Puddle-Duck, Pigling Bland and the Black Berkshire Pig, Tabitha Twitchit, Jeremy Fisher the Frog, Squirrel Nutkin, and Peter Rabbit. The montage sequence of the young girl who was Beatrix Potter, rebelling against her restricted upbringing by escaping with her paintbrush into an imagined world of whimsical animals, is also in pantomime; the clock, the mice in the cage, the Victorian parents, all are wordless.

The enchantment of the whole film is in its *look*: the masks, the costumes, the dances performed on a green meadow in England's lovely Lake District. And don't you believe for a moment that there is no audience for a pigs' *pas de deux*, if the pigs are wearing masks by Rostislav Doboujinsky and costumes by Christine Edzard translated to the screen from Miss Potter's watercolor drawings. A great many little girls will rise on their toes to contradict you.

The Pink Panther

United Artists 1964. 113 min., col. (d) Blake Edwards (sp) Maurice Richlin, Blake Edwards (ph) Philip Lathrop (m) Henry Mancini (c) David Niven, Peter Sellers, Robert Wagner, Capucine, Claudia Cardinale. (UAS)

"Inspector Clouseau Strikes Again—and Again and Again" was the headline on the *Times* advance story for the fifth (perhaps the last) movie in the highest-grossing comedy series ever made. Each sequel to THE PINK PANTHER—A SHOT IN THE DARK, 1964; RETURN OF THE PINK PANTHER, 1975; THE PINK PANTHER STRIKES AGAIN, 1976; REVENGE OF THE PINK PANTHER, 1978—has delighted vast audiences, from critic Vincent Canby to every kid on the block.

Great fun in the series: Richard Williams's animated titles; Blake Edwards's directing; Herbert Lom's playing of Dreyfus, the Sûreté man who is a mental case because of Clouseau's bungling; the outlandish Sellers accents and disguises, and the zany plots. The predictable always occurs, very satisfyingly. No matter what jewel thief, beggar, or suspicious French maid turns up; no matter how many thugs appear at Le Club Foot, Inspector Clouseau is going to display the ineptitude that has made his name a glorious beacon of hilarity in the murky world of crime fiction. "A man of great dignity who is unfortunately accident prone" (Sellers's description) doesn't begin to do justice to the facets of the character he has created.

Children seem to pass right over the more sophisticated elements in the stories. "The bedroom scenes are played for laughs, so they are quite inoffensive," said the editor of *Film Information* (National Council of Churches of Christ).

Pinocchio*

RKO 1940. 88 min., col. animation. (prod) Walt Disney (d) Ben Sharpsteen, Hamilton Luske (sp) From the story by Collodi (Carlo Lorenzini) (m) Leigh Harline, Ned Washington (voices) Dickie Jones, Cliff Edwards, Evelyn Venable, Walter Catlett, Frankie Darro. (THEATERS)

In many people's judgment, the best Disney feature of them all—for innovative animation, characters, musical score.

Compared with Collodi's original, which has many frightening elements, the Disney story is restrained. There are delightful additions: J. Worthington Foulfellow, a con-man fox; his henchman, Gideon, an avaricious cat; a juvenile delinquent named Lampwick. The cricket was developed into one of Disney's most famous animated characters, Jiminy Cricket (voice of Cliff Edwards). Songs like "Give a Little Whistle" and "When You Wish Upon a Star" brighten the tale.

The special effects in PINOCCHIO are striking, and the animation and backgrounds are of a high order. It would take pages to name all the gifted studio craftsmen responsible, but one can spot, in the credits, the late John Hubley and the distinguished illustrators Gustav Tenggren and Martin Provensen, who executed some of the many brilliant watercolor studies for the scenes.

The fantasy of PINOCCHIO— the boy transformed into a donkey, the man living on a boat inside a whale—inspired Disney to make a film of which Archer Winsten wrote, "In reviewing PINOCCHIO, you are limited only by your power of expressing enthusiasm. . . .this film is fantastically delightful" (New York Post).

Planet of the Apes

Fox 1968. 112 min., col. (d) Franklin J. Shaffer (sp) Rod Serling, Michael Wilson from the novel Monkey Planet *by Pierre Boulle (ph) Leon Shamroy (c) Charlton Heston, Roddy McDowall, Kim Hunter, Maurice Evans, James Whitmore, James Daly, Linda Harrison. (FNC)*

In the final (fifth) film of the Planet Ape series (BATTLE FOR THE PLANET OF THE APES, 1973), the last shot reveals the famous ape Caesar shedding a tear. He's saying goodbye to "one of the best science-fiction fantasies ever to come out of Hollywood. . . . Extraordinarily constructed, very efficient and craftsman like—so sit back and enjoy it" (Pauline Kael, *The New Yorker*).

The praise is most deserved by the original film, PLANET OF THE APES. No *Penguin Island*, it is still amusing entertainment with a hint of satire. Three American astronauts led by Charlton Heston, whose space ship is lost, drop in on a planet where everyone is an ape. It is 2500 years from now, and the apes are much brighter than Heston. The story is suspenseful and sometimes allegorical, and there are lines like "Human-see, human-do," and "I never met an ape I didn't like." What sets the film apart is the quality of its fascinating anthropoid masks. You don't get a chance every day to watch Maurice Evans or Kim Hunter in such creative makeup design (by John Chambers). The sequels introduced James Franciscus (BENEATH THE PLANET OF THE APES, 1970) on a rescue mission to find Heston, now living in a post-bomb New York City; Bradford Dillman (ESCAPE FROM THE PLANET OF THE APES, 1972); Ricardo Montalban and Don Murray (CONQUEST OF THE PLANET OF THE APES, 1972); and Claude Akins (BATTLE FOR THE PLANET OF THE APES, 1973). Roddy McDowall is in all five films; the baby chimp born in ESCAPE, he grows up to lead a revolt. The war between man and ape ends peaceably, by the way.

Pollyanna

Disney 1960. 134 min., col. (d) David Swift (sp) David Swift from the novel by Eleanor H. Porter (c) Hayley Mills, Jane Wyman, Richard Egan, Karl Malden, Nancy Olson, James Drury, Adolphe Menjou, Donald Crisp, Agnes Moorehead. (GEN)

Times have changed since Mary Pickford was the "Glad Girl." Hayley Mills at thirteen is quite inoffensive and seems like a good kid to know. She proves that, if a born actress is in the leading role, a good movie entertainment can be made from a book that has been embalmed in molasses for years. The youngster who warms up a whole town with her slant on living is not really Pollyanna-ish; she's Hayley. In this bit of nostalgic Americana, her performance was awarded a special Oscar as the best of the year by a juvenile. No contest.

The Popeye Follies: His Times and Life

Max Fleischer 1973. 85 min., b/w and col. animation. Max Fleischer, Robert Clampett (c) Popeye, Olive Oyl, Bluto, Wimpy, Sweet Pea, James Cagney, Rita Rio, Cab Calloway, Zachinni, Al Jolson, Will Rogers, Laurie Beecool, Gogart. (UAS)

Popeye, the mumbling sailor man with the heart of gold, is having his fiftieth birthday—he's settled a lot of arguments since he was created by cartoonist E. C. Segar in 1929. In addition to the works in progress as we go to press (an animated Popeye feature by Hanna-Barbera, sixteen CBS half-hour programs, and a live movie from Paramount), here is "An Outrageous Animated Anthology of Works by Max Fleischer" ready to enjoy.

Ever since Elzie Segar's character was brought imaginatively to the screen by producer Max Fleischer and director Dave Fleischer

(1933-1943), it's been fun for cartoon buffs. The selection in THE POPEYE FOLLIES includes some of the best two-reelers. There is also live-action footage of the 1930s. Appearing as they did at the time are James Cagney in FOOTLIGHT PARADE, Al Jolson singing "Mammy," Will Rogers making a famous speech, the first human cannonball, etc. Until kids can see the promised glories in the future films (Dustin Hoffman and Lily Tomlin as Popeye and Olive Oyl? Maybe.), THE POPEYE FOLLIES is their meat. Or their spinach, which stood the dockside hero in much better stead.

The Prisoner of Zenda

United Artists 1937. 100 min., b/w with Sepiatone. (prod) David O. Selznick (d) John Cromwell, W. S. Van Dyke (sp) John Balderston, Wills Root and Donald Ogden Stewart from the novel by Anthony Hope and the play by Edward Rose (m) Alfred Newman (c) Ronald Colman, Madeleine Carroll, Douglas Fairbanks, Jr., Mary Astor, C. Aubrey Smith, Raymond Massey, David Niven, Montagu Love, Ben Webster. (FNC)

Of the three film versions of THE PRISONER OF ZENDA (four, if you count the parody in THE GREAT RACE), the 1937 Selznick production is the nonpareil.

In 1922, Lewis Stone and Raymond Novarro starred in the version directed by Rex Ingram. In 1952, Stewart Granger, Deborah Kerr, and James Mason starred in a color version, directed by Richard Thorpe, that was almost a scene-by-scene remake of the Selznick film.

What distinguishes the 1937 version is its incomparable cast. Ronald Colman is just what he should be in the dual role of the Englishman Rudolph Rassendyl and his royal cousin and identical double, King Rudolf V. Madeline Carroll is the perfect Princess Flavia. The young readers who still like Anthony Hope's novel will become as involved with the machinations of Black Michael (Raymond Massey) and his henchman, Rupert of Hentzau (Douglas Fairbanks, Jr.), as ever. For the kingdom of Ruritanian romance is ageless, and in this film it is inhabited by players who know their way around.

Pygmalion

Britain 1938. 90 min., b/w. (prod) Gabriel Pascal (d) Anthony Asquith, Leslie Howard (sp) W. P. Lipscombe, Cecil Lewis, Ian Dalrymple, based on the play by George Bernard Shaw; additional dialog by

*Shaw (ph) Harry Stradling (m) Arthur Honegger (c) Wendy Hiller,
Leslie Howard, Wilfred Lawson, Marie Lohr, Scott Sunderland, Esme
Percy, David Tree. (JAN, LCA)*

Yes, children, long before MY FAIR LADY there was a wonderful
movie called PYGMALION, also based on Shaw's famous play about
a professor of phonetics who teaches a Cockney flower seller to
speak educated English and become a lady and who ends by falling in love with his own creation. What's more, Anthony Asquith's
"straight version" remains for many people the most satisfying
and perfectly cast film of the original.

The roots of Shaw's delightful entertainment go a long way
back. There's W. S. Gilbert's comedy *Pygmalion and Galatea*,
which may or may not be descended from William Morris's *The
Earthly Paradise*, which was certainly based on John Marston's
1598 *Metamorphosis of Pygmalion*, based on Ovid's *Metamor-
phoses*, based on the Greek legend about the sculptor who fell
in love with the statue of Aphrodite to which he had given
life. . . .It's *always* been a great story.

Brilliant, witty, skillfully played, the Asquith film has Wendy
Hiller's perfect Eliza Doolittle, Wilfred Lawson's delightful Doolittle, and Leslie Howard's charming Henry Higgins. The screenplay won an Oscar in 1938.

A lot of fun, not the least bit overshadowed by MY FAIR LADY.
You can't have too much of a good thing.

The Quiet Man

*Republic 1952. 129 min., col. (d) John Ford (sp) Frank S. Nugent from
a story by Maurice Walsh (ph) Winton C. Hoch (m) Victor Young;
traditional Irish songs (c) John Wayne, Maureen O'Hara, Barry Fitzgerald, Victor McLaglen, Ward Bond, Mildred Natwick, Arthur
Shields, Eileen Crowe. (AIM, BUD, MAC, ROA, TWY)*

"My first love story," John Ford called this lovely picture, which
is as much about his love for Ireland as it is about Sean Thornton's
love for a fiery colleen. THE QUIET MAN is a sweet Irish song on
the beauty of County Galway, on love at first sight, and on the
humor and excitement of life among some inimitable Irish characters. They cook up a plot as thick and tasty as Irish oatmeal, full
of races and courtings, a wedding, and a magnificent donnybrook
that makes everything right at the end.

Sean Thornton (John Wayne), a retired American-Irish boxer
with his own reason for avoiding a fight with any man, returns
to the land of his people. He falls in love with red-haired Mary
Kate Danaher (Maureen O'Hara) and is the Petruchio to her Kate.

Mary Kate's guardian is her brother, Squire Will Danaher (Victor McLaglen), a hard nut to crack. The Yank and the Danahers, until they work it out, have very different slants on dowries and honor.

The movie introduces you to some of the most delightful people you'll ever meet: the matchmaker, Michaeleen Oge Flynn (Barry Fitzgerald); the Widow Tillane (Mildred Natwick); and two clergymen cut from surprising cloth, Father Lonergan (Ward Bond) and the Reverend Cyril ("Snuffy") Playfair (Arthur Shields).

The over-twelves will enjoy themselves. THE QUIET MAN won two Academy Awards, for the color cinematography and the direction.

Raggedy Ann and Andy*

Fox 1977. 84 min., col. Live action & animation. (prod) Richard Horner/Osterman Prods./Bobbs-Merrill (prod super-d) Richard Williams (assoc d) Gerald Potterton (sp) Patricia Thackray, Max Wilk, based on the characters created by Johnny Gruelle (m)(lyr) Joe Raposo (ph) Al Rezek (anim art) Grim Natwick, Art Babbitt, Emory Hawkins, Tissa David, Gerald Potterton, Gerry Chiniquy (c) Claire Williams (voices) Didi Conn, Mark Baker, Fred Stuthman, Niki Flacks, George S. Irving. (FNC)

Under the imaginative direction of British animation artist Richard Williams (the Pink Panther films; the Oscar-winning animated A CHRISTMAS CAROL), this visually charming cartoon story with music reacquaints children with two old friends from their fairy-tale days. Created fifty years ago by Johnny Gruelle and still loved, Raggedy Ann and Andy have their own personalities and lots of friends.

The film opens and closes with live action, with director Williams's daughter Claire as Marcella Gruelle, for whom her father wrote the stories. The dolls come to life, and the animated story revolves around the efforts of Raggedy Ann and Andy to rescue a French doll, Babette, who has been kidnapped by pirates.

Because the script is not too juvenile, the adventures hold one's attention, and there are sixteen songs in an amusing score by Joe Raposo ("Sesame Street"). "But the star of the film is really Richard Williams. . .a worthy successor to Walt Disney" (Ken Wlaschin, Program, London Film Festival). A number of animation artists who worked for Disney, as well as Gerald Potterton of YELLOW SUBMARINE fame, contributed their talents to the film.

A Raisin in the Sun

Columbia 1961. 128 min., b/w. (d) Daniel Petrie (sp) Lorraine Hansberry from her play (m) Laurence Rosenthal (c) Sidney Poitier, Claudia

McNeil, Ruby Dee, Diana Sand, Ivan Dixon, John Fiedler, Louis Gossett. (GEN)

"Of all the films I've done," said Sidney Poitier at a Fordham Film Study Conference in 1967, "I like RAISIN the best. It is the most representative of black ghetto life—the hopes, fears, aspirations, frustrations of the people."

Lorraine Hansberry's screenplay from her own stage work and Daniel Petrie's direction have won some accolades from cinema buffs, and the movie has won not only a Cannes Festival award for "outstanding human values" but a lasting place in the experience of mature youngsters who respond to compassionate realism on the screen. They come away from this story of a Chicago family's "upward thrust" with insight into character as well as into the problems of race. The original Broadway cast, particularly Claudia McNeil as the mother who knows life "ain't no crystal stair," is very effective.

The Red Badge of Courage

MGM 1951. 69 min., b/w. (d) John Huston (sp) John Huston from the novel by Stephen Crane (ph) Harold Rosson (c) Audie Murphy, Bill Mauldin, Douglas Dick, Royal Dano, John Dierkes, Arthur Hunnicutt, Tim Durant. (FNC)

In its sixty-nine minutes, John Huston's movie is what Hemingway called Stephen Crane's novel, "all as much of one piece as a poem is." It's not surprising that the director of battle documentaries like SAN PIETRO and REPORT FROM THE ALEUTIANS should create a brilliant picture of a Civil War episode in the engagement of one regiment of Fighting Joe Hooker's Army of the Rappahannock at Chancellorsville.

Huston and photographer Harold Rosson have given us more than shots of discarded haversacks and bloody bayonets on grassy meadows or the chaos of yelling men and plunging horses in the line of fire. The film evokes the sum of a battle experience from the infinitesimal, significant details that an individual soldier knows. Henry Fleming is not only a recruit, but he is the Youth, green and growing, and the red badge he wins is the intimation of his maturity.

Perhaps because there is very little mechanized warfare in this war movie without kiss-kiss or bang-bang, the young viewer may be able to retain the image of the human being: the flaxen-mustached lieutenant, exhausted, sleeping against the trunk of a tree, or the Loud Soldier (Bill Mauldin) suddenly out of bluster.

The Red Shoes

Britain 1948. 133 min., col. (d) (sp) Michael Powell and Emeric Press-burger (ph) Jack Cardiff (m) The Royal Philharmonic Orchestra conducted by Sir Thomas Beecham (chor) Robert Helpmann (c) Moira Shearer, Anton Walbrook, Marius Goring, Leonide Massine, Robert Helpmann, Albert Basserman, Ludmilla Tcherina, the Sadler's Wells Corps de Ballet. (BUD, CWF, LCA, MAC, TWY)

A small boy we know, usually entranced by baseball, fell under a spell of enchantment during THE RED SHOES. It is full of magic—the color, Leonide Massine, and the twice-told tale, backstage and in the ballet, of the girl who comes to grief when she tries to slip out of her dancing shoes into something more comfortable.

In a romantic drama, dancer and musician are pitted against impresario, while the volatile artists of the Lermontov Ballet Company rehearse and perform at Monte Carlo, Covent Garden, and the Paris Opera. Director Michael Powell has said that in real ballet there's too much "allez-oop," while in film ballet you can cut out the *allez* and get on with the *oop*. As the camera changes ballet into fantasy in Robert Helpmann's "Ballet of the Red Shoes," the pleasure is in the *oop*, in such images as Moira Shearer's dance with a swirling abstract figure made of newspaper which turns into Robert Helpmann and back in a few seconds.

Children will enjoy the way the camera lifts Miss Shearer into a wisp, a feather, of painted motion. Four of the craftsmen who collaborated with Hans Christian Andersen to fashion this lovely film won Academy Awards: photographer Jack Cardiff (BLACK NARCISSUS), art director Hein Heckroth, set designer Arthur Lawson, and music scorer Brian Easdale.

Ride a Wild Pony*

Disney 1975. 91 min., col. (d) Don Chaffey (sp) Rosemary Anne Sisson from the novel A Sporting Proposition by James Aldridge (ph) Jack Cardiff (m) John Addison (c) Robert Bettles, Eva Griffith, John Meillon, Michael Craig. (GEN)

Scriptwriter Rosemary Anne Sisson, who did so well by the pit ponies in THE LITTLEST HORSE THIEVES, here makes a wild, white, and Welsh pony the object of a tug-of-love between a poor boy, Scotty Pirie (Robert Bettles), who has lost it, and a spoiled little rich girl, the crippled daughter of a rancher, Josie Eyre (Eva Griffith), who claims it. The pony responds in turn to the names Taff (Scotty's) and Bo (Josie's). Which child will he choose?

The audience becomes very much involved in the warm human drama. Despite several predictable Disney touches, there is an added dimension in the treatment of the characters. The story is set in the Australian outback of the 1930s, and (as in THE LITTLEST HORSE THIEVES) we are made aware of social and economic barriers. The beauty of the color photography by Jack Cardiff (THE RED SHOES) and the performances of John Meillon as a local lawyer and Robert Bettles as headstrong Scotty contribute to the film's quality.

Ring of Bright Water*

Britain 1969. 107 min., col. (d) Jack Couffer (sp) Jack Couffer and Bill Travers from the autobiographical novel by Gavin Maxwell (ph) Wolfgang Suschitzky (c) Bill Travers, Virginia McKenna, Peter Jeffrey, Jameson Clark, Helena Gloag, Roddy McMillan. (FNC)

Time magazine said this provided children with their prime requisites for a movie: "1) a star with fur, 2) adults who look foolish, and 3) no love scenes except those between otter and otter." Bill Travers and Virginia McKenna, once in love with Elsa (BORN FREE), are now in love with Mijbil, a natural scene-stealer. After enlivening their days, Mijbil loses his life and bequeaths a female otter and three cubs to them to bring up in a small cottage.

Whether or not children know Gavin Maxwell's trilogy about his experiences with otters, they will find the movie entertaining and refreshing. The approach to both otters and people is not cute but civilized. Director Jack Couffer, who previously worked on several of Walt Disney's animal films (NIKKI, THE LEGEND OF LOBO, WILD DOG OF THE NORTH, THE LIVING DESERT), shot this mostly in the beautiful highlands of western Scotland. The camera work of Wolfgang Suschitzky (ULYSSES) is outstanding.

Road to Bali

Paramount 1952. 91 min., col. (d) Hal Walker (sp) Frank Butler, Hal Kanter, and William Morrow (c) Bop Hope, Bing Crosby, Dorothy Lamour, Dean Martin, Jerry Lewis, Jane Russell, Humphrey Bogart. (BUD, MAC, TWY)

The sixth ROAD picture is the funniest and the only one in color. Bing and Bob are at the top of their form, and Dorothy is in a pink sarong. The two song-and-dance men on the run are stranded in Australia, get mixed up with an island prince, sunken treasure, a lovesick gorilla, headhunters, cannibals, and Miss Lamour. Don't be surprised to see Bogey coming out of the swamp in his boat from THE AFRICAN QUEEN. Gags at split-second intervals, and songs by James Van Heusen and Johnny Burke.

Romeo and Juliet

Britain-Italy 1968. 138 min., col. (d) Franco Zeffirelli (sp) Franco Brusati, Masolino D'Amico and Franco Zeffirelli from the play by Shakespeare (ph) Pasquale De Santis (m) Nino Rota (c) Leonard Whiting, Olivia Hussey, Milo O'Shea, Michael York, John McEnery, Pat Heywood, Natasha Parry. (PAR)

With thirteen movies of ROMEO AND JULIET between 1908 and 1968 to choose from, there's a style for almost everyone. Traditionalists admire Leslie Howard and Norma Shearer (1936); others find pleasure in Renato Castellani's Renaissance settings (1954) or in the two ballet films, the Bolshoi BALLET OF ROMEO AND JULIET (1954) with Ulanova, and the Royal Ballet film (1966) with Rudolph Nureyev and Margot Fonteyn.

Zeffirelli's movie is the teenager's favorite. "I wanted to bring the story to the attention of young people," he has said. "The story is of two urchins crushed by a stupid, banal quarrel with origins even the adults don't know. In love the young people found an ideal—one they could die for—and youth today is hungry for ideals." Unquestionably, today's young audiences identify with the sixteen-year-old Juliet (Olivia Hussey) and the seventeen-year-old Romeo (Leonard Whiting), who flatten the verse and seldom rise to any heights but who are indisputably the "urchins" crushed by adults.

This is a movie for adolescents to see, not because it is Shakespeare but because it is a love story with color, vivid action, and frequent visual beauty. When they come to their "Required Reading" chore, it will not be a chore at all; waiting for them is the discovery of the poetry and wit that the movie lacks. Until then, Zeffirelli's rich fifteenth-century tapestry and Nino Rota's music are a good introduction to the deathless young lovers.

Rookie of the Year

ABC/TV 1975. 47 min., col. (d) Lawrence B. Elikann (sp) Gloria Banta from the book Not Bad for a Girl by Isabella Taves (ph) Richard Francis (c) Jodie Foster, Ned Wilson. (TIM)

Eleven-year-old Sharon (Jodie Foster) plays baseball like a pro. Should she be allowed to fill in for an injured player on an all-boys' Little League team? The supportive coach (Ned Wilson) says yes, and so do her parents, but her brother, who's also on the team, though he doesn't play as well as Sharon, is hostile: why can't she stick to softball like the other girls? When Sharon joins the team, her brother isn't the only one who feels threatened. Irate adults pull their sons off the team and threaten to fire the coach. Sharon's girl friends stop inviting her to parties. When she goes up at bat, there are catcalls: "Give her a pink bat! Go home to Mommy, you're getting your hair dirty!" Of course, Sharon saves the coach's job and wraps up the final game for her team. The catcalls are still heard in the stands, but our girl steals that last base, home plate, and her brother admits she's great.

Though it's no longer illegal to recruit a girl for a contact sport, ROOKIE OF THE YEAR isn't dated; many a suburban town is still populated by holdouts, and many role-playing stereotypes still plague a girl who's having more than her share of peer and adult pressures and identity conflicts.

Jodie Foster handles her bat and her banter with liveliness and expertise, never once suggesting a PAPER MOON–style brat. Kids should enjoy this Emmy and festival award-winning "ABC After-school Special," and should root for Sharon as she comes home free in every sense.

Ruggles of Red Gap

Paramount 1935. 90 min., b/w. (d) Leo McCarey (sp) Walter De Leon and Harland Thompson from the novel by Harry Leon Wilson (c) Charles Laughton, Mary Boland, Charles Ruggles, Zasu Pitts, Roland Young. (MMA, TWY, UNI)

There's still a lot of mileage in Harry Leon Wilson's homespun comedy about the gentleman's gentleman who was exported to a frontier town. Edward Everett Horton, 1923; Bob Hope (FANCY PANTS), 1950; the musical, 1969—but Leo McCarey's film is tops, nice and easy, with a cast of pros working warmly together.

There are two Ruggleses: Charlie Ruggles as Cousin Egbert, the former sourdough turned millionaire, and Charles Laughton as *the* Ruggles, the British butler to end all British butlers. Both before and after his Western thaw he is a pleasure to watch, and the famous scene in which he recites the Gettysburg Address is not a bit embarrassing, but low-key and moving. A favorite scene of the kids is the Earl of Burnstead (Roland Young) fumbling "Pretty Baby" on the drums.

Run Wild, Run Free

Columbia 1969. 100 min., col. (d) Richard C. Sarafian (sp) David Rook from his novel The White Colt *(ph) Wilkie Cooper (m) David Whitaker (c) Mark Lester, John Mills, Sylvia Syms, Gordon Jackson, Bernard Miles, Fiona Fullerton. (BUD, CWF, MAC, SWA, TWY)*

Ten-year-old Philip, played by Mark Lester of OLIVER!, is so emotionally troubled as a result of an early traumatic experience that he hasn't been able to speak a word for years. Caring only for the wild animals on the moor, he sets his heart on capturing and taming a beautiful white colt. In the tradition of MY FRIEND FLICKA, the colt becomes the symbol of the boy's strength and the means of his recovery. Threads in Philip's story are reminiscent of other child-and-animal movies. The parents fail to communicate with their son, and except for "The Moorman" (John Mills), a retired Army colonel, the adult world is alien to him. Philip, a neighbor's little girl, the colt, and a pet kestrel live quite apart, in complete rapport.

Filmed in Dartmoor, Devonshire, England, the movie has many beautifully photographed scenes of the animals and children on the moors, a fine cast, and overall sensitivity and taste.

The Russians Are Coming, The Russians Are Coming

United Artists 1966. 126 min., col. (d) Norman Jewison (sp) William Rose from Nathaniel Benchley's novel The Off-Islanders *(c) Carl Reiner, Eva Marie Saint, Alan Arkin, Brian Keith, Jonathan Winters, Theodore Bikel, Paul Ford, John Phillip Law, Andrea Dromm, Tessie O'Shea, Ben Blue. (UAS)*

Take a pair of topnotch writers: novelist Nathaniel Benchley, whose *The Off-Islanders* brims over with comic invention, and scriptwriter William Rose (GENEVIEVE, THE LADY KILLERS), who knows that nothing is funnier than ordinary people in an extraordinary situation. (A pig-headed commander of a Russian submarine grounded on a sandbar off a New England island has trouble getting away because the islanders are heated up by the Cold War.) Add a pride of comic players: Theodore Bikel, all in Russian; Carl Reiner, a Thurberish wonder; Alan Arkin, never better than in this first screen role. Spice with hilarious developments running the gamut from high satire to Ben Blue burlesque (the Paul Revere ride that never came off). The result is a picture that can be seen again and again with unremitting joy. Perhaps that is because it is one of those rare movies where we like all the people we are laughing at. For the young, who will never dream that it is highly moral, it is full of lessons in human nature, international relations, child rearing, the art of comedy, and the nature of English-Russian idiom. For instance, there is the scene where the Russian sailors in "disguise" try to tell the New Englanders to get off the streets. . . .

Safety Last*

Hal Roach/Pathé 1923. 81 min., b/w. (d) Fred Newmeyer, Sam Taylor (sp) Hal Roach, Sam Taylor, Tim Whelan (ph) Walter Lundin (c) Harold Lloyd, Mildred Davis, Bill Strothers, Noah Young, Westcott Clarke, Mickey Daniels, Anna Townsend. Silent with music and sound effects. (PAR)

Say "Harold Lloyd" to almost anyone with a store of film memorabilia and he sees the comedian dangling precariously from the hands of a giant clock ten stories off the city street. As Walter Kerr has said, that classic image persists in the public mind like a race memory. Youngsters will enjoy discovering it in SAFETY LAST, the most famous feature of the "King of Daredevil Comedy."

Harold is a go-getter trying to make good as a clerk in a department store. He has trouble at a sale, attacked by a horde of lady shoppers, but it's nothing to the trouble he gets into when The Girl (Mildred Davis) arrives on a visit. He's pretended to be the manager. To impress her, he puts on quite a show. His climbing the store building as a publicity stunt is the climax.

Filming the climb with minimal deception and a minimum of safety devices—no rear-projection or process shots are involved—Lloyd did it mostly by himself, with "Human Spider" Bill Strothers doubling only in the extreme long shots. Harold's desperate acrobatics provide some of the most hilarious moments on the screen. (On the same program with SAFETY LAST are the prize-turkey and new-car gag sequences from his 1924 film HOT WATER.)

The Sea Hawk

Warners 1940. 130 min., b/w. (d) Michael Curtiz (sp) Howard Koch and Seton I. Miller from the novel by Rafael Sabatini (ph) Sol Polito (m) Erich Wolfgang Korngold (c) Errol Flynn, Brenda Marshall, Claude Rains, Donald Crisp, Flora Robson, Alan Hale, Henry Daniell, Una O'Connor, James Stephenson, Gilbert Roland, William Lundigan. (UAS)

In a performance of splendid panache, Errol Flynn sweeps through one of the great Warners sea epics. It presents the rousing spectacle, backed by a glittering musical score and Michael Curtiz's directorial flair, of the undeclared war against Spanish shipping waged in the sixteenth century by the English sea captains loyal to Queen Elizabeth. The climax is reached when Queen Elizabeth is warned, in time, of the coming Armada. Historically, the deadliest of these "sea hawks" was Sir Francis Drake. In the movie he is symbolized by Flynn as Captain Geoffrey Thorpe.

Not in the Sabatini original, but in the spirit of 1940, the production date, are the script's several veiled references to the need for opposition to military aggression.

The Secret Life of Walter Mitty

RKO 1947. 110 min., col. (d) Norman Z. McLeod (sp) Ken Englund and Everett Freeman from the short story by James Thurber (m) Sylvia Fine (c) Danny Kaye, Virginia Mayo, Boris Karloff, Fay Bainter, Ann Rutherford, Florence Bates, Thurston Hall, Reginald Denny. (AIM, MAC, TWY)

When you can have Danny Kaye as a timid proofreader who stars himself in dream sequences as Wing Commander Mitty, the scourge of the Luftwaffe, and Surgeon Mitty, and Mississippi gambler Mitty, what more can you ask? Samuel Goldwyn has thrown in the Goldwyn Girls, and the scriptwriters have padded Thurber's story without strengthening it, but this is a hugely entertaining movie just the same. Thanks to songwriter Sylvia Fine ("Sylvia has a good head on my shoulders," Kaye once said of his wife), it has at least one gem not in the original, Danny performing "Symphony for Unstrung Tongue."

Serengeti Shall Not Die

Allied Artists 1959. 83 min., col. (prod)(d)(ph) Michael Grzimek (assoc prod) Dr. Bernhard Grzimek (sp) Michael and Bernhard Grzimek from their book (ed) Klaus Dudenhofer (m) Wolfgang Zeller (comm) Holger Hagen. (BUD)

Winner of the Academy Award for best documentary feature of 1959, this straightforward film says clearly that African wild game will soon be as extinct as the great North American herds unless we save them.

SERENGETI SHALL NOT DIE is the joint effort, based on their book, of Dr. Bernhard Grzimek, director of the Frankfurt Zoo, and his son, Michael. It was completed by Dr. Grzimek after his son, who appears in much of the film, was killed when a vulture struck his plane. The two naturalists have photographed the vast roaming herds of the Serengeti National Park in Tanganyika, the largest wild animal preserve in the world. They establish that the herds, usually estimated at a million animals, are fast decreasing. By capturing and marking zebra, wildebeest, and other game, they can trace the herd migrations and judge the number of animals who would have to leave the preserve or starve, under certain government boundaries then proposed.

Critic Pauline Kael praised the "moral beauty" of this documentary. "And the solid information it provides, to children and adults, and its undisguised message of indignation and its cry for help are an appeal to our intelligence. It demonstrates that there are good, brave causes left" (*Kiss Kiss Bang Bang*, "Movies for Young Children").

Seven Brides for Seven Brothers

MGM 1954. 102 min., col. (d) Stanley Donen (sp) Albert Hackett, Frances Goodrich, and Dorothy Kingsley from Stephen Vincent Benet's story "The Sobbin' Women" (ph) George Folsey (m) Johnny Mercer and Gene de Paul (chor) Michael Kidd (c) Howard Keel, Jeff Richards, Jane Powell, Julie Newmar, Russ Tamblyn, Tommy Rall, Marc Platt, Jacques d'Amboise, Nancy Kilgas, Betty Carr, Ruta Kilmonis, Norma Doggett. (FNC)

This zestful, buoyant, and enormously attractive musical puts its best foot forward every bit of the way. There are fourteen dancing and singing roles. The songs serve mainly as accompaniment to the dances, and the "best foot" belongs to superb young dancers from the ballet theater and the musical stage. The whole beautifully integrated entertainment is a tribute to talent: Stanley Donen, the director (FUNNY FACE, THE PAJAMA GAME, DAMN YANKEES); Michael Kidd, the choreographer (WHERE'S CHARLEY, GUYS AND DOLLS); and Adolph Deutsch and Saul Chaplin, winners of an Oscar for their musical scoring.

Stephen Vincent Benet's story "The Sobbin' Women" is as delightful a source for a dance movie as one could find. The Oregon Territory in 1850 is the setting for a boisterous updating of Plutarch's account of the Romans' seizing of the Sabine women, with opportunities for such colorful bits of Americana as a barn-raising. Among the numbers to enjoy are "Bless Your Beautiful Hide," "Goin' Courtin'," and "Sobbin Women." But then it's all there to enjoy—the best dance musical between SINGIN' IN THE RAIN and WEST SIDE STORY.

Shane

Paramount 1953. 117 min., col. (d) George Stevens (sp) A. B. Guthrie, Jr., from the novel by Jack Schaefer (ph) Loyal Griggs (m) Victor Young (c) Alan Ladd, Van Heflin, Jean Arthur, Brandon de Wilde, Jack Palance, Ben Johnson, Edgar Buchanan. (FNC)

In the dream factory of Hollywood, there is no more legendary hero than the drifter Shane, the ex-gunfighter, as he is seen through the eyes of a nine-year-old boy. As Robert Warshow says in *The Immediate Experience*, Shane "is hardly a man at all, but something like the Spirit of the West, beautiful in fringed buckskins." He comes mysteriously out of the landscape, destroys the villain who is terrorizing the homesteaders, and fades away again into the more distant horizon, his day over, "leaving behind the wondering little boy who might have imagined the whole story."

The poetic quality of the film is achieved through the direction of George Stevens (A PLACE IN THE SUN, GIANT) and the color photography of Loyal Griggs, whose beautiful shots of the Teton range in Wyoming won him an Academy Award. From the opening sequence, with the lone rider emerging from the West and young Joey stalking the deer, SHANE is the kind of movie which makes a myth for the eye to remember.

Shenandoah

Universal 1965. 105 min., col. (d) Andrew V. McLaglen (sp) James Lee Barrett (c) James Stewart, Doug McClure, Glenn Corbett, Patrick Wayne, Phillip Alford, Katharine Ross. (UNI)

Directed by Victor McLaglen's son, Andrew V. McLaglen (THE WAY WEST), this film received several awards at home and abroad when it first appeared, and since then has built a warm reputation. Many people think it's one of James Stewart's best roles. A tough-minded Virginia farmer, a widower with five sons and a daughter, he is indifferent to the course of the Civil War, but when his youngest son is captured by the Union Army by mistake and the family goes in search of him, all the Andersons are drawn into the last Confederate stand. The movie keeps its eye on the younger members of the cast; an example is the reunion between two boys, one white and one black, in the thick of battle. For what it says about involvement, the family, and the Civil War, the story has much for youngsters.

Singin' in the Rain

MGM 1952. 103 min., col. (d) Gene Kelly and Stanley Donen (sp) Adolph Green and Betty Comden (m) Lennie Hayton, Arthur Freed, Nacio Herb Brown (ph) Harold Rosson (c) Gene Kelly, Donald O'Connor, Debbie Reynolds, Rita Moreno, Cyd Charisse, Jean Hagen, Millard Mitchell. (FNC)

If this exuberant muscial weren't so gloriously entertaining, we might stress its educational value—for it is an excellent record of moviemaking in the twenties, when Hollywood was making the transition from silents to sound. But never was education so much fun.

More than any other musical most people can agree on, SINGIN' IN THE RAIN has what Pauline Kael says American movies have recently lacked: "Energy, originality and excitement; the sense of the rhythm of American life; a freshness of spirit that makes them unlike the films of any other country." For its color, timing, choreography, writing, directing, and acting, it's tops. Much of the credit for its style goes to co-director Stanley Donen (FUNNY FACE, SEVEN BRIDES FOR SEVEN BROTHERS). Donald O'Connor dancing up a wall, Gene Kelly dancing up a storm, Comden and Green wittily spoofing the old silent movie stars—for high spirits, grace, and polish, they're all pretty hard to beat.

Snow White and the Seven Dwarfs*

RKO 1937. 82 min., col. animation. (prod) Walt Disney (d) David Hand (sp) credit, based on the Grimm fairy tale (anim super) Hamilton Luske, Vladimir Tytla, Fred Moore, Herman Ferguson (m) Frank Churchill, Leigh Harline, Paul Smith. (THEATERS)

There were special Oscars for it, presented by Shirley Temple: one big one, and seven little ones—for Happy, Grumpy, Sneezy, Doc, Bashful, Sleepy, and Dopey. Pare Lorentz said that years from its release, he'd still have to report that Walt Disney's first full-length cartoon was the most important film activity of its year. The reviewer in the *New York Times* called it "The ten best films of the year."

Of course, it's not perfect. There are a few horrific moments, like the witch's brew and the Wicked Queen's disguise as an old woman. Its wooden Prince and too-cute Snow White are far inferior in taste and execution to the wonderful dwarfs, or Snow White's animal friends.

But there are a few movies whose faults don't matter, because you're too busy enjoying their radiance to notice. SNOW WHITE is pure gold for children, for any number of reasons—seven, to begin and end with, for the dwarfs are inspired creations; half a dozen more if you remember songs like "Just Whistle While You Work" or "Heigh Ho."

Recommended, whenever it comes around again. It's a perennial at holiday time, for what could bring more joy, to discover or rediscover?

Sons of the Desert
(a.k.a. Fraternally Yours)

Hal Roach/MGM 1934. 77 min., b/w. (d) William A. Seiter (sp) Frank Craven, Byron Morgan (ph) Kenneth Peach (c) Stan Laurel, Oliver Hardy, Charlie Chase, Mae Busch, Dorothy Christie, Lucien Littlefield. (BUD, CON, MAC, SWA)

"A thoroughly fresh and delightful comedy, quite certainly the best and subtlest of all their features. Straightforward slapstick is limited to a relatively few gags, and the humor derives principally from situations and characterizations. . . .Thanks largely to Seiter's handling, it has that indefinable quality of charm which broadens its appeal beyond the legions of Laurel & Hardy devotees" (William K. Everson, *The Films of Laurel and Hardy*). What so many find charming in Stan and Ollie is their relationship as a duo. They are so patient, even dignified, in accepting the most outrageously violent events.

The plot of SONS OF THE DESERT is as zany as usual. Stan and Ollie pretend to their wives that they're going on a long sea voyage but instead attend a fraternal convention. The ship they supposedly sailed on is wrecked, and their wives see, in a newsreel, the pair cavorting at the convention. Hiding out and concocting a fantastic alibi of escape at sea are too much for Stan, who confesses; Ollie tries to brazen it out to the end.

Sounder

Fox 1972. 105 min., col. (d) Martin Ritt (sp) Lonne Elder III from the novel by William H. Armstrong (ph) John Alonzo (m) Taj Mahal (c) Cicely Tyson, Paul Winfield, Kevin Hooks, Carmen Matthews, Taj Mahal, Janet MacLachlan, James Best. (FNC)

When we saw SOUNDER, the audience burst into applause at the end. Thank you, they were saying, for these people whom we respect and love, this father and son, wife and husband, black child growing into manhood in his father's absence, black teacher and white friend. As *Time* said, SOUNDER manages as no other movie has done to make the special pride and trial of being black into an experience that can be shared by anyone.

The young black sharecropper and his wife in Louisiana during the Depression are determined that their son should "beat the life they got laid out for you"—beat it by going to school. To director Martin Ritt (EDGE OF THE CITY, HUD) this was also the determination of his own parents, like other immigrants working their hearts out to give their kids an education. The movie is part of our history, of our whole black heritage, a testimony to the black woman as she has never been shown on the screen before.

The sensitive screenplay is by dramatist Lonne Elder III (*Ceremonies in Dark Old Men*) from William H. Armstrong's 1970 Newbery Medal novel. Director Ritt and photographer John Alonzo shot the picture (produced by Robert B. Radnitz [AND NOW MIGUEL, MY SIDE OF THE MOUNTAIN]) on location in the East Feliciana and St. Helena parishes of Louisiana, where the look and accents of the people, and Taj Mahal's playing of his own songs, ring true. Paul Winfield and Kevin Hooks are admirable as the father and son. As Rebecca, the mother, Cicely Tyson is a total revelation of the artistry of a great actress and the nobility of a woman. A film not of sentiment but of deep feeling, SOUNDER cannot help but enrich a child.

Star Wars

Fox 1977. 121 min., col. (d)(sp) George Lucas (ph) Gilbert Taylor (spec eff) John Stears, John Dykstra, Richard Edlund, Grant McCune, Rob-

ert Blalack (cost) John Mollo (art) John Barry, Norman Reynolds, Leslie Dilley, Roger Christian (m) John Williams (c) Mark Hamill, Carrie Fisher, Alec Guinness, Harrison Ford, Anthony Daniels, Kenny Baker. (THEATERS)

". . .may be the best comic strip Hollywood has ever made, a movie of brilliant technical achievements. . . . One of its subsidiary joys is that it seems to be so many things to so many people. . . . those of us who fall under its spell more or less feel compelled to justify our fondness for something that is sheer fun" (Vincent Canby).

Director-writer George Lucas wanted to do a movie of "dreams and fantasies" and STAR WARS is truly an old-fashioned, simple story in which good triumphs over evil, "a long time ago in a galaxy far, far away. . ." Everything is stylized (including the violence) in a way to remind us of many sources: the old movie serials of Flash Gordon and Buck Rogers; the Edgar Rice Burroughs movies; the aircraft adventures of the fifties; Tolkien's The Lord of the Rings; even The Wizard of Oz.

Response has been fantastic. STAR WARS is at the top of the all-time box-office polls. It won a regiment of Oscars: film editing, sound, costume design, art direction, original score, visual effects; even one for its little robot-computer hero, R2D2, who was also named Most Promising New Actor by Time. Countless spin-offs, a number of sequels, are in the works. It's an international phenomenon; in France, the children bid each other goodbye with Que la force soit avec toi, "May the force be with you."

The Stone Flower*

USSR 1946. 85 min., col. (d) Alexander Ptushko (sp) Pavel Bazhov, I. Keller (ph) F. Provarov (m) Lev Schwartz (art) M. Bogdanov, G. Myasnikov (c) Vladimir Drushnikov, Elena Derevschikova, Tamara Makarova. Russian dialog with English subtitles. (MAC)

A delightfully entertaining film from the USSR, based on "The Malachite Casket" and other legends of the Urals, and directed by Alexander Ptushko (SADKO) with a fine sense of visual fantasy. It tells the story of Danila, a young stone carver who dreams of creating a perfect flower in stone. He journeys from the real world of folk songs, fairs, and weddings to the mountains where the Lady of the Copper Mountain is reputed to guard such a flower. In a realm of unearthly beauty, Danila carves his masterpiece—which he realizes, alas, that no man will see.

". . .told with gentleness and charm. . .directed, played, and set to music with tender adroitness. . .can be highly recommended to children of the broadest possible age brackets (say four to twice 40)" *(Time).*

Storm Boy

Australia 1976. 89 min., col. (d) Henri Safran (sp) Sonia Borg, based on the novel by Colin Thiele (ph) Geoff Burton (m) Michael Carlos (c) Greg Rowe, Peter Cummins, Judy Dick, Gulpilil. (AUS)

Gulpilil, who played the aborigine in WALKABOUT, gives a fine performance as the aborigine "Fingerbone Bill" who becomes a close friend of ten-year-old Mike Kingley, who lives with his fisherman father near the Coorong sanctuary on the South Australian coast. Master of his environment, Fingerbone knows everything about the things that really interest the boy ("You kill pelican, the sky come up with a storm"). Fingerbone teaches Mike the mysteries of the wild; they raise orphaned pelicans together.

"With its simple, direct story-line, fine acting and marvellously photographed scenes of natural beauty, STORM BOY is the best movie of its kind for some little while" *(Monthly Film Bulletin,* British Film Institute).

The Sundowners

Warners 1960. 141 min., col. (d) Fred Zinnemann (sp) Isobel Lennart from the novel by Jon Cleary (ph) Jack Hildyard (m) Dmitri Tiomkin (c) Deborah Kerr, Robert Mitchum, Peter Ustinov, Michael Anderson, Jr., Glynis Johns, Chips Rafferty, Dina Merrill, Mervyn Johns. (GEN)

Fred Zinnemann's robust and sensitive film is about a family of itinerant sheepherders in the Australian outback of the 1920s; Paddy Carmody (Robert Mitchum), the footloose drover who delights in his freedom, and his wife and son, who long for a farm to settle on.

"It is not a film of escape," critic Paul V. Beckley said, "but a film of life." The life brims over with openness and vitality: father and son shearing sheep with the other drovers or following their horse at the bush-country tracks; the windblown mother envying the woman who owns a stove and helping to put out a "crown fire" or bring a neighbor's baby into the world.

Deborah Kerr's portrait of Paddy Carmody's wife is a work of love and art; it was cited by the New York Film Critics as the best of the year. Peter Ustinov, as a literate vagabond who attaches himself to the family, is a pleasure, and so is Glynis Johns as an outback lady innkeeper. The color photography of Jack Hildyard (THE BRIDGE ON THE RIVER KWAI; SUDDENLY, LAST SUMMER) carries us on our own gypsy tour of the Snowy River Mountains of New South Wales and the dry salt pans of South Australia.

Sunrise at Campobello

Warners 1960. 144 min., col. (prod)(sp) Dore Schary, based on his play (d) Vincent J. Donehue (m) Franz Waxman (ph) Russell Harlan (c) Ralph Bellamy, Greer Garson, Hume Cronyn, Jean Hagen, Ann Shoemaker, Alan Bunce, Tim Considine, Zina Bethune, Lyle Talbot. (BUD, CHA, ROA, TWF, WHO)

For the over-twelves, "The most positive, unswervingly upbeat family-type movie anybody could ask for" (*New York Herald Tribune*). The upbeat note, of course, is struck by FDR's courage in the face of terrible odds. From 1921, when he was stricken by polio, to his "Happy Warrior" speech in 1924 at the Democratic Convention where he nominated Al Smith, he fought an hourly battle against apathy and despair.

Shot on location in Hyde Park and on Campobello Island, the film stresses the family life of the Roosevelts, with an especially convincing portrayal of Eleanor Roosevelt by Greer Garson, who was nominated for an Academy Award.

Swiss Family Robinson*

Disney 1960. 128 min., col. (d) Ken Annakin (sp) Lowell S. Hawley, based on the novel by Johann Wyss (ph) Harry Waxman, Paul Beeson (m) William Alwyn; Muir Mathieson (c) John Mills, Dorothy McGuire, James MacArthur, Janet Munro, Sessue Hayakawa, Tommy Kirk, Kevin Corcoran, Cecil Parker. (GEN)

A great many liberties have been taken with the old-fashioned novel by Johann Wyss on which this film is based, but few children will mind. A tree house, chases through the jungle, an invasion by pirates—here's adventure and to spare, not to speak of animals both friendly and wild, and Tarzan-like vines to climb on.

A wilderness story, a family story, and a romantic fantasy, SWISS FAMILY ROBINSON is beautifully photographed. By casting it with seasoned and attractive actors, said Arthur Knight in the *Saturday*

Review, "Disney has avoided the one-dimensionality that afflicts most children's films. And by playing it tongue-in-cheek—including a pirate attack in which everyone is blown up but nobody dies—director Ken Annakin has dodged both the cloying sweetness and the bloody horror of earlier Disney efforts in this field."

A Tale of Two Cities

MGM 1935. 128 min., b/w. (prod) David O. Selznick (d) Jack Conway (asst d) Val Lewton, Jacques Tourneur (sp) W. P. Lipscomb, S. N. Behrman, based on the novel by Charles Dickens (ph) Oliver T. Marsh (m) Herbert Stothart (c) Ronald Colman, Elizabeth Allan, Edna May Oliver, Blanche Yurka, Reginald Owen, Basil Rathbone, Henry B. Walthall, Donald Woods, Walter Catlett, Fritz Leiber, H. B. Warner, Claude Gillingwater, Billy Bevan, Isabel Jewell, Tully Marshall, E. E. Clive. (FNC)

It has always been one of Dickens's most popular novels for its complex and exciting story and its romantic melodrama, though it is lacking in Dickensian humor. His main concern was not to rewrite history (he thought Carlyle's *French Revolution* was definitive); he wanted to play a large cast of heroic and villainous characters against the background of a time tumultuous with injustice, tyranny, and the horror of the Reign of Terror. His sympathies were with the British and French, who became the victims of the revolution.

In terms of Dickens's theme, style, and fast-paced narrative, the Selznick film is faultless, though it is less history than Victorian melodrama. Ronald Colman is the only Sydney Carton imaginable, once you have seen him, as Edna May Oliver is the only Miss Pross and Blanche Yurka is the only Madame DeFarge.

A TALE OF TWO CITIES was filmed creditably in 1958, by J. Arthur Rank (directed by Ralph Thomas, with Dirk Bogarde as Carton; 117 min., b/w, TWY), but it does not have the fans of the earlier film. In its way, MGM had made a classic of a classic; not high art but stirring popular entertainment.

The Thief of Baghdad*

United Artists 1940. 109 min., col. (d) Zoltan Korda, Michael Powell, Tim Whelan, Ludwig Berger (sp) Miles Malleson and Lajos Biro (ph) Georges Périnal (art) Vincent Korda (c) Sabu, Conrad Veidt, June Duprez, Rex Ingram. (UAS)

"Everything is possible," says the Elder in the Land of Legend, "when seen through the eyes of youth"—and when transformed by the camera's magic. Alexander Korda's production, not to be confused with the Douglas Fairbanks film in 1924 or Steve Reeves's dubbed Italian version in 1961, is the classic fantasy out of the Arabian Nights. The fables of the Prince of Baghdad and his love, the Princess of Basra; Abu, the small thief; the Grand Vizier; the flying horse; the giant genie; the All-Seeing Eye; and the Magic Carpet are brought to life in a style which was awarded four Oscars. Outstanding are the trick photography (production designer William Cameron Menzies), art direction (Vincent Korda), color cinematography (Georges Périnal), and special effects (Lawrence Butler and Jack Whitney). A delight for all ages.

Third Man on the Mountain

Disney 1959. 105 min., col. (d) Ken Annakin (sp) Eleanore Griffin from the book Banner in the Sky *by James Ramsey Ullman (ph) Harry Waxman (m) William Alwyn and Muir Mathieson (c) Michael Rennie, James MacArthur, Janet Munro, Herbert Lom, James Donald, Nora Swinburne, Laurence Naismith. (GEN)*

This mountain-climbing adventure, based on a novel, really parallels the first ascent of the Matterhorn, when one of the survivors was a Swiss youth. The movie centers around an eighteen-year-old Swiss boy in 1865 who swears he will scale the Citadel, an unconquered peak that took his father's life.

Shot while climbing the Matterhorn, looking down on Zermatt, the movie has truly spectacular scenery, and the advantage of direction by Ken Annakin (THOSE MAGNIFICENT MEN IN THEIR FLYING MACHINES). There is the thrill of the ascent, plenty of suspense, and a couple of underlying moral questions for kids to ponder. (How much truth is there in what Elizabeth tells Rudi's mother, "A man must do what he feels he must do, or else he's not a man"? And at what point does Rudi really become the "hero of the mountain"?)

The Thirty-Nine Steps

Britain 1935. 80 min., b/w. (d) Alfred Hitchcock (sp) Alma Reville, Ian Hay, and Charles Bennett from the novel by John Buchan (c) Robert

Donat, Madeleine Carroll, Godfrey Tearle, Peggy Ashcroft, John Laurie, Helen Haye, Wylie Watson. (BUD, EMG, JAN, WHO)

Vintage Hitchcock. "The most original, literate and entertaining melodrama of 1935" (*The New York Times*) is one of the most original, literate, and entertaining melodramas you're likely to see on today's television or screen. Nobody has yet caught up with Richard Hannay, chasing the "Maguffin" (Hitchcock's term for the object of the chase in any of his films) across the Highlands, with beautiful Madeleine Carroll in tow and a band of urbanely menacing international spies lying low. The humor is fresh, the characters three-dimensional, the camera full of surprises, and the timing perfect. We'd give a lot to be ten years old and discovering for the first time the man with the missing finger or "Mr. Memory" in the music hall.

Those Magnificent Men in Their Flying Machines

Britain 1965. 138 min., col. (d) Ken Annakin (sp) Jack Davies and Ken Annakin (ph) Christopher Challis (m) Ron Goodwin (cost) Osbert Lancaster and Dinah Greet (c) Stuart Whitman, Sarah Miles, James Fox, Alberto Sordi, Robert Morley, Gert Frobe, Jean-Pierre Cassel, Terry-Thomas, Irina Demick, Flora Robson, Sam Wanamaker, Red Skelton, James Robertson Justice (narrator). (FNC)

The animated cartoon titles of Ronald Searle and the costumes of Osbert Lancaster, those two inimitable British cartoonists, set the style for TMMITFM's extravagantly funny and nostalgic series of flight gags. Jack Davies, writer of comedy for Norman Wisdom and the "Doctor" series, and director Ken Annakin present a burlesque history of the early days of aviation, presumably about a fictitious international air race in 1910 for a prize of ten thousand pounds. (The subtitle is "How I Flew from London to Paris in 25 hours and 11 Minutes.") Actually, it is about two hours of thrills and spills, chases, running gags, slapstick, romance, and caricature.

The stars of the picture are the planes themselves, the Demoiselles, Bristol Box-Kites, and Bleriots, fragile charmers shown in beautiful flight after they have been milked for as many laughs as Mack Sennett's tin lizzies. Thanks to Christopher Challis's color photography and a cast of international aces (Terry-Thomas is a standout as "That bounder, Sir Percy"), the movie stays up in the air. It may or may not be educational. "Its only message," Stan Margulies, the producer, has said, "is don't go up in a 1910 airplane."

The Three Caballeros*

RKO 1945. 72 min., col. (d) Harold Young (m) Paul Smith, Charles Wolcott, Edward Plumb (spec eff) Ub Iwerks (c) Aurora Miranda, Carmen Molina, Dora Luz (voices) Sterling Holloway, Clarence Nash, Jose Oliveira, Fred Shields. (GEN)

There's so much going on every minute in this follow-up to SALUDOS AMIGOS that the 1945 critics called it a melange of bad taste and good fantasy. Today, it's a favorite with Disney buffs for its visual puns, off-beat Donald Duck dream sequences, and integration of the live action and animation.

For children under twelve, there's Donald Duck making love to a live senorita; Pablo the Penguin, a dropout from the Arctic; an araquin bird who steps out of the film frame to shake hands with Donald; Little Gauchito, who enters a winged burro in a race; Joe Carioca, the Brazilian parrot of SALUDOS AMIGOS; and a ride through Latin America on a magic serape.

There is authentic Latin American music by prominent South American composers and songs by three leading female stars of Mexico and Brazil are among the sixteen in the film. Two, "You Belong to My Heart" and "Baia," became top hits.

The Time Machine

MGM 1960. 103 min., col. (d) George Pal (sp) David Duncan from the novel by H. G. Wells (c) Rod Taylor, Alan Young, Yvette Mimieux, Sebastian Cabot. (FNC)

Since the director is George Pal (DESTINATION MOON, WHEN WORLDS COLLIDE, THE WAR OF THE WORLDS), H. G. Wells's visual imagination if not his social allegory gets prime treatment. A master of trick photography for adventure films, Pal won a special Oscar in 1943 "for the development of novel methods and techniques." He has a subject to his taste in Wells's first successful novel (1895), a tale about a Victorian "Time Traveler," a scientist who journeys in his time machine to the year 802,701 A.D.

Based on the first section of the book only, the movie concentrates on the struggle between the effete Eloi and the bestial Morlocks, and has a happier ending than the original. (Rod Taylor gets Yvette Mimieux and is allowed to go home.) Though the story may seem old-fashioned to more sophisticated young science-fiction buffs, it's what the small fry cut their teeth on.

Recommended for its ingenious visualization of time travel, for which the special-effects directors, Gene Warren and Tim Baar, received an Academy Award.

Toby Tyler, or Ten Weeks with a Circus*

Disney 1960. 96 min., col. (d) Charles Barton (sp) Bill Walsh and Lillie Hayward from the book by James Otis Kaler (ph) William Snyder (m) Buddy Baker (c) Kevin Corcoran, Richard Eastham, Henry Calvin, Tom Fadden, Barbara Beaird. (GEN)

Entirely faithful to an old-fashioned but still popular book, this has the virtue not only of Kevin ("Moochie") Corcoran's Toby, which won the award for the year's best juvenile performance, but of a shiningly simple production. Without artificial additives, the flavor of the circus comes through.

Kevin, to begin with, looks like a kid who'd run away from uncle and aunt on the farm to join the circus for a wonderful interlude as "Monsieur Toby, Equestrian Extraordinaire." But then he looked right in THE SHAGGY DOG and POLLYANNA, too. Col. Castle's Great American Circus, at the turn of the century, isn't the greatest show on earth; it's a one-ring traveling troupe. But it has the kindly clowns, the oily concessionaires, the gruff strong man with a warm heart, the wildly mischievous monkey named Mr. Stubbs, and Monsieur Ajax the bareback rider and his beautiful partner, Mademoiselle Jeanette.

This "minor classic among children's movies" (Paul B. Beckley, *New York Herald Tribune*) offers unadulterated romanticism. Who doesn't want to run away to join the circus for just a little while—and to be the star of its one ring?

Tom Brown's School Days

Britain, 1951. 94 min., b/w. (prod) Brian Desmond-Hurst (d) Gordon Parry (sp) Noel Langley from the novel by Thomas Hughes (c) John Howard Davies, Robert Newton, James Hayter. (UNI)

When United Artists released this British film from Thomas Hughes's classic novel in 1952, we didn't take our resident American schoolboy to see it. Too antique (1834) and too British, we thought. Well, we were wrong. When the later BBC-TV series, all 240 minutes, of TOM BROWN'S SCHOOL DAYS was shown on PBS in 1976, it absorbed many youngsters completely. Maybe the pattern of the new boy at school is clear through the ages; maybe we care more about rugby and soccer than we used to.

As Tom (John Howard Davies) valiantly holds his own against the bully Flashman, and noble headmaster Dr. Arnold (Robert Newton) expels that blackguard from Rugby, some over-twelves may squeal, sniffle, and cheer almost as pleasurably as their prototypes did when the novel was fresh from the printer and nobody had heard of the movies. On the screen, hazing comes on strong, though it's bastinadoing and "roasting" instead of Hell Week.

Like so many other British films, TOM BROWN'S SCHOOL DAYS has excellent period detail. You can see Big Brooke playing rugby in the original fashion, which makes ice hockey look like a rather genteel sport; and a paper chase with hare and hounds, straight out of the mezzotint engravings, that looks as if it still might be fun.

Treasure Island

Disney 1950. 96 min., col. (d) Byron Haskin (sp) Lawrence Edward Watkin from the novel by Robert Louis Stevenson (c) Robert Newton, Bobby Driscoll, Basil Sydney, Finlay Currie, Geoffrey Wilkinson, Denis O'Dea. (GEN)

A well-read boy was once asked by his teacher why he always made his book reports on *Treasure Island.* "But that's the *best,*" replied Fred. He was not disappointed in Disney's movie, made in England with a superb English cast and Bobby Driscoll, the sole Hollywood contribution, as a fine Jim Hawkins.

From the first moments in the Admiral Benbow Inn to the skull-duggery aboard the *Hispaniola* and in the stockade on Skeleton Island, it has the lifeglow of Stevenson's pirates and adventurers. Robert Newton is so clearly the Long John Silver of everyone's imagination that he was snapped up for the feature LONG JOHN SILVER and a series of Australian television programs based on the character.

Caught up in every scene, as the beautiful square-rigger plows across the Atlantic from Bristol to the treasure, one knows this is the best filming the novel could have. (Much less stirring is Victor Fleming's 1934 movie, with Jackie Cooper and some familiar MGM faces. But Jackie was the first *boy* to play Jim Hawkins; in the two earlier versions, the part was acted by a girl.)

A Tree Grows in Brooklyn

Fox 1945. 128 min., b/w. (d) Elia Kazan (sp) Tess Slesinger and Frank Davis from the novel by Betty Smith (ph) Leon Shamroy (c) Dorothy McGuire, Joan Blondell, James Dunn, Lloyd Nolan, Peggy Ann Garner, Ted Donaldson, James Gleason. (FNC, MAC, ROA)

Elia Kazan's first movie re-creates lovingly and realistically the tenements and slum streets of Brooklyn's Williamsburg, sixty years ago. But it is the tenderness with which he realizes the love of twelve-year-old Francie Nolan for her weak but charming father that makes this movie from Betty Smith's autobiographical novel so moving for young people. Life in the big city has changed, and slums are being shown more realistically in contemporary films. But Francie's hunger to grow, in the dust of her home, is timeless, and so are the relationships between the parents and the two children in the Nolan family.

"A more interesting and likable movie than most," was James Agee's verdict in 1945, and it stands up well. Peggy Ann Garner and James Dunn, as her father, both won Academy Awards for their performances.

20,000 Leagues Under the Sea

Disney 1954. 127 min., col. (d) Richard Fleischer (sp) Earl Felton, based on the novel by Jules Verne (ph) Franz Lehy, Ralph Hammeras, Till Gabbani (c) Kirk Douglas, James Mason, Peter Lorre, Paul Lukas. (GEN)

It still grips the imagination—Verne's futurist fantasy of the mad Captain Nemo in his atomic-powered submarine; the man-eating sharks; the buried treasure; the giant squid wrecking the propeller. The *Nautilus* adventures have been spectacularly filmed underwater in the Bahamas, in Jamaica, off San Diego, and in studio tanks; the special effects won an Academy Award.

The cast is excellent. Altogether, a production worthy of its source. Verne would have liked the battle between the crew and the squid and Captain Nemo (James Mason) savagely destroying the nitrate ship.

2001: A Space Odyssey

Britain-US 1968. 160 min., col. (d) Stanley Kubrick (sp) Stanley Kubrick and Arthur C. Clarke from Clarke's story "The Sentinel" (ph) Geoffrey Unsworth and John Alcott (spec eff) Stanley Kubrick, Wally Veevers, Douglas Trumbull, Con Pederson, Tom Howard (m) Richard and Johann Strauss, Gyorgy Ligeti, Aram Khachaturian (c) Keir Dullea, William Sylvester, Leonard Rossiter, Gary Lockwood (voice) Douglas Rain. (FNC)

Completed four years and 10 million dollars after DR. STRANGE-

LOVE, this spectacular fantasy has the most remarkable models, constructions, and perspectives that Stanley Kubrick could design and special-effects craftsmen could create. To most young people, Arthur C. Clarke fans especially, every aspect of the film's vision is fascinating, and its imagery conveys magnificently what Kubrick says he hoped to convey: "The grandeur of space and the myriad mysteries of cosmic intelligence."

What happens when a strange monolith, throwing off mysterious rays, is found at the bottom of a moon excavation? Kubrick, at great length and with a minimum of conventional plot lines, pictures an "odyssey" in new worlds of imagination. His invention and mastery of special effects, which won an Academy Award, are superb; there are even elements of humor in his use of the computer, Hal, as protagonist. The sweep of color, the entry of the astronaut into unknown space-time dimensions, the intricate and immensely intriguing space hardware—all realized with a great filmmaker's understanding of the newest possibilities of the screen image—make this a mind-blowing experience for science-fiction lovers in the age of space flight.

The Vanishing Prairie

Disney 1954. 71 min., col. (d) James Algar (sp) James Algar, Winston Hibler, Ted Sears (narr) Winston Hibler. (GEN)

This "True-Life Adventure" has fascinating glimpses of the almost extinct buffalo, bighorn sheep, cougar, and antelope. We see the birth of a buffalo, the courtship and nesting of western grebes, and the escape of a gopher from a falcon swooping down on it. For those who like to see Mother Nature wearing a funny hat, there are trick sequences of mountain rams banging their heads together to the tune of the Anvil Chorus, and whooping cranes doing a "dance." For those who prefer Thoreau's approach to wildlife, the Disney photographers are most admirable when they are spending quieter moments with their cameras, as deliberately as nature, rediscovering "how many creatures live wild and free though secret." Like its predecessor, THE LIVING DESERT, this won an Academy Award for best documentary feature.

Way Out West

Hal Roach/MGM 1936. 77 min., b/w. (d) James Horne (sp) Jack Jevne, Charles Rogers, James Parrott, Felix Adler (ph) Art Lloyd, Walter Lun-

din (c) Stan Laurel, Oliver Hardy, Sharon Lynne, James Finlayson, Chill Wills, The Avalon Boys, Rosina Lawrence. (GEN)

Laurel and Hardy come to Brushwood Gulch—way, way out as the West goes—to deliver the deed to a gold mine to the daughter of their dead partner. Saloonkeeper Mickey Finn (James Finlayson) palms off a false heiress to whom Laurel and Hardy hand over the deed. When they finally give it to the real heiress, a kitchenmaid at Finn's, they're run out of town.

Undiluted Laurel and Hardy, with song and dance, a strongly propelled plot, spoofs of the stereotyped sagebrush characters, and lots of running gags. Admirers of Stan and Ollie will relish such typical routines as Stan's being tickled into helplessness by the bar owner's wife, and the duo's putting their mule into Mickey Finn's apartment.

When Hal Roach reissued WAY OUT WEST theatrically in 1969, Vincent Canby of the *New York Times* called it the funniest show in town: "What must be one of the most consistently funny Laurel and Hardy features."

West Side Story

United Artists 1961. 155 min., col. (d) Robert Wise and Jerome Robbins (sp) Ernest Lehman from the Broadway musical by Arthur Laurents (ph) Daniel L. Fapp (m) Leonard Bernstein (lyr) Stephen Sondheim (chor) Jerome Robbins (c) Natalie Wood, Richard Beymer, Russ Tamblyn, Rita Moreno, George Chakiris, William Bramley, Ned Glass, (voices) Marni Nixon, Jimmy Bryant. (UAS)

This is the film that got nine Academy Awards—best picture, best supporting actor, best supporting actress, directing, art, cinematography, costume design, editing, and music scoring—and still sets the standard for dance and music on the screen. It moves with the animal energy of the Jets and the Sharks, the two gangs whose racial tensions on Manhattan's Upper West Side explode into violent warfare. Though often compared with ROMEO AND JULIET, it is not a story of youthful innocence stained by society, unless you really believe that those teenage hoods and their rumbles are romantic, and it is certainly not a serious study of slum violence or juvenile delinquency.

What it is—and promises to be for years—is a superb utilization of all cinematic means. The dance numbers of Jerome Robbins have never been matched for the exciting way they play to the camera. As thrilling as the pictorial quality is the musical thrust of Leonard Bernstein's score, with Stephen Sondheim's clever lyrics in "Gee, Officer Krupke," "Dance at the Gym," "Jet Song," "Tonight," and "I Feel Pretty." From visual high point to visual high point, this is electric entertainment.

Where the Lilies Bloom

United Artists 1974. 97 min., col. (prod) Robert B. Radnitz (d) William Graham (sp) Earl Hamner, Jr., from Vera and Bill Cleaver's 1969 Newbery Award novel (ph) Urs Furrer (m) Earl Scruggs (c) Julie Gholson, Harry Dean Stanton, Sudie Bond, Tom Spratley, Alice Beardsley, Jan Smithers, Matthew Burrill, Helen Harmon. (UAS)

In the genre of family-oriented films of Robert B. Radnitz (SOUNDER, AND NOW MIGUEL) and Earl Hamner, Jr. ("The Waltons" on TV), WHERE THE LILIES BLOOM is about four orphans, aged five to sixteen, who survive on their 200-year-old farm in the Appalachians by sharecropping and "wildcrafting"—collecting and selling roots and bark for medicinals. Their poverty is not the poverty of spirit; they are loving and enterprising children who grow in strength with their discoveries of others.

Mary Call Luther (Julie Gholson), fourteen, wants to be a writer and longs for the day when she will have time to be "all the things inside me no one else can see." Like Francie in A TREE GROWS IN BROOKLYN, she adores her shiftless father. She promises him to keep the family together, and after his death, although she is not the oldest, she copes very sturdily. Things get very involved, but they end happily. Storekeeper Connell, blood brother to Ike Gadsey of "The Waltons," dances to a Watauga County fiddler's tune at the wedding of Kiser Pease, the Luthers' neighbor, and pretty Devola, Mary Call's sister.

The Luthers, especially Mary Call, are an attractive bunch whom other youngsters enjoy watching. The film is rich in local color. Photographed by the late Urs Furrer in the Blue Ridge Mountains, it is lovely to look at, with all sorts of interesting regional humor, diet, customs, and dialect. Did you know that "lamb's quarters" are a kind of spinach?

Where the Red Fern Grows

Doty-Dayton 1976. 100 min., col. (d) Norman Tokar (sp) Douglas Stewart and Eleanor Lamb from the novel by Wilson Rawls (m) Lex De Azevedo; songs written by the Osmonds, sung by Andy Williams (ph) Dean Cundey (c) James Whitmore, Beverly Garland, Jack Ging,

Lonny Chapman, Stewart Petersen, Jill Clark, Jeanna Wilson. (MOD, SWA)

The true story of an Ozark boy's ambition to own a pair of raccoon-hunting hounds, his struggle to save the money, and the long and sometimes funny business of training them. Lynn Minton, in *McCall's* magazine, which gave it a "Movie of the Month Award," noted that in addition to its adventure and suspense, it has "love and loyalty between parents, children, and grandfather. All in all, the kind of movie that restores faith in the word 'heartwarming.' "

The restraint and appeal of the actors transcend the film's tendency to overstress the difference between the good guys and the bad guys. (The latter chew tobacco and taunt the young hero.) Stewart Petersen is fine as the boy, Billy Coleman; and James Whitmore is great as Grampa. The Ozarks and the hounds make pleasant company, too.

White Wilderness*

Disney 1958. 72 min., col. (prod) Ben Sharpsteen (d)(sp) James Algar (ph) James Simon, Hugh Wilmar, Lloyd Beebe, Herb and Lois Crisler. (GEN)

This "True-Life Adventure" won an Academy Award for best documentary feature, a Berlin Festival prize, and a *Family Magazine* medal. After three years of scouting their photographic prey from the Canadian and Alaskan timber lines to the edge of the polar ice cap, the Disney group made a most informative and revealing picture of animal life in the North American Arctic.

Here are polar bears and their cubs, walruses, ermines, jaegers, musk oxen, ring seals, migrant reindeer and caribou, eider ducks, and wolves. Among the wonderful things in the film are a colony of lemmings making their death march to the sea, white Beluga whales swimming underwater, and a wolf pack invading a herd of caribou—most wonderful is the evidence of nature equipping each species for its battle to survive in the vast frozen wild. Although the narration and soundtrack are intrusive, the visuals are so interesting that one bears with the rest.

The Wizard of Oz*

MGM 1939. 101 min., col. (d) Victor Fleming (sp) Noel Langley, Florence Ryerson, and Edgar Allan Woolf from the book by L. Frank Baum

(m) Herbert Stothart, E. Y. Harburg, and Harold Arlen (c) Judy Garland, Frank Morgan, Ray Bolger, Bert Lahr, Jack Haley, Billie Burke, Margaret Hamilton. (FNC)

"A bigger job than merely creating something real descended upon us all," confided producer Mervyn LeRoy to the *New York Times* about THE WIZARD, "the task of putting realism into the fantastic." Mr. LeRoy was worried about making believable Munchkins out of midgets and shooting the inside of a cyclone, but he needn't have bothered.

What lifts one over the rainbow today, as it did then, is the magic of the music and the performers. Herbert Stothart's prize-winning score, "Yip" Harburg and Harold Arlen's lyrics, and Judy Garland's radiance are the most special of "special effects." And where is one to find another trio like the Tin Woodsman (Jack Haley), the Scarecrow (Ray Bolger), and the Cowardly Lion (Bert Lahr)? "Mr. Lahr's lion is fion," said Frank S. Nugent, in one of film criticism's understatements of all time. You remember him— the last of the great clowns, as the king of beasts who didn't have the prowess of a meow-ess.

World Without Sun

France 1964. 91 min., col. (d)(sp)(narr) Jacques-Yves Cousteau (ph) Pierre Goupil (m) Serge Baudo, Henri Crolla, Andre Hodeir (c) Cousteau, Simone Cousteau, and the Oceanauts. Narrated in English. (BUC, BUD, MAC, SEL)

Winner of the 1964 Academy Award for best documentary feature, this breathtakingly lovely film of underwater exploration is one part science, one part poetry, and one part magical adventure.

Cousteau's expedition set out to explore the resources of the ocean and observe marine life. At a depth of forty-five feet on the continental shelf—an underwater ledge in the Red Sea off Port Sudan—a dual cylindrical construction became the home of the "Oceanauts." In its five rooms they spent a month, supplied with food and electricity from their ship, *Calypso*, anchored above. The base also contained a fantastic garage for "Denise," a kind of diving saucer propelled by jets capable of diving to depths of 1,000 feet. (Jules Verne would have loved it.)

Skin divers in silver suits gliding into caverns beneath the sea, and surrealistic fish and plants—all the physical wonders caught in their mesmerizing colors and rhythms—make WORLD WITHOUT SUN a feast for the eye. "One day," Cousteau has predicted, "man will walk on the sea bed as we now walk on the boulevards." Until then, let Cousteau's cameras walk for you.

Wuthering Heights

United Artists 1939. 104 min., b/w. (d) William Wyler (sp) Ben Hecht and Charles MacArthur from the novel by Emily Brontë (ph) Gregg Toland (c) Merle Oberon, Laurence Olivier, David Niven, Geraldine Fitzgerald, Flora Robson, Hugh Williams, Donald Crisp, Leo G. Carroll. (BUD, MAC, TWY, WHO)

In 1939, the year of GONE WITH THE WIND, the New York Film Critics named WUTHERING HEIGHTS best picture of the year. Its reception was warm from the start. Alexander Woollcott gave the imperial nod to producer Samuel Goldwyn, "Sam has done right by our Emily," and the Brontë Society, somewhat to its own surprise, had nothing but praise for the Hecht-MacArthur screenplay. Laurence Olivier, who had begun as a most reluctant Heathcliff, ended by saying his first realization of the possibilities of cinema dated from his association with William Wyler. His Heathcliff is superb, one of the classic romantic roles. Gregg Toland's black-and-white photography, which received an Academy Award, is outstanding; Yorkshire's stone walls and heather are brought to life in California, with famous shots of Oberon and Olivier on windy Peniston Crag.

Prime romance for the over-twelves.

The Yearling

MGM 1946. 135 min., col. (d) Clarence Brown (sp) Paul Osborne from the novel by Marjorie Kinnan Rawlings (ph) Charles Rosher and Leonard Smith (m) Herbert Stothart (c) Gregory Peck, Jane Wyman, Claude Jarman, Jr., Forest Tucker, Henry Travers, Margaret Wycherly, Chill Wills, Clem Bevans. (FNC)

Marjorie Kinnan Rawlings's Pulitzer Prize novel about a boy's love for a pet fawn, which his parents are forced to shoot, is saved from movie sentimentality by the quality of the writing and direction. Clarence Brown directs Paul Osborne's script with sensitivity and power. When the boy Jody (Claude Jarman, Jr.) returns home after his heartbroken flight into the swamp, his father (Gregory Peck) shares a new understanding with him. "Every man wants life to be fine and easy," he says to his son. "It *is* fine, but it's *not* easy." There is deep, inarticulate tenderness in the relationships between the adults and the boy in this family, and the pioneer living of early Florida settlers is well filmed. The interior sets and the art direction received Academy Awards.

Yellow Submarine

Britain 1968. 85 min., col. (d) George Dunning (sp) Lee Minoff, Al Brodax, Jack Mendelsohn, and Erich Segal from an original story by Lee Minoff based on the song "Yellow Submarine" by John Lennon and Paul McCartney (ph) John Williams (des) Heinz Edelman (m) The Beatles (voices) The Beatles, John Clive, Geoffrey Hughes, Peter Batten, Paul Angelus, Dick Emery, Lance Percival. (BUD, CWF, MOD, SEL, TWY)

"Nothing is Real," says the subtitle; the Blue Meanies might be right out of Lewis Carroll. This glorious anthology of the art of animation is an invitation to let your imagination soar. Most of the musical numbers come from the Beatles' album *Sgt. Pepper's Lonely Hearts Club Band,* with three new songs. The Beatles appear as cartoon characters, with their own singing voices, except for an appearance in person at the end.

The great achievement of the film is its visual style: "Exactly right" (Stanley Kauffmann); "A thorough audiovisual sauna" (John Simon). There are thousands of drawings which remind one of Dr. Seuss, Aubrey Beardsley, Picasso, Peter Max, art nouveau, Saul Steinberg, Warhol, Trnka, Lenica, Borowczyk, newsreels, sing-along footage. The animators have used every conceivable technique of animation art: rotoscoping, pixillations, live-action superimpositions, cutouts. Heinz Edelmann (design), George Dunning (direction), and Charles Jenkins (special effects) are among the many brilliant international artists responsible for the mind-expanding, wild, fantastic fun.

Young Mr. Lincoln

Fox 1939. 100 min., b/w. (prod) Kenneth Macgowan (d) John Ford (sp) Lamar Trotti (ph) Bert Glennon (m) Alfred Newman (c) Henry Fonda, Alice Brady, Marjorie Weaver, Eddie Collins, Pauline Moore, Richard Cromwell, Ward Bond, Donald Meek. (FNC)

The film has come to be recognized as the richest work in John Ford's prewar period and Henry Fonda's beautifully developed performance as perhaps his finest. Film-study professors analyze it; young people drink it in effortlessly, with the pleasure of complete acceptance evoked by films that are mythic and deeply true. The most American of films, it is the one film by another director that Sergei Eisenstein wished he had made himself.

"The idea of the picture," Ford said, "was to give the feeling that even as a young man you could sense there was going to be something great about this man. I had read a good deal about Lincoln, and we tried to get some comedy into it too, but everything in the picture was true."

It was also a lyrical vision; the dramatic trial to save the two innocent boys from a lynch mob is built up by Ford until it culminates finally in a dissolve to the Lincoln Memorial in Washington. Children will find fact, history, legend, and faith in the picture. The very human portrait of Lincoln's early years in Illinois, the shambling, charming, homespun lawyer of unfailing humor, will stay with them as long as any other portrait in cinema.

Featurettes

The Amazing Cosmic Awareness of Duffy Moon

ABC-TV 1976. 32 min., col. (prod) Daniel Wilson (d) Larry Elikann (sp) Thomas Baum, based on the book The Strange but Wonderful Cosmic Awareness of Duffy Moon *by Jean Robinson (m) Joe Weber (lyr) Zoey Wilson (c) Lance Kerwin, Ike Eisenmann, Jim Backus, Jerry Van Dyke. (TIM)*

Duffy Moon, who is eleven, is "The Shrimp" of the sixth grade. Although he can tame a pet raven, is a member of the American Begonia Society, and reads lots of books, he's regularly singled out for bullying by bigger boys in the neighborhood; he's small, and he's "different."

Duffy is lucky, however, in having a good friend in Peter, an athlete and class leader. When Duffy reads *Cosmic Awareness*, he's sure he has the magic powers to become a human dynamo. He and Peter set up a neighborhood odd-jobs company which is very successful in competition with the company run by Duffy's tormentors. Troubles start—but on the day of reckoning, Duffy realizes that he doesn't need his friend Peter, or a book, or his old excuses about being small; his growth and his success are his own doing.

". . .Characters close to the truth, and edges of realism not usually associated with children's programs. More, the film does it all with a neat sense of humor. . . .Engaging and inventive" (*Variety*).

Beware, Beware, My Beauty Fair*

1973. 29 min., col. (prod) National Film Board of Canada (d)(sp)(ed) Peter Svatek, Jean LaFleur (ph) Douglas Kiefer. (PNX)

Played by youngsters from the Children's Theater, Montreal, this engrossing mystery-fantasy has humor and a happy ending in its play-within-a-play. During the presentation of a school play, an adventure about beauty and the beast, the audience sees only the play on stage, but the film audience becomes involved in a chillingly real mystery behind the scenes.

Big Henry and the Polka Dot Kid

NBC-TV 1976. 33 min., col. (prod) Linda Gottlieb (d) Richard Marquand (sp) W. W. Lewis, based on the story "Luke Baldwin's Vow," by Morley Callaghan (c) Chris Barnes, Ned Beatty, Estelle Parsons. (LCA, MMM)

Luke is ten and an orphan whose new home is in Cree River, in the north woods of Ontario, with his uncle and aunt, who own a logging camp. He loves Ol' Dan, a blind, injured dog, that his Uncle Henry considers an extravagance and plans to have put away. Not that Uncle Henry is an unkind man; he's "practical." As widowed neighbor Edwina tells Luke, Big Henry's bark is worse than his bite. His sternness, like Luke's compassion, is part of his tradition. Luke wins the battle to save Ol' Dan; he convinces his uncle that there are more important values than "practicality." The boy and the man, who have been unable to communicate before, are ready to cross the barriers; they need and love each other.

Chris Barnes (THE BAD NEWS BEARS) is a sensitive Luke, and the film sustains the interest of the original Morley Callaghan story. This NBC "Special Treat" program won an Emmy in 1977, as well as several American festival awards.

Bim*

France 1952. 47 min., b/w. (prod) Georges Derocles (d)(sp) Albert Lamorisse (ph) André Costey. Commentary written and spoken by Jacques Prévert. Dubbed in English. (CON, WHO)

Once upon a time, a Bedouin boy named Abdullah cherished the handsome little donkey Bim, which had been given him according to custom. When it was stolen, he had many perilous adventures before he recovered it. Poet-screenwriter Jacques Prévert's commentary adds charm to this little film by Albert Lamorisse (THE RED BALLOON), which was selected for the Cannes and Edinburgh festivals.

Blind Bird*

USSR 1963. 45 min., col. (d) Boris Dolin (sp) Anatoli Jedan, Boris Dolin (ph) Youri Berenstein (c) Oleg Jakov. (MEG, CON)

Shown in the sixties and again in 1971 on the CBS Children's Film Festival program, this Venice prizewinner, told with a minimum of dialog, is for the under-tens. Vassia walks the streets of his town carrying a plywood box containing his friend Pelka, a pink pelican blinded as a result of a head injury. After many obstacles and a journey to Moscow, Pelka's sight is restored and Vassia sets the bird free.

Bolero

USA 1973. 26 min., col. (prod) Allan Miller (d) Allan Miller, William Fertik (ph) William Fertik (ed) Sarah Stein. (PYR)

"Kids get close to a baseball or football team because they know the players on the team as persons. If we had that same relationship with our musicians, we'd be that much closer to music," says Allan Miller (producer and co-director, with William Fertik, of BOLERO).

How close this superb film brings us to the appreciation of an orchestra is shown by the honors it's won: the 1973 Academy Award for best live-action short subject; prizes at the Buenos Aires, Chicago, and American film festivals. It humanizes music, and it's exciting fun; we become involved and entertained as we learn. In informal rehearsals and talks with the members of the Los Angeles Philharmonic Orchestra, we hear about the joys, and the problems, of being musicians. Then with a magnificent sweep we are into a complete performance by the orchestra of Ravel's *Bolero* conducted by Zubin Mehta.

"One of the finest music appreciation films ever made. A thrilling experience" (ALA, *Booklist*).

Boy With Glasses*

Japan 1959. 45 min., b/w. (d)(sp) Tukichi Uno. (CON)

Produced with great simplicity, this CBS Children's Film Festival presentation deals with something common to many children and should appeal especially to the under-tens. Susumu, a shy little boy who needs glasses, won't wear them, for all the reasons kids know. Images of all the people he dislikes run through his mind (all bespectacled); lies to his teacher pile up ("I left my glasses home by mistake"). Susumu is in a bad way. But he gets help from his older brother, his friends, and his teacher, and he learns that his classmates and everyone else like him just as much with glasses as they did without.

The Bridge of Adam Rush

ABC-TV 1975. 47 min., col. (d) Lawrence S. Elikann (sp) Lee Kalcheim (ph) Richard Francis (m) Roger Gerstein, John Scott (c) Lance Kirwin, James Pritchett, Barbara Andres. (TIM)

Winner of a Writers Guild of America award for best children's script, this outstanding ABC "Afterschool Special" film "gives us not only an idea of what life was like at the turn of the nineteenth century but also of the timeless challenges of adjusting to new people, places and expectations." (*Los Angeles Times*).

Twelve-year-old Adam Rush's happy life in Philadelphia in 1801 is disrupted by the death of his father and the marriage of his mother to a poor farmer. Adam is transplanted to a rural home in upstate New York. Here he struggles to adjust to rough living, and most of all to his stepfather. When Adam and his stepfather take on a man-sized job together one summer, building a bridge, they grow in understanding and respect for each other. Adam realizes that Thomas Rush needs him and likes him, and he comes to like this quiet, hardworking man.

Modern children who have to adapt to new and difficult situations (death, moving away, divorce, stepparents) will respond sympathetically to this well-produced story.

A Christmas Carol*

ABC-TV 1971. 26 min., col. animation (exec prod) Chuck Jones (prod) Richard Williams. From the story by Charles Dickens (narr) Sir Michael Redgrave (voices) Alastair Sim, Michael Hordern, Joan Sims, Diana Quick. (XER)

Winner of the 1972 Academy Award for best animation short, this is highly imaginative and visually faithful to nineteenth century engravings of London and the John Leech illustrations in the first edition of Dickens's story.

The text, which is also faithful, is narrated by Sir Michael Redgrave in the words of the original. Richard Williams's cinematic style is inventive; a line intimating that Christmas is everywhere has been animated as a fifteen-second sequence in which Scrooge and the Ghost of Christmas Present fly all over the world. The voice of Scrooge is that of the late Alastair Sim, who was convinced this might be the definitive version of the story. It is surely one of the best, along with the live-action feature A CHRISTMAS CAROL directed by Brian Desmond-Hurst in 1951, in which Alastair Sim played Scrooge to Mervyn Johns's Bob Cratchit (q.v.).

The End of the Game

USA 1975. 28 min., col. (prod) Robin Lehman, Claire Wilbur (d)(ph) Robin Lehman (asst ph) Glen Tracy (ed) Jacqueline Lecompte. (PNX)

This 1975 Academy Award winner and 1977 American Film Festival Blue Ribbon winner is another testament to Robin Lehman's notable cinematography. Filmed in Zaire, Kenya, and Tanzania, the documentary takes us from deep inside an anthill to the majestic giraffes suckling their young—a microscopically detailed view of the interdependence of animal life in nature. The drama of the jungle (African storms, beetle ritual dances, feeding time and playtime) is shattered by the sound of a rifle shot. A most absorbing film, THE END OF THE GAME makes its point for ecology, animal life, and environmental studies.

Follow the North Star

ABC-TV 1975. 47 min., col. (prod) Harve Sherman (d) Eric Till (sp) Alvin Boretz (c) Chris Valentine, Dennis Hines, Louise Stubbs, Mel Profit, Jon Granik. (TIM)

Benjy (Chris Valentine), an idealistic northern boy whose father is a "stationmaster" on the underground railroad before the Civil War, dreams of helping Harriet Tubman bring slaves across the Mason-Dixon Line to freedom. His family gives shelter to a slave woman separated from her son, David, and forced to leave him behind when she fled. Benjy, imbued with his father's religious and social convictions, risks his life to make a long journey alone to Maryland to find David, bring him to freedom, and reunite him with his mother. On the trip back, the boys are pursued by a bounty hunter. During their experience together, both boys grow in insight. David (Dennis Hines) learns that great risks sometimes earn great rewards. Benjy finds, to his surprise, that there may be contradictory elements in the human beings on the other side of the slavery issue; he comes to trust and respect a slaveowner who appears to be moral and humane in certain relationships.

"A briskly paced yarn, minus the preachment of sentimentality. . .conveys much about justice and decency. . . ." (*The New York Times*), FOLLOW THE NORTH STAR won a Christopher Award. It was originally an ABC "Afterschool Special."

Free To Be. . .You and Me

ABC-TV 1974. 42 min., col. (prod) Marlo Thomas, Carole Hart (d) Bill Davis (m) Stephen Lawrence, Shelley Miller, Carol Hall, et al. (c) Marlo Thomas, Alan Alda, Harry Belafonte, Mel Brooks, Rita Coolidge, Billy DeWolfe, Roberta Flack, Roosevelt Grier, Michael Jackson,

Kris Kristofferson, Shel Silverstein, Bobby Morse, The New Seekers, Tom Smothers, Cicely Tyson, The Voices of East Harlem, Dionne Warwick. (MCG, CON)

Based on the bestselling record and book, FREE TO BE. . .YOU AND ME is an Emmy award winner with a string of other honors for its celebration of the human potential. "Marlo Thomas and Friends," in songs and stories, involve young people in exploring their personalities without regard to role-stereotyping. The themes are varied, like the talents and backgrounds of Marlo's friends. Mel Brooks offers a comic baby's-eye view of you, me, and the world. In the animated "Ladies First," Marlo gives prim little heroine Shel Silverstein a comeuppance. "It's All Right to Cry," sings Roosevelt Grier, to all boys afraid to show their feelings. "When We Grow Up" is a speculation about things to come by Roberta Flack and Michael Jackson.

Entertaining and fast-paced, the film conveys its message very clearly. Be yourself; relate to others; fulfill your talents and goals without concern for sexist clichés. "We're saying to a child," said Marlo Thomas of her film, "Make your life choices based on what *you* want."

A Gallery of Children

WETA-TV 1970. 30 min., col. (prod) National Gallery of Art, Washington, DC, Extension Services (narr) Joan Kennedy. (NGA)

In the National Gallery of Art, Washington, a group of children are introduced to other children depicted in paintings dating from the Renaissance through the nineteenth century. Their guide is Joan Kennedy.

Got to Tell It: A Tribute to Mahalia Jackson

CBS-TV 1974. 34 min., col. (prod)(d)(sp) Jules Victor Schwerin (comm)(narr) Studs Terkel. (PNX)

A moving documentary about the "queen of the gospels," the late singer Mahalia Jackson, whose records and concert appearances brought the religious music of American blacks to vast audiences throughout the world.

In his commentary, the writer Studs Terkel emphasizes the joys and triumphs of Miss Jackson's life as she communicated them in her songs. Eleven of them, taken from old performances, are in the film, including "Go Tell It on the Mountain," "Didn't It Rain," "When the Saints Go Marching In," "A Closer Walk with Thee," "He's Got the Whole World in His Hand," and "Move On Up a Little Higher." There is also footage of Miss Jackson's slave-like living quarters when she was growing up, and of her 1972 funeral attended by more than 40,000 people.

Harriet Tubman and the Underground Railroad

CBS-TV 1964. 54 min., b/w. documentary. (c) Ethel Waters, Ruby Dee, Ossie Davis, Brock Peters (narr) Van Heflin. (CAL, BUD, MCG/CON)

Originally produced for the CBS "Great Adventure" series under the title GO DOWN, MOSES, this is a moving and suspenseful documentary reenactment, by a fine cast, of the first of nineteen trips into the South before the Civil War during which Harriet Tubman led runaway slaves along the underground railroad to freedom in the North.

Children will respond to this excellent portrayal of a strong black woman, important in our history as leader in the fight against slavery. Arguments for and against slavery and an explanation of the Fugitive Slave Law are included in the film.

Helen Keller in Her Story

USA 1954. 48 min., b/w. (prod) Nancy Hamilton (tech d) Richard Carver Wood (ph) Joe Lipkowitz (m) Morgan Lewis (comm) James Shute (narr) Katharine Cornell (consultant) Nella Braddy Henney (c) Helen Keller. (PNX)

The original title of this documentary portrait of Helen Keller at seventy-four, THE UNCONQUERED, communicates its affirmation of hope and serenity. When the off-screen narrator, actress Katharine Cornell, quotes the line, "I cried when I had no shoes—until I met a man who had no feet," the message will not be lost on youngsters. Reviewing the distinguished career of the woman who overcame blindness, deafness, and muteness, the film is a joyous tribute to courage.

Absorbing and cheerful are the glimpses of Miss Keller herself in her home in Connecticut, touching her beloved flowers during a walk in the woods or seen in close-ups with Polly Thompson (her "eyes" and loyal companion after Annie Sullivan Macy). Included are photographs of her infancy and early girlhood, footage of an earlier film she made, and news shots of her extensive travels, when she met many famous people.

The Horse with the Flying Tail*

Disney 1960. 47 min., col. (prod)(d) Larry Lansburgh (ph) Hannis Staudinger, Robert Carmet, Sidney Zucker, Larry Lansburgh, Werner Kurz, James Bauden (m) William Lava (narr) George Fenneman, Dorian Williams. (GEN)

Winner of the Academy Award for the best documentary feature, this true-life story of a horse is spirited and eventful. The proud palomino named Nautical has happy days as a yearling in New Mexico, is afterward victimized by a horse trader, then wins one of the great international show events in London (the King George V Cup), and takes time out to frolic in the English Channel on holiday.

To film THE HORSE WITH THE FLYING TAIL, cameras rolled in five different countries within two years when the U.S. Equestrian Team, headed by America's top four Olympic equestrians, headed for European competitive events. We see Nautical tested first in Paris against Europe's top jumpers, then in Aachen, Ostend, and London. The "Flying Foursome," the four American equestrians, pilot their horses through difficult training maneuvers. The film also focuses on the U.S. contestants in the pre-Olympic international show at Aachen in which they garnered forty placings.

"I Have a Dream. . .": The Life of Martin Luther King

CBS-TV 1968. 35 min., b/w. documentary. (prod) CBS News. (BFA)

By telling the story of Dr. King—his life and dedication, and the forces that brought him to the leadership of his people—"I HAVE A DREAM. . ." not only introduces youngsters to a great American but explores the civil rights movement of the 1950s and 1960s in which he played such an important role. This CBS News documentary uses actual news film footage of historic events and speeches.

I'll Find a Way

National Film Board of Canada 1978. 26 min., col. (prod) Kathleen Shannon, Yuki Yoshida (d) Beverly Shaffer (ph) Hideaki Kobayashi (m) Larry Crosley (c) Nadia De Franco. (MEG)

Ten-year-old Nadia De Franco was born with spina bifida; she needs a brace and crutches and has spent a lifetime in physiotherapy. At the close of this film, when she is asked what she would do if other kids stared or made cracks, she says, "I don't know how I'll deal with them. But I'll find a way."

It's not hard to see why I'LL FIND A WAY won the 1978 Academy Award for best short live-action picture. Photographer Hideaki Kobayashi and director Beverly Shaffer have done a beautiful job of showing a charming and alert little girl. Nadia is a lovely child as well as an inspiring one. She introduces us to her friends ("My friends never feel sorry for me") and family, and to her classmates, most of whom are more severely handicapped than she is. We watch Nadia and her friends play basketball, sing, take field trips, study, and learn. The warmth and strength they project in this lively documentary are good to feel—and it should not be lost on any child who experiences I'LL FIND A WAY that Nadia and other handicapped children want to be like all children, loved and accepted and not treated like a race apart.

The Incredible Flight of the Snow Geese

Survival Anglia, Ltd. 1975. 50 min., col. (d)(sp)(ph)(comm) Jen and Des Bartlett (m) Glen Campbell. (PIC)

"Magnificent photography and a remarkable subject have combined to produce a memorable film," wrote the ALA *Booklist* about this multiple-award-winning documentary by the world famous naturalist-cinematographers Jen and Des Bartlett. It should be a treat for anyone who loves birds, nature, and such breathtaking camerawork as close shots of a curtain of migrating birds' simultaneous flapping into flight over crystalline trees in the frozen Arctic tundra.

The Bartletts—with humor, close observation, and humanity—capture the 2,500-mile flight of the snow geese from their home near Hudson Bay to the National Wild Life Refuge on the Gulf shore of Texas. We see courting rituals, the birth of the goslings, the birds' closeknit family life, and the Bartletts' efforts to teach some of their adopted orphan chicks how to swim, fly, and get through U.S. Customs.

Lonely Boy

1962. 27 min., b/w. (prod) National Film Board of Canada (d) Wolf Koenig, Roman Kroitor (c) Paul Anka. (CON, NFB)

Winner of nine international awards—a brilliant *cinema verité* study of Paul Anka, teenage idol, singer, and songwriter of the fifties. Provides a candid look, from both sides of the footlights, at the creation of an "image," the modern phenomenon of celebrity, and the adolescents who buy that image. "I'm just a lonely boy," sings Anka.

The Morning Spider

Britain 1976. 22 min., col. (prod) Mark O'Connor (d) Claude and Julian Chagrin. (PYR)

Another imaginative *tour de force* by Julian and his wife Claude Chagrin. In 1975, British pantomimist and comic Julian Chagrin performed the role of a fir tree (THE CHRISTMAS TREE) and won top international festival awards for a fantasy of a London musician (THE CONCERT). In the mime-fantasy THE MORNING SPIDER, which was nominated for an Academy Award, Julian Chagrin plays a morning spider.

Morning Spider is a nice fellow who works hard but can't seem to cope. In a busy twenty-four hours, he lets a jackhammer wasp dig right across his threshold, lets a blue fly get away because he can't bring himself to eat her, and lets a centipede spend the night, waiting till dawn for all 120 shoes to drop. But then Morning Spider follows a mysterious cord through the underbrush and comes upon exquisite Red Spider—for a very, very happy ending.

My Hands Are the Tools of My Soul

USA 1977. 54 min., col. documentary (prod) Swannsway Productions (d) Arthur Barron (ed) Zina Voynow. (TEX)

This documentary introduces children not only to the rich culture of the North American Indian but to the concept that a people's art is part of its life, part of the relationship between man and his environment.

The Indian sense of the harmony of nature permeates the script. We see the masks and carvings, pottery and sand paintings as forms arising from daily living, from the activities of eating, sleeping, hunting, talking, and praying. When the Iroquois mask-maker, Jake Thomas, carves a mask from a standing tree, he asks the Great Spirit for assistance and we learn the functions of the mask: to drive away evil, disease, and high winds. We learn that the Katchina dolls represent the spirits of Katchina energy and force. The soundtrack consists of traditional and modern poetry and statements by Indians. Music of the Southwest and Plains tribes is arranged and performed by Indian singers and musicians. In its spiritual insight and in the variety of its presentation, the film is an illumination of the art of a people and of the process of all artistic creation.

Mzima: Portrait of a Spring

USA 1974. 53 min., col. documentary. (prod) Alan and Joan Root. (MCG/CON)

Distinguished by a good script and excellent photography, this multiple-award winner is an outstanding nature documentary. Kenya's Mzima Springs, a microcosm of the jungle world, illustrates the interdependence of animals—hippos, crustaceans, fish, cormorants, snake birds, otters, crocodiles, eagles, kites. In rare underwater footage, a crocodile devours an antelope that ventured too far into the springs.

"The fascinating study of a universe in miniature. . .a place of beauty and drama, a source of never-ending wonder" (*Scholastic Teacher*).

Portrait of Grandpa Doc

ABC-TV 1977. 28 min., col. (prod) Diane Baker (d)(sp) Randal Kleiser (ph) Harry Winer, John Monsour (m) Charles Albertine (c) Melvyn Douglas, Barbara Rush, Anne Seymour, Bruce Davison, Keith Blanchard. (PNX)

How much does grown-up Greg, the painter, owe to his grandfather's influence? Sifting photos and home movies of their summer vacations, the man realizes what a very special relationship existed between Grandpa Doc and the boy Greg. As he transposes the scenes to canvas, we see in flashbacks the loving strength of the bond between the two. "I see in you the seeds of what you can become. I'll be very glad to help those seeds grow," said the retired doctor to the boy who gave promise of being an artist.

Companion, teacher, mentor, storyteller, friend, and above all, listener, Grandpa Doc (superbly played by Melvyn Douglas) is a memorable figure.

This ABC "Short Story Special" is the tribute of writer-director Randal Kleiser (GREASE) to his own grandfather, and it was partly photographed in Seaside Park, New Jersey, the home of their close family. Like Kleiser's earlier film PEEGE, it also deals with the youngster's coming to terms with the death of a loved one. For children there is wisdom about the generations, as well as about themselves, and the real pleasure of spending some time with somebody as special as Gandpa Doc.

The Red Balloon*

France 1956. 34 min., col. (prod)(d)(sp) Albert Lamorisse (ph) Edmond Séchan (m) Maurice Le Roux (ed) Pierre Gillette (c) Pascal Lamorisse. (MAC)

A lovely miniature, a poetic fantasy about a small boy and a red balloon in the gray streets of Paris, so revealing in its sense of a child's imagination that it has been a classic since it won the Grand Prix at Cannes in 1956. There is no dialog, only music. The boy (the director's son) discovers and "tames" the balloon, playing with it and taking it to church and school, where adults do not feel about it as Pascal does. When some street urchins try to snatch it, Pascal wins for a little while, but in the end the balloon is destroyed; it "dies," a limp, red rag in his hand. But suddenly all the balloons in Paris leave their owners and come to Pascal, lifting him joyously into the sky.

THE RED BALLOON can mean anything you want it to. Meanwhile, there is the beauty of Edmond Séchan's photography and Lamorisse's concept.

Red Sunday

USA 1975. 28 min., col. (prod) Robert Henkel, James Graff. (d) James B. Kelly. (PYR)

"One of the best films made for the Bicentennial" (*Media & Methods*), this documentary of the controversial Battle of Little Big Horn was produced by the Montana and North Dakota Bicentennial commissions. Its impact is dramatic, as a study of live cavalry action on the historic site and as a picture of the whole Indian struggle to resist the imposition of the white man's culture on his own.

Original drawings, photographs, and paintings by both Indian and white artists—most of the Indian drawings done by actual participants in the battle—enrich the documentary. RED SUNDAY won several top awards (American Film Festival, Chicago Film Festival, C.I.N.E., etc.).

Run, Appaloosa, Run

Disney 1966. 48 min., col. (prod)(d)(ph) Larry Lansburgh (sp) Janet Lansburgh (m) Richard Shores (c) Adele Palacios, Wilbur Plaugher, Jerry Gatlin (narr)(songs) Rex Allen. (GEN)

The oldest breed known to history, the Appaloosa is a popular horse in the paddocks today, but for fifty years was a forgotten strain. The name is derived from the Palouse country in northeastern Washington, and the Nez Perce Indians of that region have been selectively breeding this colorful spotted horse for a couple of centuries. In this fictional movie, when the Appaloosa Sky Dancer wins the Hell's Mountain Stampede and Suicide Race for his young Indian owner-rider, Mary Blackfeather (Adele Palacios), it is a triumph for the tribe, too.

Larry Lansburgh (THE HORSE WITH THE FLYING TAIL, an Academy Award winner) is an old hand at horse and dog films. His track and rodeo sequences here are almost documentary. At the competition in Omak, when Sky Dancer is humiliated and almost victimized by a circuit rodeo rider, we meet the famous rodeo clown Wilbur Plaugher (played by himself).

Saludos Amigos

Disney 1943. 42 min., col. (d) Bill Roberts, Jack Kinney, Hamilton Luske, Wilfred Jackson (m) Edward Plumb, Paul Smith; Charles Wolcott, Ned Washington (narr) Fred Shields, Aloysio Oliveira (voices) Clarence Nash, Aloysio Oliveira, Pinto Colvig. (GEN)

Nine story and scriptwriters, five art supervisors, four directors, fifteen animators, etc., etc., labored to bring forth this combination of animated cartoon, live-action musical comedy, and goodwill travelog. It's amusing, in many spots. Donald Duck is a typical American tourist at Lake Titicaca, renting a llama to cross a rope bridge; Pedro is a baby plane that wants to fly the mail like papa; Goofy gets tangled up in bolas, trying to capture wild animals in "El Gaucho Goofy"; Joe Carioca tours South America with the aid of a paintbrush that fills in the background as the trip unfolds.

Disjointed as it is, SALUDOS AMIGOS is bright enough, and looks ahead to Disney's feature THE THREE CABALLEROS.

Sara's Summer of the Swans

ABC-TV 1974. 33 min., col. (d) James B. Clark (sp) Betsy Byars and Bob Rodgers from the Newbery Award book The Summer of the Swans *by Betsy Byars (ph) Bob Collins (c) Heather Totten, Chris Knight, Priscilla Morrill, Eve Plumb, Betty Ann Carr, Reed Diamond. (TIM)*

Sara, a redheaded stringbean with braces, is fourteen. She's not very well satsified with herself, or with her friends. Her pretty sister is busy with boyfriends; Sara swings from mood to mood and finds comfort only with her little brother Charlie, with whom she goes to look at the wild swans. Sara is brought up short the day Charlie gets lost. A teenage boy whom she'd previously scorned helps her find Charlie. Sara is drawn out of herself. Perhaps her unhappiness has been the result of her own attitudes? Here is the promise of a new friendship. Beginning to grow up, Sara feels that she may not be just an ugly duckling after all.

About this well-directed ABC "Afterschool Special" the reviewer for *Christian Science Monitor* wrote, "Were I in the age group for which the show has been produced, I would be flipping over the revelations, marveling at the sharing of my own problems, grateful for the help and direction offered me without any condescension."

Shark!

USA 1976. 29 min., col. documentary. (sp)(narr)(c) Peter Benchley (ph) Stan Waterman. (LCA)

The man who gave us JAWS, writer Peter Benchley, now gives us a brief documentary that demonstrates the fascination of marine study without artificial additives.

In SHARK! Benchley is the narrator and deep-sea diver reporting on his search for the White Shark off Australia's Great Barrier Reef. He and his underwater photographer encountered a great many interesting denizens of the sea before they met the ancient predator. "Will find appreciative audiences," said the ALA *Booklist.*

Silver Blaze

Britain/Canada-TV 1976. 31 min., b/w. (d) John Davies (sp) Julian Bond from a story by Sir Arthur Conan Doyle (ph) Roger Pearce (m) Paul Lewis (c) Christopher Plummer, Thorley Walters, Basil Henson, Gary Watson. (LCA)

The great racehorse, Silver Blaze, is stolen, and his trainer is murdered. Sherlock Holmes (Christopher Plummer) and the faithful Dr. Watson (Thorley Walters) set their wits to the mystery. Filmed in lovely English settings, SILVER BLAZE is good Conan Doyle and good movie adventure, acted with style.

Sittin' on Top of the World: At The Fiddlers' Convention

USA 1973. 24 min., sepia col. (prod) Sandra Sutton, Max Kalmanowicz (narr) H. P. Van Hoy. (PNX)

Exuberant performances of American mountain music and dance, both traditional and contemporary, at the oldest and largest bluegrass music festival of all, in the North Carolina Smoky Mountains. The documentary is informative about the history and structure of bluegrass music: there is a narration by the festival's producer, H. P. Van Hoy.

Ski the Outer Limits

USA 1968. 25 min., col. (prod) Summit Films. (PYR)

Wonderful ski footage, filmed at Vail, Jackson Hole, Taos, Chamonix, and Kitzbuhel, exploring downhill racing, slalom, and giant slalom. A sports documentary with an added dimension; it is "an outdoor ballet of great poetic skill" (*Media & Methods*) which also comments on our need to challenge the outer limits set by the circumstances of our lives. Multiple awards for documentary and sports achievement.

Skinny and Fatty*

Japan 1959. 45 min., b/w. (d) N. Terao (sp) S. Yoshida, M. Wakasugi. (CON)

With a minimum of dialog, the film portrays a special friendship that grows between two Japanese children. They meet at school, where Skinny helps Fatty to stand up for himself. When they are separated (Skinny's family moves away), Fatty is able to succeed on his own. He climbs a mountain and yells to his invisible friend, Skinny: *"Thank you."* Shown on the CBS-TV Children's Film Festival series, at the New York Film Festival, and at the Vancouver Film Festival (where it won the Grand Prize).

Snowbound

NBC-TV 1978. 33 min., col. (prod) Linda Gottlieb (d) Andrew Young (sp) Edward Pomerantz and Kurt Villadsen from the book by Harry Mazer (ph) Robert Young, Michael Barrow (m) Michael Kamen (c) Michael Mullins, Lisa Jane Persky, Vicky Dawson, Shirley Stoler. (LCA)

In this drama, filmed in snow country in Colorado and Massachusetts, a teenage boy and girl stranded after a blizzard survive days of privation and danger and come to understand more about life and each other. "The best of this year's offerings on NBC 'Special Treat' series," said *Film & Broadcasting Review.*

A Storm Called Maria

Disney/ABC-TV 1959. 48 min., b/w. (d) Ken Nelson (sp) James Algar and Larry Clemmons from the book Storm *by George R. Stewart (ph) Jon F. Stanton, Les Thomsen (m) Joseph S. Dubin; song "Storm" by Stan Jones (narr) Don Holt (c) George Kritsky, Walt Bowen, Leo Quinn. (GEN)*

Originally shown on the "Disneyland" television program, this documentary charts the devastation of nature in storms on land and sea, and men's efforts to minimize the wreckage. The main drama is the progress and impact of one titanic blow traced in the factual-fictional book *Storm* by George R. Stewart, professor of meteorolgy at the University of California. The Disney footage is integrated with news clips and historical film records.

Superlative Horse*

USA 1975. 36 min., col. (prod) Urs Furrer, Yanna Brandt (assoc prod) Michael Sheppard (d) Yanna Brandt (sp) Jean Merrill (ph) Urs Furrer. (PNX)

Beautifully produced children's story, with outstanding photography by the late Urs Furrer, distinguished Swiss-born American cinematographer (WHERE THE LILIES BLOOM, PART 2 SOUNDER). Based on Jean Merrill's remaking of an allegorical tale from ancient China, it tells of a powerful Duke Mu, a lover of horses, who sets an aspirant for the post of chief groom an important task: he must find a "superlative" horse. The final choice of young Han Kan is a surprise to those who judge only by outward appearances, but it turns out to be exactly right.

Universe

NASA 1976. 27 min., col. documentary. (prod)(d) Lester Novros for NASA (ph) Carl Zeiss. (narr) William Shatner. (SCR)

Winner of the 1977 American Film Festival Blue Ribbon (first place, "Physical Sciences and Mathematics") and an Academy Award nomination for the arts and sciences best documentary short, this outstanding and imaginative overview of modern astronomy uses animation as well as footage of actual space technology taken by Skylab astronauts. Its visual impact, essentially nontechnical nature, and absorbing effect—it even gives us the *sounds* of the universe picked up by radio telescope—make it a documentary find for the over-tens. "A truly timeless film" (Hans Fickenscher, *Film News*).

A Walk in the Forest

Seymour Films 1976. 28 min., col. (prod)(d) Randall Hood (narr) Richard Harris. (PYR)

A beautiful documentary, winner of eight awards, which uses time-lapse photography to show the moods of the forest through the seasons and the balance of plants and creatures in nature. A raging forest fire underscores the need for man to learn to return what he takes from the earth. A lesson in ecology, a travel record, and an experience in the wonder of living things—all possible through photography of a high order.

The White Heron

White Heron Corp. 1978. 26 min., col. (prod)(d)(sp) Jane Harrison from a short story by Sarah Orne Jewett (ph) Fred Murphy (m) Richard Bell (c) Ruth Rogers, Gary Stine, Mary Pike. (LCA)

Sylvy, a shy young girl in her early teens, lives alone with her grandmother in the Maine woods in 1896. Her life is centered around the birds, the plants, and her cow, Mistress Moolly. "Sylvy is afraid of folks," says her grandma, who knows that Sylvy is counted as one of them by the wild things to whom she is so close. One day an attractive young hunter from the city asks Sylvy to help him find the rare white heron for his collection. His kindness and attentiveness—he gives her a penknife as a gesture of friendship—win her interest, and she companionably searches the forest for the heron with him. But when Sylvy, alone at daybreak, sees the beautiful white bird, she refuses to reveal its secret hiding place to the hunter.

The meaning of this lovely, quiet allegory is apparently a personal one for children. Said one fifth-grader at a preview, "Sylvy couldn't give away the bird because she would have been giving herself away." It is moving for children to share Sylvy's first interaction with other people and her refusal to act in a way inconsistent with what she loves and cares for.

Charlie Chaplin Mutual Comedies

In 1916–1917, Chaplin's fame was steadily growing, and with it his creativity. In eighteen months he made a dozen of his best comedies, for the Mutual Company. Sound tracks were added in 1932. The classic Mutual comedies, still hilarious, vividly demonstrate the essence of the character and the technique that he was to build on for the great features he made at his peak. Several of the little Mutuals were prototypes of his features. And since each is a distinctive work, it is reviewed separately.

The Adventurer*

Mutual 1917. 30 min., b/w. (d)(sp) Charles Chaplin (ph) Rollie Totheroh (c) Charles Chaplin, Edna Purviance, Eric Campbell, Henry Bergman, Albert Austin, Frank J. Coleman, Kono. (FNC)

Escaping from jail, Charlie eludes the guards with lightning ease. He saves two ladies from drowning and is invited by them to a ritzy party. After creating general havoc, he saves Edna Purviance from a jealous suitor and just has time to take off again when the guards reappear. Because of its clever slapstick, it is one of the most popular of the Mutuals.

Behind the Screen*

Mutual 1916. 30 min., b/w. (d)(sp) Charles Chaplin (ph) Rollie Totheroh (c) Charles Chaplin, Eric Campbell, Edna Purviance, Frank Coleman, Henry Bergman, Lloyd Bacon. (FNC)

It's not easy to be a stagehand on a movie set, but Charlie is ingenious and can hot-towel a bear rug or carry eleven chairs as well as the next man. Offered a job as an actor in a movie which involves pie throwing, Charlie ducks too nimbly, and the pies wind up disrupting the production on the adjoining set.

The Count*

Mutual 1916. 30 min., b/w. (d)(sp) Charles Chaplin (ph) Rollie Totheroh (c) Charles Chaplin, Edna Purviance, Eric Campbell, James T. Kelley, Leo White, Albert Austin, Charlotte Mineau, Frank J. Coleman. (FNC)

Charlie has been fired by his boss, a tailor. At the Moneybags mansion where the tailor is impersonating a guest, Count Broko, Charlie enrages his ex-boss but joins in the imposture. The funny business includes parlor magic with disappearing spaghetti and forward passes with a roast chicken. Charlie is the life of the party when he displays his skill at eating watermelon.

The Cure*

Mutual 1917. 30 min., b/w. (d)(sp) Charles Chaplin (ph) Rollie Toth-eroh (c) Charles Chaplin, Edna Purviance, Eric Campbell, John Rand, James T. Kelley. (FNC)

Alcoholic Charlie takes the water cure at the sanatorium. A revolving-door sequence, a muscle-feeling sequence, an interlude in the massage room, a mix-up in the curative waters—life at the health resort is one mad, wonderful whirl.

Easy Street*

Mutual 1917. 30 min., b/w. (d)(sp) Charles Chaplin (ph) Rollie Toth-eroh (c) Charles Chaplin, Edna Purviance, Albert Austin, Eric Campbell, James T. Kelley, Henry Bergman, John Rand. (FNC)

In this most famous of the Mutual two-reel comedies, the hobo Charlie, reformed by Edna at the Mission, becomes a cop and tames the toughest street in town. His pacification of the giant bully (Henry Bergman) is a classic. In the closing scene, the reformed Easy Streeters, including the now angelic bully and his wife in their Sunday best, walk sedately to the Mission with Charlie and Edna. Subtitle: "Love Backed by Force, Forgiveness Sweet, Bring Hope and Peace, to Easy Street."

The Fireman*

Mutual 1916. 30 min., b/w. (d)(sp) Charles Chaplin (ph) William C. Foster, Rollie Totheroh (c) Charles Chaplin, Edna Purviance, Eric Campbell, Lloyd Bacon, Leo White. (FNC)

Charlie, not much of a fireman, upsets the engine company by driving the engine out single-handed. He serves coffee and cream for the fire chief's breakfast by extracting them from the engine boiler. Interrupted by an alarm while playing checkers, Charlie silences it by stuffing it with a handkerchief. He hands the owner of a burning house a book to help him relax. Arriving finally on the scene of the fire (after losing most of the engine), Charlie makes a heroic rescue of Edna Purviance, daughter of the house.

The Floorwalker*

Mutual 1916. 30 min., b/w. (d)(sp) Charles Chaplin (ph) William C. Foster, Rollie Totheroh (c) Charles Chaplin, Edna Purviance, Eric Campbell, Lloyd Bacon, Albert Austin, Leo White, Charlotte Mineau. (FNC)

Charlie's first problem in the department store, after he's knocked over boxes with his cane and mismanaged the drinking fountain, is a bout with the escalator in which he comes off second. Because he is the spitting image of a floorwalker who's just absconded with loot from the manager's office, Charlie is bribed by the thief to change places with him. The free-for-all involves a chase down the "up" escalator, an encounter with the store elevator, and a mirror scene between Charlie and his double (the ancestor of a similar stunt in the Marx Brothers' DUCK SOUP). A famous high point is the "ballet" with which Charlie attempts to fend off the manager.

The Immigrant*

Mutual 1917. 30 min., b/w. (d)(sp) Charles Chaplin (ph) Rollie Totheroh (c) Charles Chaplin, Edna Purviance, Albert Austin, Henry Bergman, Stanley Sanford, Eric Campbell, James T. Kelley. (FNC)

Drama, sentiment, and comedy—Charlie and his immigrant sweetheart, Edna, in bad times and good. A very adroit restaurant sequence finds Charlie not without resources although he has just discovered he hasn't enough for the check.

One A.M.*

Mutual 1916. 30 min., b/w. (d)(sp) Charles Chaplin (ph) William C. Foster, Rollie Totheroh (c) Charles Chaplin. (FNC)

Except for a brief moment with a taxi driver, Charlie appears alone, in a virtuoso solo pantomime performance. At the end of a night out, man-about-town Charlie loses his key and returns home to struggle with inanimate objects—rugs, stuffed animals, a bottomless decanter, a pendulum, and a folding bed. After a mishap under the shower, he finally (with dignity unimpaired) makes his bed in the tub.

The Pawnshop*

*Mutual 1916. 30 min., b/w. (d)(sp) Charles Chaplin (ph) Rollie Toth-
eroh (c) Charles Chaplin, Edna Purviance, John Rand, Henry Bergman. (FNC)*

As clerk in a pawnshop, Charlie copes with a rival by doing a
balancing act on a ladder and sweeps up by performing a tight-
rope walk. His greatest triumphs, however, are the medical treatment of an ailing alarm clock and the balletic foiling of a robbery.

The Rink*

*Mutual 1916. 30 min., b/w. (d)(sp) Charles Chaplin (ph) Rollie Toth-
eroh (c) Charles Chaplin, Edna Purviance, James T. Kelley, Henry
Bergman. (FNC)*

A clumsy waiter when he is at work, Charlie is something else
when he spins around on roller skates. Falling in love with Edna,
he crashes a fancy skating party and turns it into a disaster area.
Marvelous gags.

The Vagabond*

*Mutual 1916. 30 min., b/w. (d)(sp) Charles Chaplin (ph) William C.
Foster, Rollie Totheroh (c) Charles Chaplin, Edna Purviance, Eric
Campbell, Leo White, Lloyd Bacon, Charlotte Mineau. (FNC)*

An emotional drama, anticipating THE KID and THE CIRCUS. Charlie
plays the violin, rescues the girl from a brutal gypsy chief, and
camps out with her. He has a rival, a handsome artist who paints
the gypsy girl's portrait, but love conquers all in the end, when
the girl (now a wealthy woman's newly found heiress) reclaims
Charlie.

Who but Charlie, in their country idyll, could have opened eggs
with a hammer or trapped flies in his pocket?

Children's Film Foundation Features

Here are thirty-six features, a representative selection of the more than 150 films of the Children's Film Foundation of Great Britain that are available for rental and sale in the United States.

For more than fifty years, the Children's Film Foundation has made films designed only for children. Although primarily intended for special matinees in 600 commercial theaters in the United Kingdom, they are in great demand in 16mm in many overseas territories. Henry Geddes, executive producer since 1964, believes that the enthusiasm generated by the CFF films is due to the fact that they really entertain: "The stories are well constructed and presented in visual terms their audiences can immediately understand." The motivating force behind the CFF has always been the reactions of children, not the notions of adults about what children enjoy. (The CFF "Chiffy" awards each year go to the films the children have liked best. Weekly reports also come in from the theaters about what's popular and what's not to the kids' tastes.)

What do they want to see? "They" in the CFF audiences are about nine or ten; the films are not for the over-twelves. They prefer action to dialog and find animals, other children ("ordinary, not too sweet or waif-like"), excitement (not violence), and humor most appealing. "Scary films but not horror"—got that?—and, of course, cowboys, westerns, mysteries, space fiction, and fantasies. An interesting qualification: the children want their detective stories to unravel progressively; they're not concerned about past mysteries.

How well do the CFF features fare in the United States? They've been a favorite on library programs for years; they've been a staple on television Saturday-morning children's film programs; they're steadily booked by theaters for morning and matinee showings. Some expert judgments:

"CFF. . .has developed a certain formula for making entertaining children's films—but this formula is also the limitation with CFF films. There's always a running gag, lots of action with lengthy chases, and kids always solve the problem. However, these films do very well on television, and have the same appeal to American audiences as in Great Britain." (Faith Frenz-Heckman, Director of Children's Programs, CBS-TV, in *Young Viewers*, Summer 1978)

"With good reason we look to the Children's Film Foundation as the leading producer of films of the highest quality made specifically for children. Its films are inevitably one of the Los Angeles International Children's Film Festival's big successes." (Richard Harmetz, Director, Center of Films for Children, Los Angeles, January 1976)

"Three hundred children can't be wrong—I listened to their uncanny silence and was deafened by their ear-splitting applause." (Harriette Lewis, Chairman, Mass Media Committee, National Council of Women, January 1976)

Henry Geddes once told Richard Harmetz that the ideal children's film would be noisy but wordless and populated entirely by children. In the cast credits for the thirty-six features in this section, only the names following a semi-colon are those of adults, "guest stars." The protagonists are played by children, members of accredited British acting schools. Some of these children have gone on, since their CFF days, to film careers: Mandy Miller, Olivia Hussey, Judy Geeson, John Moulder Brown, Jack Wild, Susan George, David Hemmings, Michael Crawford—and yes, Jean Simmons and Anthony Newley started in the children's films of the Rank Organization that preceded the productions of the CFF. Among the guest stars in the CFF casts may be noted such fine English character actors as Bernard Lee, Gordon Jackson, Janet Munro, Hattie Jacques, George Cole, Adrienne Corri, and Dandy Nichols.

In addition to Henry Geddes himself, the roster of directors includes many young men, more receptive to the requirements of children's films than industry veterans, and such distinguished directors as Basil Wright, Halas and Batchelor, Alberto Cavalcanti, Charles Frend, James Hill, and Michael Powell.

Complete, annotated lists of the CFF films available for rental may be obtained from Janus and Macmillan; of films available for sale, from Lucerne and Sterling Educational.

Adventure in the Hopfields

CFF, 59 min., b/w. (d) John Guillermin (sp) Nora Lavrin, Molly Thorp (c) Mandy Miller, Melvyn Hayes, Dandy Nichols. (JAN/LUC, STE)

A girl (Mandy Miller, CRASH OF SILENCE) accidentally breaks her mother's favorite ornament and goes hop-picking to earn money to replace it.

Anoop and the Elephant

CFF, 55 min., col. (prod) Hugh Stewart (sp) Stephen Jenkins (c) Rachel Brennock, Linda Robson, Anoop Singh, Rani. (JAN)

What would you do if a baby elephant named Rani decided to adopt you?

Blow Your Own Trumpet

CFF, 41 min., b/w. (d) Cecil Musk (sp) Geoffrey Bond (c) Peter Butterworth, Michael Crawford, Gillian Harrison. (JAN/LUC, STE)

In spite of his father's opposition, a boy learns to play the trumpet and competes for a place in the town band.

The Boy Who Turned Yellow

CFF, 54 min., col. (d) Michael Powell (sp) Emeric Pressburger (c) Mark Dightam, Lem Kitaj, Robert Eddison, Brian Worth, Helen Weir, Esmond Knight. (JAN)

John unaccountably turns yellow and receives a visit from a strange being, Nick (short for electronic), who appears from the television set and embarks with him on a chain of adventures. (CFF Chiffy, 1977)

Bungala Boys

CFF, 61 min., col. (d)(sp) Jim Jeffries (c) Peter Cauldwell, Alan Dearth, John Dennis, Julie Youatt. (JAN/LUC, STE)

On an Australian beach, the new lifesaving surfers' club succeeds against obstacles. (Venice Festival 1962 special award)

The Christmas Tree

CFF, 52 min., b/w. (d) James Clark (sp) Michael Barnes (c) William Burleigh, Anthony Honour, Kate Nicholls. (JAN/LUC, STE)

Gary and his sister and brother plot to get a tree for a hospital Christmas Eve party. (La Plata Festival 1967, honourable mention)

The Clue of the Missing Ape

CFF, 58 min., b/w. (d) James Hill (sp) Frank Wells, Donald Carter, Comdr. H. Jones (c) Roy Savage, Nati Banda, Patrick Boxill, George Cole. (JAN/LUC, STE)

A girl from Gibralter and a sea cadet foil the plans of enemies of the British fleet in Gibralter. (Venice Festival 1954 joint first prize, best entertainment film for children)

The 'Copter Kids

CFF, 57 min., col. (d) Ronald Spencer (sp) Patricia Latham (c) Sophie Neville, Jonathan Scott-Taylor, Kate Dorning, Paul Chambers. (JAN)

Helicopter pilots help children track down cattle rustlers.

Cry Wolf

CFF, 58 min., col. (d) John Davis (sp) Derry Quinn (c) Anthony Kemp, Mary Burleigh, Martin Beaumont; Judy Cornwell, Ian Hendry, Adrienne Corri, Janet Munro, Wilfred Brambell, Pat Coombes. (JAN)

Because a highly imaginative boy has involved his friends in so many false alarms, he can't get help in a dangerous situation.

Cup Fever

CFF, 63 min., b/w. (d)(sp) David Bracknell (c) Dennis Gilmore, Raymond Davies, Amanda Humby, Olivia Hussey. (JAN)

How Barton United wins the Manchester Junior Football League Cup, after a major setback. (Venice Festival 1966 Silver Gondola Award, Golden Capricorn, CFF Chiffy, 1976.)

Danger Point

CFF, 56 min., col. (d) John Davis (sp) Patricia Latham (c) Raymond Hoskins, Veronica Purnell, Bernard Lee, Sidney Tafler, Hattie Jacques. (JAN)

Teenagers in a borrowed Sea Scouts yacht endangered by a sea mine off Bradda Head.

Daylight Robbery

CFF, 57 min., b/w. (d) Michael Truman (sp) Derry Quinn (c) Trudy Moors, Darryl Read, Janet Hannington; Janet Munro, Gordon Jackson, Ronald Fraser, Patricia Burke, Zena Walker, James Villiers. (JAN)

Three children accidentally locked in a supermarket over the weekend tangle with a gang tunneling into the bank vaults next door. (Venice Festival 1965 special award)

Egghead's Robot

CFF, 56 min., col. (d) Milo Lewis (sp) Leif Saxon (c) Keith and Jeffrey Chegwin, Kathryn Dawe, Roy Kinnear, Patricia Routledge. (JAN)

"Egghead" Wentworth programs his father's robot paratrooper to perform his chores, but forgets to program it to keep him out of trouble. (CFF Chiffy, 1975)

Fern, The Red Deer

CFF, 58 min., col. (d)(sp) Jan Darnley-Smith (c) Candida Prior, Craig McFarlane, Mark Eden, Diana Eden, John Leyton. (JAN/LUC)

A young deer is adopted by Exmoor children.

The Glitterball

CFF, 56 min., col. (d) Harley Cokliss (sp) Howard Thompson (c) Ben Buckton, Keith Jayne, Ron Pember, Marjorie Yates, Barry Jackson. (JAN/LUC)

An animated silver ball from outer space creates havoc with R.A.F. Strike Command. (Ruby Slipper, Top Award, Los Angeles Children's Film Festival, 1977; 2nd Prize, Moscow Festival, Children's Films, 1977)

Go Kart Go

CFF, 55 min., b/w. (d) Jan Darnley-Smith (sp) Michael Barnes (m) Ron Goodwin (c) Graham Stark, Wilfrid Brambell, Gladys Henson, John Moulder Brown. (JAN/LUC, STE)

Rival groups in the exciting local Go-Kart races. (Venice 1964 Medal)

GLITTERBALL (CFF)

MAURO THE GYPSY (CFF)

ROBIN HOOD JUNIOR (CFF)

Headline Hunters

CFF, 60 min., col. (d) Jonathan Ingrams (sp) Geoffrey Bond (c) Leonard Brockwell, Susan Payne, Malcolm Epstein; Bill Owen, Reginald Marsh, David Lodge, Dermot Kelly, Glynn Houston. (JAN/STE)

While the editor is ill, his children keep the local newspaper running.

The Johnstown Monster

CFF, 54 min., col. (d)(sp) Olaf Pooley (c) Connor Brennan, Simon Tully, Kim McDonald, Derek Farr. (JAN)

A youngster takes a photograph which seems to show that the legend of the Johnstown Monster may not be only a legend after all. (La Bourboule Festival 1975: President's Prize)

Kadoyng

CFF, 60 min., col. (d) Ian Shand (sp) Leo Maguire (c) Leo Maguire, Adrian Hall, Teresa Codling, Bill Owen, Frieda Knorr. (JAN)

When Kadoyng arrives from extraterrestrial spheres, he saves the village of Byway from a threat. (CFF Chiffy, 1975)

The Last Rhino

CFF, 55 min., col. (d)(sp)(prod) Henry Geddes (m) Edwin Astley (c) David Ellis, Susan Millar-Smith. (JAN, MAC/LUC, STE)

Two children prevent the destruction of a wounded rhino, the last in an East Africa game reserve. (Gijon Festival 1963, Gold Medal)

Mauro the Gypsy

CFF, 58 min., col. (d) Laurence Henson (sp) Patricia Latham (c) Graeme Greenhowe, Fiona Kennedy, Andrew Lyatt, Katie Gardiner. (JAN)

Mauro and his gypsy family are suspected of wrongdoing, but things are not always what they seem. (Moscow Festival 1973, Special Award, Contribution to Racial Tolerance)

The Monster of Highgate Pond

CFF, 59 min., b/w. (prod) Halas & Batchelor Cartoon Films Ltd. (d) Alberto Cavalcanti (sp) Mary Cathcart Borer from Joy Batchelor's story (m) Francis Chagrin (c) Rachel Clay, Michael Wade, Terry Raven, Philip Latham. (MAC, JAN/LUC, STE)

Three children are given an unidentified egg from Malaya which hatches in the town pond, with astonishing results.

Mystery on Bird Island

CFF, 57 min., b/w. (d) John Haggarty (sp) Mary Dunn (c) Mavis Sage, Vernon Morris, Jennifer Beech, Nicky Edmett. (JAN/LUC, STE)

A battle of wits between smugglers and four children who are trying to get a bird-watcher on a Channel Islands bird sanctuary. (Venice Festival 1955 Silver Gondola, best children's film)

One Wish Too Many

CFF, 55 min., b/w. (prod) Basil Wright, Realist Film Unit Ltd. (d) John Durst (sp) Norah Pulling (c) Anthony Richmond, Rosalind Gourgey, John Pike, Gladys Young. (JAN/LUC, STE)

All their wishes are granted by the magic marble, but Peter and his friends have some surprises. (Venice Festival 1956 Silver Gondola, best children's film)

Paganini Strikes Again

CFF, 59 min., col. (d) Gerry O'Hara (sp) Mike Gorell Barnes (c) Philip Bliss, Andrew Bowen, Simon Thompson, Julie Dawn Cole, Jean Marlow. (JAN)

Young musicians witness the only clue to a robbery and pursue the case on their own.

The Rescue Squad

CFF, 54 min., b/w. (d) Colin Bell (sp) Malcolm Stewart (c) Christopher Brett, Shirley Joy, Malcolm Knight, Gareth Tandy, Lindy Leo, Danny Grove. (JAN/LUC, STE)

Six children who are trapped in a high tower where they've lost a toy plane are rescued by a donkey. (Venice Festival 1963, two awards)

Robin Hood Junior

CFF, 61 min., col. (prod)(d) Matt McCarthy, John Black (sp) Matt McCarthy (c) Keith Chegwin, Mandy Tulloch, Keith Jayne, Rachel Brennock. (JAN/LUC)

Children foil the Norman barons, in Sherwood Forest. (Moscow Festival 1975 Special Diploma; CFF Chiffy, 1977)

Runaway Railway

CFF, 55 min., b/w. (d) Jan Darnley-Smith (sp) Michael Barnes from the story by Henry Geddes (c) John Moulder Brown, Kevin Bennett, Leonard Brockwell, Roberta Tovey, Sidney Tafler, Ronnie Barker. (MAC, JAN/LUC, STE)

When their favorite engine is about to be broken up, the young railway enthusiasts take things in hand, inadvertently becoming involved in a mail-train robbery.

The Sky-Bike

CFF, 62 min., col. (d)(sp) Charles Frend (c) Spencer Shires, Ian Ellis, John Howard; Liam Redmond, William Lucas. (JAN)

A boy intrigued by flying teams up with an old inventor and they compete against unscrupulous rivals in a man-powered flying machine contest.

Smokey Joe's Revenge

CFF, 57 min., col. (d) Ronnie Spencer (sp) Patricia Latham (c) Kay Humblestone, Nicky Cox, Donny Martyne, Margaret Lacey, John Barrett. (JAN/LUC)

An antique traction engine consigned to the scrap heap by an ungrateful owner gets its own back. (CFF Chiffy, 1976)

Supersonic Saucer

CFF, 50 min., b/w. (prod)(sp) Frank Wells (d) S. C. Fergusson (m) Jack Beaver (c) Marcia Monolescue, Fella Edmunds, Gillian Harrison, Donald Gray. (JAN/LUC, STE)

A group of children adopt a baby supersonic saucer from Venus, which causes many misunderstandings but comes to the aid of their school.

Tim Driscoll's Donkey

CFF, 56 min., b/w. (d) Terry Bishop (sp) Mary Cathcart Borer (c) David Coote, Carole Lorimer, Anthony Green. (JAN/LUC, STE)

Young Tim, from the hills behind Dublin, pursues his pet donkey to its new owners in England. (Venice Festival 1955, first prize for best children's film; Montevideo Festival 1956, special award)

Toto and the Poachers

CFF, 50 min., col. (prod) Henry Geddes (d) Brian Salt (sp) Henry Geddes, Johnnie Coquillon, Brian Salt (c) John Aloisi. (JAN)

A young African boy, taken on safari to look after the camp of the game warden, with the aid of his monkey helps to capture ivory poachers. (Venice Festival 1958, second prize for best children's film)

Where's Johnny?

CFF, 58 min., col. (d) David Eady (prod)(sp) Mike Gorell Barnes (c) Raymond Boal, Kim Clifford, Perry Benson, Graham Stark, Patrick Newell. (JAN)

What happens to Johnny after he becomes invisible.

Wings of Mystery

CFF, 55 min., b/w. (d) Gilbert Gunn (sp) H. K. Lewenhak (ph) David A. Holmes (c) Judy Geeson, Hennie Scott, Francesca Bertorelli, Graham Aza. (JAN/LUC, STE)

Children discover the identity of the person in the steelworks selling secrets abroad and use a racing pigeon to help capture him.

The Zoo Robbery

CFF, 64 min., col. (prod)(d)(sp) Matt McCarthy and John Black (c) Karen Lucas, Paul Gyngell, Walter McKone, Luke Batchelor. (JAN)

When Yen-Yen the Yeti, star attraction of the London Zoo, is kidnapped, her friends in a canal barge have quite a time rescuing her. (CFF Chiffy, 1977)

A Supplementary List of Features

"Not Prime but Choice"

Across the Great Divide

Pacific International 1977. 100 min., col. (d)(sp) Stewart Raffill (ph) Gerard Alcan, Fred R. Krug (m) Gene Kauer, Douglas Lackey; song, Beau Charles (c) Robert Logan, Heather Rattray, Mark Edward Hall, George "Buck" Flower, Hal Bokar, Frank F. Salsedo. (PFI)

Against the spectacular backdrop of Utah and British Columbia scenery, this robust children's western enfolds the adventures of two spunky, self-reliant preteenagers, a brother and a sister, whom a charming gambler guides to Oregon in 1876 to reclaim their inheritance, encountering on the way some very fierce animals and (for a change) some very friendly Indians.

The Adventures of Chico*

(prod)(d)(sp)(ph) Stacy and Horace Woodard, 1938. 55 min., b/w. documentary. English narration. (IVY)

A beautiful documentary, filmed in Northern Mexico, about twelve-year-old Chico, the son of a peon, and his love for his world of "friends," the birds and animals he has fed and reared. Brilliant photography, and the patient, natural shots of living creatures in exciting as well as humorous moments.

The Adventures of Huckleberry Finn

MGM 1960. 107 min., col. (d) Michael Curtiz (sp) James Lee from the novel by Mark Twain (c) Tony Randall, Eddie Hodges, Archie Moore, Josephine Hutchinson, Neville Brand, Mickey Shaughnessy, Andy Devine, Buster Keaton, Finlay Currie, John Carradine, Royal Dano, Sterling Holloway. (FNC)

There's never been a movie about the most famous boy in American literature, the "great-spirited boy among mean-spirited men," that was more than a vehicle for a child star, like Mickey Rooney (1939) and Eddie Hodges here, who scored in Capra's A HOLE IN THE HEAD (1959); but until a better one comes along, this version will do for entertaining the youngsters, provided you follow it up by introducing them to the book.

211

Huckleberry Finn

United Artists 1974. 118 min., col. (d) J. Lee Thompson (sp)(m)(lyr) Richard M. Sherman, Robert B. Sherman (ph) Laszlo Kovacs (c) Jeff East, Paul Winfield, Harvey Korman, David Wayne, Arthur O'Connell, Gary Merrill, Lucille Benson. (UAS)

This musical version was variously described by the critics as "a lavish bore" (*The New York Times*) and "drearily elephantine . . . a morass of treacle" (*Monthly Film Bulletin*, British Film Institute). Even the competent playing of Paul Winfield as Jim fails to rise above the dismaying level of this completely tasteless production.

The Adventures of Sherlock Holmes

Fox 1939. 85 min., b/w. (d) Alfred Werker (sp) Edwin Blum and William Drake from the play Sherlock Holmes by William Gillette (c) Basil Rathbone, Nigel Bruce, Ida Lupino, Alan Marshal, Terry Kilburn, George Zucco, Henry Stephenson, E. E. Clive. (FNC, LCA)

"Sherlock," announces Professor Moriarty (George Zucco), "I am about to commit the most incredible crime of my career." From then on, it's nonpareil Conan Doyle: the plot against the Star of Delhi; the clubfooted gaucho armed with a bola in the London fog; Ida Lupino's terror on receiving a sketch of a man with an albatross around his neck—and Basil Rathbone (Holmes) explaining it all to Nigel Bruce (Dr. Watson).

The Adventures of the Wilderness Family*

Pacific International 1975. 94 min., col. (d)(sp)(ph) Stewart Raffill (m) Gene Kauer, Douglas Lackey (c) Robert F. Logan, Susan Damante Shaw, Hollye Holmes, Ham Larsen. (PFI)

Based on a true story and filmed in the Uinta Mountains, Utah, this follows a young father, mother, and two children in their flight from urban traumas in Los Angeles today to pioneer living in a remote wilderness log cabin, where they collect a raccoon, bear cubs, and a variety of adventures with nature and animals.

The African Lion

Disney 1955. 72 min., col. (d) James Algar (ph) Alfred G. Milotte, Elma Milotte (sp) James Algar, Winston Hibler, Ted Sears, Jack Moffitt (m)

Paul J. Smith (narr) Winston Hibler. (GEN)

Singled out by Pauline Kael as a choice documentary for children, though she never liked the others in the True-Life series, THE AFRICAN LION avoids gimmickry. The Milottes (BEAVER VALLEY) spent three years near Mount Kilimanjaro in patient filming of the spontaneous actions of the lion family and other wildlife, with absorbing results.

All Creatures Great and Small

Britain 1974. 90 min., col. (prod) David Susskind, Duane Bogie (d) Claude Whatham (sp) Hugh Whitemore from the book by James Herriot (ph) Peter Suschitsky (m) Wilfred Josephs (c) Simon Ward, Anthony Hopkins, Lisa Harrow, Brian Stirner, Freddie Jones, T. P. McKenna, Brenda Bruce. (TIM)

True pictures of work among animals, with the humor and warmth of James Herriot's bestselling book. His experiences from the beginning of his days as a veterinary surgeon, to his marriage and the outbreak of World War II, have been filmed in the lovely settings of the Yorkshire hills and dales.

All Things Bright and Beautiful

Britain/Reader's Digest 1978. 94 min., col. (prod) David Susskind, Margaret Matheson (sp) Alan Plater from James Herriot's books (d) Eric Till (c) John Alderton, Colin Blakely, Lisa Harrow. (TIM)

The appealing mixture as before, scenes from the life of veterinary surgeon James Herriot in the North Yorkshire dales. ". . . Small, sometimes funny, sometimes moving dramas played out in a picturesque countryside with British eccentricities and style adding charm and authenticity. Nothing slick. The film's most graphic episode . . . is the birth of a calf, forcefully and skillfully shown—all part of the life of one who likes life and wins respect and love in return" (*Film Information*, National Council of Churches of Christ).

Almost Angels

Disney 1962. 93 min., col. (d) Steve Previn (sp) Vernon Harris (m) Strauss, Schubert, Brahms; "Greensleeves" (c) Vienna Boys Choir,

Peter Weck, Vincent Winter, Sean Scully, Hans Holt, Bruni Lobel, Fritz Eckhardt. (AIM, BUC, MAC, TWY)

Good choral music, views of Vienna and the Danube, and a brisk and pleasant story about the Vienna Boys Choir, focusing on the boys' singing, and their life in and out of school. European-made production; English dialog.

Anchors Aweigh

MGM 1945. 103 min., col. (prod) Joe Pasternak (d) George Sidney (sp) Isobel Lennart from a story by Natalie Marcin (ph) Robert Planck, Charles Boyle (m) Sammy Cahn, Jule Styne; Ralph Freed, Sammy Fain (c) Gene Kelly, Kathryn Grayson, Frank Sinatra, José Iturbi, Dean Stockwell, Carlos Ramirez, Henry O'Neill, Leon Ames, Rags Ragland, Edgar Kennedy, Henry Armetta, Billy Gilbert. (FNC)

Easy and pleasant song-and-dance performances by Gene Kelly and Frank Sinatra as two gobs on shore leave in Hollywood, with a famous, charming sequence à la Disney in which Kelly does a whimsical adagio with a little cartoon character. Miss Grayson's singing and José Iturbi's playing Tschaikovsky *and* a boogie-woogie version of "The Donkey Serenade" are part of the entertainment.

Animal Crackers

Paramount 1930. 97 min., sepiatone. (d) Victor Heerman (sp) Morrie Ryskind, Pierre Collings, based on the Marx Brothers musical by George S. Kaufman, Bert Kalmar, Morrie Ryskind, and Harry Ruby (ph) George Folsey (c) Groucho, Harpo, Chico, and Zeppo Marx, Margaret Dumont, Lillian Roth. (FNC, SWA)

It has a heavy, intricate plot that drags. But it also has Groucho's greatest monologue; his most famous character (Captain Geoffrey T. Spaulding); wonderful encounters with Chico (Signor Emanuel Ravelli); Harpo's famous silverware-dropping routine, and Kalmar and Ruby's song "Hooray for Captain Spaulding."

The Bears and I*

Disney 1975. 89 min., col. (d) Bernard McEveety (sp) John Whedon, based on the book by Robert Leslie (ph) Ted Landon (m) Buddy Baker (c) Patrick Wayne, Chief Dan George, Andrew Duggan, Michael Ansara, Robert Pine, Val DeVargas. (FNC)

Saccharine but occasionally wholesome concoction, one of the packaged wilderness-diet foods, about a war veteran in the Canadian Rockies who finds meaning in bringing up three orphaned bear cubs and settling a dispute between an Indian tribe and the Parks Commission. For younger children, who will enjoy the three bears' fight with an elk and a wolverine, and their crazy slide down a snowy mountain on a runaway sled.

Beau Geste

Paramount 1939. 114 min., b/w. (d) William Wellman from the novel by Percival Christopher Wren (c) Gary Cooper, Robert Preston, Ray Milland, Brian Donlevy, Susan Hayward, Broderick Crawford, Donald O'Connor. (UNI, TWY)

Not the sixties remake (adventure without style) or the seventies remake, released by comedian Marty Feldman (spoof without adventure), but the McCoy—or rather, the P. C. Wren, with the Foreign Legionnaries, the fortress, the note to Scotland Yard; intrigue and derring-do in the best old romantic vein of the thirties.

Bedknobs and Broomsticks

Disney 1971. 117 min., col. (d) Robert Stevenson (sp) Bill Walsh and Don DaGradi from a book by Mary Norton (ph) Frank Phillips (m) Richard M. and Robert B. Sherman (spec eff) Danny Lee, Eustace Lycett, Alan Maley (c) Angela Lansbury, David Tomlinson, Sam Jaffe, Reginald Owen, Tessie O'Shea. (TWY, MAC, FNC, ROA, SWA)

In the same vein, though not in the same class, as MARY POPPINS, this live-action plus cartoon-sequences fantasy is about three Cockney youngsters, refugees from the London blitz, who are billeted in a country village with a Miss Eglantine Price (delightfully played by Angela Lansbury), who turns out to be an apprentice witch. Their many adventures include a visit to the land of Naboombu, where the animals are smarter than people. The special effects won an Academy Award.

Bethune

1964. 58 min., b/w. documentary. (prod) National Film Board of Canada (d)(ph) Donald Brittain, John Kemeny, Guy Glover. (CON, NFB)

A documentary of the remarkable career of Dr. Norman Bethune, who gave up his medical practice in Canada to serve with the Loyalists during the Spanish Civil War, and with the North Chinese Army during the Sino-Japanese War. He is a legendary figure, for his pioneering of the world's first mobile blood-transfusion service, in Spain, and his battlefront treatment of the wounded, in China. Multiple international awards.

The Blue Bird

USA/USSR 1976. 97 min., col. (d) George Cukor (sp) Hugh Whitemore, Alfred Hayes from the play by Maurice Maeterlinck (ph) Freddie Young, Ionas Gritzus (m) Irwin Kostal, Andrei Petrov (chor) Igor Belsky, Leonid Jakobson (cost) Edith Head, Marina Azizian (c) Elizabeth Taylor, Jane Fonda, Ava Gardner, Cicely Tyson, Robert Morley, George Cole, Harry Andrews, Will Geer, Mona Washbourne, Nadejda Pavlova, George Vitzin, Margareta Terechova, Oleg Popov, Leonid Nevedomsky. (FNC)

The first American-Soviet co-production: a musical based on Maeterlinck's classic about Tyltyl and Mytyl, the children whom a benign witch sends on a quest for the blue bird which will bring happiness to a sick child. Extravagant, lush, and star-studded, it is an "intermittently beautiful but rather earthbound fantasy" (*Film & Broadcasting Review*). Its best features are all the child actors; Nadejda Pavlova of the Bolshoi Ballet, as the blue bird; the exterior shots of the outskirts of Leningrad and the city of Riga; the clown Oleg Popov; and the title and production graphics by the British illustrator of children's books, Brian Wildsmith.

Boy of Two Worlds

Denmark 1960. 88 min., col. (d) Astrid Henning-Jensen (sp) Astrid Henning-Jensen and Bjarne Henning-Jensen (ph) Henning Bendtsen (m) Herman D. Koppel and the Danish State Symphony Orchestra (c) Jimmy Sterman, Edvin Adolphson. (BUD, IVY, MAC, WCF)

Little Paw is of mixed races and knows more about animals and the jungle than about the manners of his blonde and blue-eyed classmates in the Danish town in which he is an outsider. Sensitively and movingly made by the distinguished Danish filmmakers the Henning-Jensens (PALLE ALONE IN THE WORLD, DITTE CHILD OF MAN), and widely honored here and abroad, BOY OF TWO WORLDS is a good story, recommended for its insight into conflicts of race and culture on the level of a small boy's experience.

Brian's Song

Screen Gems 1971. 75 min., col. (d) Buzz Kulik (sp) William Blinn from the book I Am Third by Gale Sayers with Al Silverman (ph) Joe Biroc (m) Michel Le Grand (c) James Caan, Billy Dee Williams, Jack Warden, Bernie Casey, Shelley Fabares, David Huddleston, Judy Pace, Abe Gibron, Jack Concannon, Ed O'Bradovich; players, coaches, and staff of the Chicago Bears. (GEN)

The inspiring story of the friendship between Brian Piccolo and Gale Sayers. When they were rookie football players at the Chicago Bears summer camp in 1965, they were the first racially mixed roommates in the NFL; and they were supportive and compassionate friends until Brian's death in 1970.

Many awards and citations, including five Emmys, brotherhood awards, and the first *Black Sports* magazine award "for interracial understanding through the medium of sports."

Cat Ballou

Columbia 1965. 96 min., col. (d) Elliot Silverstein (sp) Walter Newman and Frank R. Pierson, based on the book by Roy Chanslor (ph) Jack Marta (c) Jane Fonda, Lee Marvin, Michael Callan, Dwayne Hickman, Nat King Cole, Stubby Kaye, Reginald Denny, Arthur Hunnicutt, Bruce Cabot, Jay C. Flippen. (MAC, SWA, TWY)

"Outrageous" is the word most often used, and always cheerfully, about this hilarious spoof of westerns. From Academy Award winner Lee Marvin, riding his inebriated palomino, to schoolmarm Jane Fonda, whose outlaw band includes, among other originals, an Indian who denies he's Hebrew, it is great fun. Its way-out comedy is sure to be relished by the kids, if not by the very refined among their elders. Multiple award winner (acting, directing, comedy).

Charlotte's Web*

Paramount 1973. 94 min., col. animation. (prod) Joseph Barbera, William Hanna (d) Charles Nichols, Iwao Takamoto (sp) Earl Hamner, Jr., based on the book by E. B. White (m)(lyr) Richard M. and Robert B. Sherman (art) Bob Singer. (FNC)

The animated-cartoon version of E. B. White's classic about Charlotte, the spider who weaves words into her web trying to save the life of her friend Wilbur the pig, who is facing the threat of the sausage factory. Charlotte is the voice of Debbie Reynolds; Wilbur, of Henry Gibson; Templeton, of Paul Lynde; Mrs. Arable, of Martha Scott; the goose, of Agnes Moorehead; Fern Arable, of Paul Ferdin. The narrator is Rex Allen.

Cheyenne Autumn

Warners 1964. 156 min., col. (d) John Ford (sp) James R. Webb from the book by Mari Sandoz (ph) William Clothier (m) Alex North (c) Richard Widmark, Carroll Baker, Karl Malden, Sal Mineo, Dolores Del Rio, Ricardo Montalban, Gilbert Roland, Arthur Kennedy, John Carradine, Victor Jory, Edward G. Robinson, James Stewart, Patrick Wayne, Elizabeth Allen, George O'Brien, John Qualen. (GEN)

Slow but very moving story of the tragic flight of 286 Cheyenne men, women, and children, pursued by the cavalry, from a barren Oklahoma reservation to their native Yellowstone country 1,800 miles away. The film of the heroic pilgrimage (which included a Quaker schoolmistress) is one of the most deeply felt of director John Ford, who said, "I had wanted to make it for a long time. I've killed more Indians than Custer, Beecher and Chivington put together . . . . I wanted to show their point of view for a change."

Christopher Columbus

Britain 1949. 103 min., col. (prod) A. Frank Bundy (d) David MacDonald (sp) Muriel and Sydney Box, Cyril Roberts (c) Fredric March, Florence Eldridge, Francis L. Sullivan, Linden Travers. (GEN)

A panoramic and often visually striking British biography of the explorer and navigator, with a minimum of departures from history, such as the rich young widow who falls in love with Columbus and tries to dissuade him from his attempt to find a sea route to India.

Davy Crockett, King of the Wild Frontier*

Disney 1955. 93 min., col. (d) Norman Foster (sp) Tom Blackburn (ph) Charles P. Boyle (m) George Bruns (c) Fess Parker, Buddy Ebsen, Basil Ruysdael, Hans Conried. (GEN)

If it seems a little episodic, it's because this feature was spliced together from three "Frontierland" episodes on the Disneyland TV show, as a response to the overnight national excitement about the legendary giant of the Tennessee backwoods. Suddenly, every boy and girl in America was singing "The Ballad of Davy Crockett," conning the folks for coonskin hats, and acting out the tales of the Indian fighter who tracked down Chief Red Stick but did not kill him. Still popular.

Destination Moon

Eagle-Lion 1950. 91 min., col. (prod) George Pal (d) Irving Pichel (sp) Robert A. Heinlein, Rip van Ronkel and James O'Hanlon from Heinlein's book Rocketship Galileo *(ph) Lionel Lindon (art) Chesley Bonestell (des) Ernest Fegté (c) John Archer, Warner Anderson, Erin O'Brien Moore, Tom Powers. (GEN)*

George Pal's pre-moonwalk, pre–STAR WARS success which inspired so many imitations. Designer Fegté and rocketeer Hermann Oberth achieved a sense of realism for the moon surfaces. Of interest historically, and of interest to Heinlein readers.

Doctor Dolittle*

Fox 1967. 152 min., col. (d) Richard Fleischer (sp) Leslie Bricusse from the stories by Hugh Lofting (ph) Robert Surtees (m) Lionel Newman, Anthony Courage; songs, Leslie Bricusse (c) Rex Harrison, Samantha Eggar, Anthony Newley, Richard Attenborough, Peter Bull, Geoffrey Holder. (FNC)

The sight of urbane Rex Harrison, in top hat and cane, as Doctor Dolittle, surrounded by a flock of sheep with whom he is carrying on an animated conversation, is one of the better moments in an uneven musical production based on the popular Hugh Lofting stories. Leslie Bricusse won an Academy Award for his song "Talk to the Animals."

A Dog of Flanders*

Warners 1959. 97 min., col. (d) James B. Clark (sp) Ted Sherdeman from the novel by Ouida (m) Paul Sawtell, Bert Shefter; St. Cecilia Academy of Rome Orchestra and Chorus (c) David Ladd, Donald Crisp, Theodore Bikel. (FNC)

The art-enchanted youngster in Ouida's famous story who names his mongrel pet after the dog of his idol, Rubens, is lovingly portrayed against authentic settings in the Netherlands and Belgium, in this award-winning production by Robert B. Radnitz (SOUNDER).

Do You Keep a Lion at Home?*

Czechoslovakia 1964. 81 min., col. (d) Pavel Hobl (sp) Sheila Ochova, Buhumil Sobotka (ph) Jiri Vojta (m) William Bukovy (c) Ladislav Ocenasek, Josef Filip, Olga Machoninova, Jan Brychta. English dialog. *(MAC)*

Two boys who find their nursery school closed decide to roam around Prague on their own. Through photographic tricks and various animation techniques, inventive use of music and color, and the director's whimsy, the adventures become great fun— making friends with a talking dog, meeting ghosts in armor, and winning a race in a little auto.

Drums Along the Mohawk

Fox 1939. 105 min., col. (d) John Ford (sp) Lamar Trotti and Sonya Levien from the Walter D. Edmonds novel (ph) Bert Glennon, Ray Rennahan (c) Claudette Colbert, Henry Fonda, Edna May Oliver, Eddie Collins, John Carradine, Jessie Ralph, Arthur Shields, Ward Bond, Chief Big Tree, Mae Marsh. (FNC)

Ford's first film in color, about the experiences of a young couple in the Mohawk Valley of upstate New York before and during the American Revolution, is a carefully documented historical film well above the average and a piece of authentic Americana. The drums are those of Iroquois Indians paid by the British to fight the colonists.

The Eleanor Roosevelt Story

Landau 1965. 90 min., b/w. (prod) Sidney Glazier (d) Richard Kaplan (sp) Archibald MacLeish (m) Ezra Laderman (narr) Archibald MacLeish, Eric Sevareid, Frances Cole (Mrs. Roosevelt's cousin). (BUD, IVY, TWY, MAC)

Winner of the Academy Award for best documentary feature, this moving portrait of a very great lady and of her times is worthy of its subject. Vivid, compassionate, yet not sentimental, Archibald MacLeish's script is fact touched by the poet's insight.

An Elephant Called Slowly

Britain 1969. 91 min., col. (d) James Hill (sp) Bill Travers, James Hill (ph) Simon Trevor (m) Bert Kaempfert (c) Virginia McKenna, Bill Travers, George Adamson. (BUD, MOD, SEL, TWY, WRS)

The two stars of BORN FREE return to the Kenya bush country, where one of a herd of friendly elephants, named Pole Pole (Swahili for "slowly"), shares their adventures with gamekeeper Adamson. Swinging safari music, lovely African landscapes, and lots of wild animals.

End of the Trail

NBC-TV 1967. 54 min., b/w. (prod)(d) Donald B. Hyatt (sp) Philip Reisman, Jr. (ed) Silvio D'Alisera, James Pallan (m) Robert Russell Bennett (narr) Walter Brennan. (CON)

The life and fate of the Plains Indians during the great westward movement of the 1870s. Walter Brennan is storyteller on and off camera; the production (an NBC-TV "Project 20" special) combines Montana location shots with historic photographs brought to life by the "still-pictures-in-action" technique. Most of the story is told in the words of the Plains Indians themselves, one of the most underestimated of all peoples culturally (in the view of the producer-director), who were tragically caught up and buried in the white man's expansion.

The Endless Summer

USA 1966. 95 min., col. (prod)(d)(sp)(ed)(narr) Bruce Brown (ph) Bruce Brown, R. Paul Allen, Bob Bagley, Paul Witzig (m) The Sandals (c) Bruce Brown, Mike Hynson, Robert August. (SWA, TWY, MAC, BUD)

Testing beaches from California to Ghana, in Australia, New Zealand, Tahiti, and Hawaii, filmmaker Bruce Brown and two friends set out on a three-month, 35,000-mile trip in search of "the perfect wave." The adventures and discoveries of surfing in an exciting documentary.

Everybody Rides the Carousel

CBS-TV 1975. 72 min., col. animation. (prod)(des)(d) John and Faith Hubley. Adapted from the works of Erik H. Erikson. (m) William Rosso. (PYR)

"New insight as well as a smile" (ALA *Booklist*) is promised viewers of the Hubleys' delightful animation of Erik H. Erikson's abstractions about the life cycle. Cicely Tyson introduces it. The visual metaphor for the life cycle is a carousel upon which there are eight rides: infancy, toddler, childhood, school, adolescence, young adulthood, maturity, and old age. Recognizable human forms and situations, sparse and nontechnical narration, emotions and life processes enhanced by the Hubleys' imagination— something to enjoy in EVERBODY RIDES THE CAROUSEL for everybody over ten. (Blue Ribbon winner at the American Film Festival, other awards.)

Finian's Rainbow

Warners 1968. 140 min., col. (d) Francis Ford Coppola (sp) E. Y. Harburg and Fred Saidy, based on their musical play (m) Burton Lane (lyr) E. Y. Harburg (ph) Philip Lathrop (c) Fred Astaire, Petula Clark, Don Francks, Keenan Wynn, Tommy Steele, Al Freeman, Jr. (GEN)

Here are Fred Astaire as the Irishman who steals a pot of gold from a leprechaun; Tommy Steele and Petula Clark in the "Something Grandish" number; Keenan Wynn as the bigoted white senator turned black by a magical spell—and the magical spell of the rollicking tunes themselves: "How Are Things In Glocca Morra?" and "Look to the Rainbow" and "If This Isn't Love" and "Old Devil Moon."

Fire Over England

Britain 1937. 81 min., b/e. (prod) Erich Pommer (d) William K. Howard (sp) Clemence Dane, Sergei Nolbandov from the novel by A. E. W. Mason (ph) James Wong Howe (m) Richard Addinsell (art) Lazar Meerson (c) Laurence Olivier, Vivien Leigh, Flora Robson, Leslie Banks, Raymond Massey, Robert Newton, James Mason. (JAN, BUD)

In its genre—the patriotic-historical romance—this is as fine and stirring as you can imagine. The intrigues in the courts of England and Spain that climaxed in the Spanish Armada have been re-created with the finest talents available; the results are superior, in script, cinematography, special effects (in the model-ship sequences), direction, music, and acting.

The 5,000 Fingers of Dr. T

Columbia 1953. 88 min., col. part animation. (d) Roy Rowland (sp) Ted Geisel ("Dr. Seuss"), Allan Scott from a book by Dr. Seuss (m) Frederick Hollander (c) Peter Lind Hayes, Mary Healy, Hans Conried, Tommy Rettig. (MAC, TWY, SWA, BUD)

Famous humorist-cartoonist Ted Geisel, known to millions of readers of children's books as Dr. Seuss, concocts a fantasy about a ten-year-old who falls asleep at the piano and dreams he's in a magical castle where Dr. Terwilliker keeps 500 small boys to play a concerto for 5,000 fingers at an enshrined keyboard—one of many surrealistic sets in the film.

Flight of the Doves

Columbia 1971. 101 min., col. (d) Ralph Nelson (sp) Frank Gabrielson and Ralph Nelson from the novel by Walter Macken (ph) Harry Waxman (m) Roy Budd (c) Ron Moody, Jack Wild, Dorothy McGuire, Stanley Holloway. (BUD, MAC, SWA, TWY)

Pleasant adventure tale, photographed in Ireland, of two children running away from their cruel stepfather to their grandmother's cottage. In close pursuit, in addition to the stepfather, is a magician-uncle (Ron Moody), a master of many disguises; encountered on the way are gypsy tinkers, country moonshiners, and an Irish rabbi.

Flipper*

MGM 1963. 90 min., col. (d) James B. Clark (c) Chuck Connors, Luke Halpin, Connie Scott, Kathleen Maguire. (FNC)

So many people enjoy watching Flipper, the grinning dolphin charmer who dances on his tail, that the sequel to the original film was followed by the popular television series. Experienced animal-film director James B. Clark's charming little movie shows Flipper getting himself in and out of scrapes.

Friendly Persuasion

Allied Artists 1956. 139 min., col. (d) William Wyler (sp) Based on the novel by Jessamyn West (m) Dmitri Tiomkin, Paul F. Webster (cost) Dorothy Jeakins (song) Pat Boone (c) Gary Cooper, Dorothy McGuire, Marjorie Main, Anthony Perkins, Walter Catlett, Richard Eyer, Phyllis Love. (CIN)

Cracker-barrel Americana in a loosely connected series of stories about Jessamyn West's Birdwells, a family of Quakers living on a farm in southern Indiana at the time of the Civil War. Neighbors, friends, rustic adventure, and the conflict of principles when son Josh wants to shoulder a gun after Morgan's Raiders appear on the scene.

Gilbert and Sullivan

Britain 1953. 112 min., b/w. (prod) Frank Launder, Sidney Gilliat (d) Sidney Gilliat (sp) Gilliat and Leslie Baily from Baily's The Gilbert and Sullivan Book (ph) Christopher Challis (m)(lyr) Sir Arthur Sullivan and W. S. Gilbert; The London Symphony Orchestra, conducted by Sir Malcolm Sargent (c) Robert Morley, Maurice Evans, Eileen Herlie, Peter Finch, Isabel Dean, Wilfred Hyde-White, Martyn Green, members of the D'Oyly Carte Opera Company. (ROA, WRS)

Excerpts from *Trial by Jury, H.M.S. Pinafore, The Pirates of Penzance, The Mikado, The Gondoliers, Iolanthe, Ruddigore,* and *The Yeomen of the Guard,* excellently performed in the traditional style by Martyn Green and members of the D'Oyly Carte Opera Company, may whet the taste of young people for the Gilbert and Sullivan music and lyrics. The biographical drama is not gospel truth, but is divertingly played in an attractive Victorian setting.

Go for It

USA 1975. 90 min., col. (prod) Richard Rosenthal, Wilt Chamberlain, Hal Jepson (d) Paul Rapp. (PYR)

The thrills and excitement of high-risk sports—superstar men and women athletes, both professional and amateur, in their endless quest for mastery, trying to define why they "go for it." Interviews, narration, and action footage bring us the experience of surfing, skiing, hang gliding, kayaking, and mountain climbing against the background of natural environments from the California coast to Canada's Cariboo Mountains.

The Good Earth

MGM 1937. 138 min., b/w and sepia. (prod) Irving G. Thalberg, Albert Lewin (d) Sidney Franklin (sp) Talbot Jennings, Tess Schlesinger and Claudine West from the novel by Pearl S. Buck and the play by Owen Davis (ph) Karl Freund (mont) Slavko Vorkapich (m) Herbert Stothart (c) Paul Muni, Luise Rainer, Walter Connolly, Tillie Losch, Key Luke, Jessie Ralph, Charley Grapewin, Soo Young, Chingwah Lee. (FNC)

Faithful to Pearl S. Buck's Pulitzer Prize novel of 1932, about the China of fifty years before our time, this would be dated except for the strong dramatic interest of ageless human character. Wang Lung and O-lan struggle with the land, and depend on it and their sudden wealth causes greed and strife within the family. Many of the backgrounds were filmed in China; the locust plague is one of the special effects, and Karl Freund's photography and Luise Rainer's characterization won Oscars.

Gulliver's Travels*

Paramount 1939. 77 min., col. (prod) Max Fleischer (d) Dave Fleischer (sp) Edmond Seward, based on the novel by Jonathan Swift (anim) Graham Place (ph) Charles Schettler (m) Victor Young. (IMA, IVY, MAC, BUD, TWF)

The first attempt by the Fleischer brothers, Max and Dave—creators of Popeye—to make a feature-length animated film, in the wake of the success of Disney's SNOW WHITE AND THE SEVEN DWARFS. Their version of Swift has the popular song "It's a Hap Hap Happy Day," and enough humor to please the under-twelves.

Hand in Hand

Britain 1959. 75 min., b/w. (d) Philip Leacock (sp) Diana Morgan from Leonard Atlas's adaptation of Sidney Harmon's story (ph) Frederick A. Young (m) Stanley Black (c) Loretta Parry, Philip Needs, John Gregson, Derek Sydney, Sybil Thorndike, Finlay Currie. (GEN)

Winner of many awards, yet not unanimously admired (contrived, its detractors say), this is still one of the few features dealing with children's attitudes toward religion and makes for good discussion. A bond springs up between two eight-year-olds, a Roman Catholic boy and a Jewish girl, who are close companions until older children and some adults point out their religious differences. After reassurances from a priest and a rabbi who are friends like themselves, the children come to greater understanding.

Hans Christian Andersen*

Goldwyn 1952. 104 min., col. (d) Charles Vidor (sp) Moss Hart, based on a story by Myles Connolly (ph) Harry Stradling (m) Frank Loesser (chor) Roland Petit (c) Danny Kaye, Farley Granger, Jeanmaire, Roland Petit. (GEN)

"A fairy tale, but quite a different one," was the dismissal given by Denmark's leading newspaper to the biographical element of the film, which has nothing to do with the real Andersen. But we think the man who loved children so much would be happy to see their pleasure in Frank Loesser's songs ("Thumbelina," "Ugly Duckling," "Wonderful Copenhagen"), Danny Kaye's infectious high spirits, and Jeanmaire's lovely dancing with the Roland Petit company.

Hue and Cry

Britain 1946. 75 min., b/w. (d) Charles Crichton (sp) T. E. B. Clarke (ph) Douglas Slocombe (m) Georges Auric (c) Alastair Sim, Jack Warner, Valerie White, and the Blood-and-Thunder Boys. (CAL, CCC)

One of the first postwar Ealing Studio comedies, it uses the London dock and bombsite locations for a delightful boys' adventure that is a spoof on authority. The "Blood-and-Thunder Boys," under the leadership of an imaginative youngster named Joe, are convinced that the boys' weekly, *The Trump*, and its odd writer (Alastair Sim) are coverups for a gang of thieves, and they persist until they bring about a gigantic roundup. A better movie than EMIL AND THE DETECTIVES, which has a similar idea.

I Remember Mama

RKO 1948. 134 min., b/w. (d) George Stevens (sp) DeWitt Bodeen from the play by John Van Druten based on Kathryn Forbes's autobiographical novel, Mama's Bank Account (ph) Nicholas Musuraca (m) Roy Webb (c) Irene Dunne, Barbara Bel Geddes, Oscar Homolka, Philip Dorn, Cedric Hardwicke, Edgar Bergen, Florence Bates, Rudy Vallee, Ellen Corby, Barbara O'Neill. (FNC)

Katrin is "the dramatic one," the observant child who misses nothing and wants to be a writer; when she becomes one, she narrates and reenacts her family drama, the joys and sorrows of her loving immigrant Norwegian-American family in San Francisco at the turn of the century.

The Incredible Journey*

Disney 1963. 80 min., col. (d) Fletcher Markle (sp) James Algar from the book by Sheila Burnford (ph) Kenneth Peach (narr) Rex Allen (c) Emile Genest, John Drainie, Tommy Tweed, Sandra Scott, Syme Jago. (GEN)

Blending fiction and elements of the True-Life series, and beautifully photographed in Canada, this charming picture about pets tells how a bull terrier, a Siamese cat, and a Labrador retriever brave the dangers of a 250-mile trek across the wilderness to (incredibly) reach home and their human family.

International Velvet

MGM 1978. 126 min., col. (prod)(d)(sp) Bryan Forbes, suggested by Enid Bagnold's novel National Velvet (ph) Tony Imi (m) Francis Lai (c) Tatum O'Neal, Christopher Plummer, Anthony Hopkins, Nanette Newman, Peter Barkworth, Jeffrey Byron. (FNC)

Tatum O'Neal is a young, orphaned American living in England with her aunt, Nanette Newman, who plays original Velvet twenty-five years older. An Olympic Gold Medal in the Equestrian Event is at stake. This sequel to NATIONAL VELVET is weak in characterization and dialog, but it is at times intoxicating "bottled horse" (Penelope Gilliatt, *The New Yorker*): its steeplechase sequences are superb, and Anthony Hopkins as the Olympic trainer makes the scenes with the foal, Arizona Pi, really exciting.

It Couldn't Be Done

NBC-TV 1970. 53 min., col. documentary. (prod)(d) Walt De Faria, with Sheldon Fay, Jr. (sp) Lee Mendelson (m) Elliot Willensky, Lee Mendelson, Sheldon Fay, Jr. (narr) Lee Marvin. (TWY, FNV)

What do the four faces at Mt. Rushmore, the Eads Bridge, the Alcan Highway, the Brooklyn Bridge, have in common? They were all made by people who tackled "impossible" projects and succeeded. This award-winning documentary gives the inside story of these and many other famous achievements that "couldn't be done."

It's in the Bag

United Artists 1945. 70 min., b/w. (d) Richard Wallace (sp) Jay Dratler, Alma Reville (c) Fred Allen, Binnie Barnes, Robert Benchley, Jerry Colonna, John Carradine, Gloria Pope, Minerva Pious; also Jack Benny, William Bendix, Don Ameche, Rudy Vallee, Victor Moore. (IVY)

Barker for a flea circus, Fred Allen comes into a bundle but has to hunt for it. During the search, he runs into a mad cross-fire of Allen gags, wit, comedy routines from the famous show—and just about every star available for a bit part or walk-on.

The Jackie Robinson Story

Eagle-Lion 1950. 76 min., b/w. (d) Alfred E. Green (sp) Lawrence Taylor, Arthur Mann (c) Jackie Robinson, Ruby Dee, Louise Beavers, Minor Watson. (FNC)

It's ancient history, the life story of the man who struck out Jim Crow, the Brooklyn Dodgers' great star who was the first Negro to make it in the major leagues. But it's still a good thing to hear Branch Rickey (Minor Watson) insist that you put a player on the field without regard to color, and to see Jackie Robinson enact his own drama with dignity and restraint.

Jane Eyre

NBC-TV/Britain 1970. 108 min., col. (d) Delbert Mann (sp) Jack Pulman from the novel by Charlotte Brontë (ph) Paul Beeson (m) John Williams (art) Alec Vetchinsky (c) George C. Scott, Susannah York, Ian Bannen, Jack Hawkins, Nyree Dawn Porter, Rachel Kempson. (FNC, MAC, TWY, PRU)

Superior to the 1944 version with Orson Welles—with color, an excellent British cast supporting George C. Scott, and the episode omitted earlier, of Jane's relationship with the Reverend St. John Rivers. For over-tens, the whole wonderful romantic story, from orphan Jane's childhood ordeal at Lowood Institution to her fascinating involvement with the master of Thornfield.

Journey to the Outer Limits

National Georgraphic Society 1974. 52 min., col. documentary. (prod)(d) Alex Grasshoff (sp) Ken Rosen, Paul Boorstin (ph) David Meyers, Mike Hoover (ed) David Newhouse. (AIM, NGE)

Winner of an Emmy, an American Film Festival Blue Ribbon, and other awards, this excellent documentary shows nineteen city-bred students of the Colorado Outward Bound School as they confront nature's challenges and learn to live together despite their disparate backgrounds. Their graduation-in-survival is a climb of an 18,715-foot mountain, the Santa Rosa Peak in the Peruvian Andes.

Kill the Umpire

Columbia 1950. 78 min., b/w. (d) Lloyd Bacon (sp) Frank Tashlin (ph) Charles Lawton, Jr. (m) Heinz Roemheld (c) William Bendix, Una Merkel, Ray Collins, Gloria Henry. (AIM, MAC, ROA, WCF)

William Bendix in top form as an ardent baseball fan who finally becomes an umpire so that he can be in the ball park every sunny afternoon and get paid for it. Slapstick comedy with a deft cast, and a few sidelights about good sportsmanship and following the ground rules.

The Life of Emile Zola

Warners 1937. 110 min., b/w. (d) William Dieterle (sp) Norman Reilly Raine, Geza Herczeg and Heinz Herald from the book Zola and His Time by Matthew Josephson (ph) Tony Gaudio (m) Max Steiner (c) Paul Muni, Joseph Schildkraut, Gloria Holden, Gale Sondergaard, Donald Crisp, Louis Calhern, Dickie Moore, Morris Carnovsky, Vladimir Sokoloff. (UAS)

"Rich, dignified, honest, and strong" (*The New York Times*), this stirring historical biography reaches its peak when writer Zola (Paul Muni) successfully defends Jewish Captain Dreyfus (Joseph Schildkraut), the victim of anti-Semitism, against the false charge of treason. Basil Wright thought, in 1937, that Muni's performance was the greatest yet in screen drama, and there were many awards for Muni, Schildkraut, the screenplay, and the production. Today, youngsters of some maturity will respond to the film's championship of individual liberty in the face of bigotry and ignorance.

The Lion Who Thought He Was People*
(a.k.a. *Christian the Lion*)

Scotia American 1976. 90 min., col. (d)(sp) James Hill, Bill Travers (c) Bill Travers, Virginia McKenna, George Adamson, John Rendall, Anthony Bourke, Terence Adamson. (FNC)

The stars of BORN FREE are seen again in the great Kenya game preserve, involved with the task of rehabilitating an affectionate and gentle tame lion cub, Christian, to survive among the wild lions of his native African habitat. Eventually, the lion assumes leadership of his own pride.

The Littlest Outlaw

Disney 1955. 75 min., col. (d) Roberto Gaveldon (sp) Bill Walsh from a story by Larry Lansburgh (ph) Alex Phillips (m) William Lava (c) Pedro Armendaria, Joseph Calleia, Rodolfo Acosta, Andres Velasquez, Pepe Ortiz. (GEN)

Filmed by the Disney company, with the facilities of the Churu-busco Studios, on location near San Miguel Allende in Mexico, this is a little more than the routine boy-horse adventure. The boy is brave, kind, ten-year-old Pablito (engagingly played); the horse is a general's prize jumper, Conquistador; they take flight from a brutal horse trainer and get to meet gypsies and outlaws, see a bullfight with Pepe Ortiz and a horse show in Mexico City, and join the blessing of the animals on the Feast of St. Anthony.

Living Free

Britain, 1972. 91 min., col. (d) Jack Couffer (sp) Millard Kaufman from the book by Joy Adamson (ph) Wolfgang Suschitzky (c) Susan Hampshire, Nigel Davenport, Geoffrey Keen, Peter Lukoye. (BUD, CWF, SWA, TWY)

After Elsa the Lioness dies, her three cubs try it on their own for a while in the Kenya wilds, but they get into trouble and have to be rescued by the Adamsons and taken to safety in Serengeti National Park, 700 miles away. Wolfgang Suschitzky's color photograph of Africa is beautiful. The *New York Times* called this sequel to BORN FREE "sensible entertainment for the children—and bright ones, too."

Madam Curie

MGM 1943. 124 min., b/w. (prod) Sidney Franklin (d) Mervyn LeRoy (sp) Paul Osborn, Paul H. Rameau, based on the book by Eve Curie (ph) Joseph Ruttenberg (m) Herbert Stothart (c) Greer Garson, Walter Pidgeon, Henry Travers, Albert Basserman, Dame May Whitty, C. Aubrey Smith, Robert Walker, Victor Francen, Reginal Owen, Van Johnson, Margaret O'Brien (narr) James Hilton. (FNC)

Given the big-studio, romanticized treatment, Eve Curie's tender biography of her mother survives because of the intrinsic interest of the dedicated, great woman of science and the unrelenting search of the Curies for the secret of radioactive substances.

The Man Who Skied Down Everest

Canada/Japan 1975. 80 min., col. (prod) Crawley Films (d) Isao Zeniya, Kenji Fukuhara (sp) Judith Crawley, based on the diary of Yuichiro Miura (ph) Mitsuji Kanau et al. (m) Lawrence Crosley (narr) Douglas Rain. (SPE)

A record of the 1970 expedition to Mount Everest by the Japanese skier Yuichiro Miura, culminating in his bid to ski down part of the mountain's upper slopes. Startling glimpses of the attempt, which was rated partly as a failure, and during which six Sherpa porters died in an ice fall. Winner of 1975 Academy Award for best documentary feature.

The Man Who Would be King

Allied Artists 1975. 129 min., col. (d) John Huston (sp) John Huston, Gladys Hill, based on the short story by Rudyard Kipling (ph) Oswald Morris (des) Alexander Trauner (m) Maurice Jarre (c) Sean Connery, Michael Caine, Christopher Plummer, Karroum Ben Bouih, the Blue Dancers of Goulamine. (CIN)

Kipling's story of the two former British Army officers (Sean Connery, Michael Caine) who have remained in India. Ne'r-do-well soldiers of fortune, they set out in the 1880s to find a country in remote Afghanistan where they can set themselves up as kings. Their adventures in Kafiristan, where Connery is taken for the son of Alexander the Great, are filmed with exotic detail and frequent excitement. Kipling himself (Christopher Plummer), as reporter for the *Northern Star*, narrates; his amazement at the adventurers' plans spotlights their craziness.

Melody

Britain 1971. 103 min., col. (d) Waris Hussein (sp) Alan Parker (ph) Peter Suschitsky (m) The BeeGees and Richard Hewson (c) Jack Wild, Mark Lester, Tracy Hyde, Sheila Steafel, Kate Williams. (FNC, BUD, TWY, WCF)

In this comedy with music about preteens in a South London grade school, three eleven-year-olds enact a love triangle of sorts, and student rebels rise against the establishment. "A witty and perceptive look at the grown-up world from a child's point of view," according to *Parents' Magazine*.

A Midsummer Night's Dream

Britain 1968. 124 min., col. (prod) Michael Birkett (d) Peter Hall (ph) Peter Suschitzky (m) Guy Woolfenden. Text by William Shakespeare. (c) David Warner, Diana Rigg, Paul Rogers, Bill Travers, Ian Richardson, Judi Dench, Barbara Jefford. (MAC)

"England's Royal Shakespeare Company, under Director Peter Hall, has turned A MIDSUMMER NIGHT'S DREAM into a richly textured color film . . . . 'For the first time,' says Paul Rogers, who plays Bottom in a blustering, John Bullish vein, 'a Shakespearean movie has been made that doesn't sacrifice the poetry' " (*Time*). Only ten lines of the original have been cut. Not only have the words been communicated but Peter Suschitzky's contemporary camera skills have given original style to the fantasy.

The Mikado

Britain/Universal 1939. 90 min., col. (d) Victor Schertzinger (super) Geoffrey Toye (m)(lyr) Sir Arthur Sullivan, W. S. Gilbert; The London Symphony Orchestra (c) Kenny Baker, John Barclay, Martyn Green, Sydney Granville, Gregory Stroud, Jean Colin, Elizabeth Paynter, Kathleen Naylor, Constance Willis. (WRS)

Since its premiere in 1885, *The Mikado* has been the most popular operetta in the Gilbert and Sullivan repertoire, and more than one film production has appeared. This one, despite the inexplicable omission of "I've Got a Little List" and "There's Beauty in the Bellow of the Blast," is the best to date—with lovely music (the chorus of the D'Oyly Carte Opera Company) and such practiced G&S artists to do justice to the fun as John Barclay (The Mikado), Martyn Green (Ko-Ko), Sydney Granville (Pooh-Bah) and

Constance Willis (Katisha). Do not confuse this with the 1967 production directed by Stuart Burge.

Napoleon and Samantha*

Disney 1972. 91 min., col. (d) Bernard McEveety (sp) Stewart Raffill (c) Johnny Whitaker, Jodie Foster, Michael Douglas, Will Geer, Ellen Corby. (GEN)

A good cast marks this pleasant movie about an eleven-year-old boy, his girl chum, and his toothless pet lion, who trek up to the mountains looking for a guardian.

Nicholas Nickleby

Britain 1947. 106 min., b/w. (d) Alberto Cavalcanti (sp) John Dighton from the novel by Charles Dickens (ph) Gordon Dines (m) Lord Berners (art) Michael Relph (c) Derek Bond, Sir Cedric Hardwicke, Mary Merrall, Sally Ann Howes, Stanley Holloway, Alfred Drayton, Dame Sybil Thorndike, Cathleen Nesbitt. (BUD, KPF, LCA, ROA)

Wackford Squeers, proprietor of the infamous Dotheboys Hall poor-boys' school; Vincent Crummles of the very funny acting troupe; love-smitten Nicholas; honest Smike and villainous Uncle Ralph Nickleby—Dickens's gallery is faithfully dramatized under Cavalcanti's direction, which deserves more notice than it won at the time of release.

The Old Curiosity Shop

Britain 1935. 105 min., b/w. (d) Thomas Bentley (sp) Margaret Kennedy and Ralph Neale from the novel by Charles Dickens (ph) Claude Friese-Greene (m) Eric Coates (c) Ben Webster, Elaine Benson, Hay Petrie, Beatrix Thompson, Gibb McLaughlin, Lily Long, Peter Penrose, Reginal Purdell, Polly Ward, Amy Veness. (JAN)

Everybody's heard of Little Nell, but too few filmgoers know the excellent British movie in which she appears, Dickens's THE OLD CURIOSITY SHOP. It is vividly and faithfully re-created, with Hay Petrie as a perfect Quilp; Ben Webster, Grandfather to the life; and the village scenes of the old coaching days filmed by director Thomas Bentley, director of more Dickens adaptations than any other British filmmaker.

The Olympics in Mexico

Columbia 1968. 112 min., col. (d) Alberto Isaac (ph) Walter Lassally and Brian Probyn. (BUD, CCC, MAC, TWY)

Nominated for the Academy Award for best documentary feature, and the recipient of Special Honor from the Helms Athletic Foundation, this account of the celebrated XIX Olympiad in Mexico City captures not only the exciting competitions but the colorful simultaneous cultural Olympiad and the behind-the-scenes dramas. It was assembled over more than a year, with cinematographer Walter Lassally (TOM JONES) surpervising eighty cameramen in documenting the events—diving, horsemanship, gymnastics, long-distance running, and many others—which will interest not only sports fans but film fans.

Part 2 Sounder

Gamma III 1976. 98 min., col. (prod) Robert B. Radnitz (d) William A. Graham (sp) Lonne Elder III from the book by William H. Armstrong (ph) Urs Furrer (c) Harold Sylvester, Ebony Wright, Taj Mahal, Annazette Chase, Darryl Young. (SWA)

The sequel to SOUNDER, without the incandescent performance of Cicely Tyson as the mother and wife, and with more didacticism, is still a sensitive picture of a black family in the Louisiana of the Depression, who are struggling to provide a schoolhouse and a teacher for their children. Top award, Virgin Islands Film Festival.

Pete's Dragon*

Disney 1977. 134 min., col. (d) Don Chaffey (sp) Malcolm Marmorstein from a story by Seton I. Miller (h) Frank Phillips (m) Al Kasha, Joel Hirschhorn (m/dir) Irwin Kostal (chor) Onna White, Martin Allen (c) Sean Marshall, Helen Reddy, Mickey Rooney, Shelley Winters, Red Buttons, Jim Dale, Jim Backus (GEN)

Twelve songs, lavish sets, special effects, and a big-name cast mark this mixture of live action and animation, suspense and broad comedy, but the true star is animator Ken Anderson's "Elliott," a playful green dragon who can fly or disappear at will. On Elliott's back, nine-year-old orphan Pete escapes from the cruel Gogans and finds refuge, after many adventures, with his new family, the lighthouse keeper and his daughter, in the little 1900 Maine fishing village of Passamaquoddy.

The Pickwick Papers

Britain 1950. 109 min., b/w. (d)(sp) Noel Langley from the novel by Charles Dickens (c) James Hayter, James Donald, Nigel Patrick, Kathleen Harrison, Hermione Gingold, Joyce Grenfell, Donald Wolfit, Athene Seyler, Hermione Baddeley, George Robey, Mary Merrall. (BUD, TWF, WHO, KPF)

"All real gentlemen are a little off," we are assured by Mrs. Leo Hunter (Joyce Grenfell), and older children with a taste for Dickensian caricature will relish this idly film's superb galaxy of gentlemen and ladies who are a little off. England's best players, directed by Noel Langley, adaptor of GREAT EXPECTATIONS and A CHRISTMAS CAROL, enliven the famous episodes: the Pickwick Club meeting, the journey, the country ball, the encounters with Mr. Jingle, the visit at Dingley Dell, the Bardell-Pickwick trial, and the stay in debtors' prison.

Pippi Longstocking*

Munich-Stockholm 1973. 99 min., col. (d) Olle Hellbom (sp) Astrid Lindgren from her books (ph) Kalle Bergholm (m) Georg Riedel (c) Inger Nilsson, Maria Persson, Pär Sundberg, Beppe Wolgers, Margot Trooger. Dubbed in English. (MAC)

After seeing Pippi's comic and fantastic adventures on film, younger children snatch from the library shelves Astrid Lindgren's books about Pippilotta Rollgardinia Victualia Peppermint Longstocking. As played by Inger Nilsson, Pippi looks like an illustration from one of the volumes: freckled, red-headed, braided, and spunky enough to give the grown-ups in an idyllic Swedish town their comeuppance and the other children, like Tommy and Annika, the time of their lives. With her dappled horse, her monkey ("Mr. Nilsson"), suitcase of gold coins, tall tales about her seacaptain father, and penchant for magic, Pippi is what every nine-year-old might like to be.

Sequels: PIPPI IN THE SOUTH SEAS (1974, 85 min.) and PIPPI ON THE RUN (1977, 97 min.).

The Point

ABC-TV 1970. 75 min., col. animation. (d)(anim) Fred Wolf (sp) Norman Lenzer, based on a story by Harry Nilsson (m) Harry Nilsson (narr) Dustin Hoffman. (GEN)

An animated musical fantasy, with seven songs sung by their composer, Harry Nilsson, about the adventures of a boy named Oblio, who is round-headed and lives in a kingdom where everyone else's head is pointed. Declared an outlaw and banished to Pointless Forest with his dog, Arrow, Oblio meets giant bees, a three-headed man, an old rock with a wonderful disposition, and a tree in the leaf-selling business—thus finding out that you don't have to be pointed to have a point in life, and prejudice is a pretty silly thing.

Pride and Prejudice

MGM 1940. 118 min., b/w. (d) Robert Z. Leonard (sp) Aldous Huxley and Jane Murfin, based on Helen Jerome's dramatization of Jane Austen's novel (art) Cedric Gibbons, Paul Goesse (c) Greer Garson, Laurence Olivier, Mary Boland, Edna May Oliver, Maureen O'Sullivan, Ann Rutherford, Frieda Inescort, Edmund Gwenn, Karen Morley, Heather Angel, Marsha Hunt, Melville Cooper. (FNC)

Only for girls over twelve who are up to Jane Austen's comedy of eighteenth-century manners, when life for Mrs. Bennet's brood of flounced young ladies turned on husband hunting at the county ball. The screenplay cleverly condenses the essential parts of the novel (with the original dialog); the charm and wit are in the Austen spirit; and the period atmosphere is delightfully evoked by the art direction, which won an Academy Award. Laurence Olivier fans treasure his Mr. Darcy as highly as his Heathcliff.

Pride of the Yankees

RKO 1942. 128 min., b/w. (d) Sam Wood (sp) Jo Swerling and Herman Mankiewicz from a story by Paul Gallico (c) Gary Cooper, Teresa Wright, Babe Ruth, Walter Brennan, Dan Duryea, Bill Dickey, Robert W. Meusel, Mark Koenig, Ernie Adams, Bill Stern. (AIM, CWF, MAC, TWY)

Producer Sam Goldwyn wanted it known that this was not so much the story of Lou Gehrig the great baseball player as of Lou Gehrig the fine and humble man—and Gehrig's film biography is a saga of American life, with the tragedy of too-early death at the height of his career. It contains some montage of American League games and personal appearances by players Babe Ruth, Bob Meusel, Bill Dickey, and Mark Koenig and by sports announcer Bill Stern.

Race for Your Life, Charlie Brown!*

Paramount 1977. 78 min., col. animation. (d) Bill Melendez (sp) Charles M. Schulz from his "Peanuts" comic strip (ph) Dickson/Vasu (m) Ed Bogas (voices) of Duncan Watson, Greg Felton, Stuart Brotman, Gail Davis. (PAR)

Charlie, Snoopy, Woodstock, Linus, Schroeder, and Peppermint Patty are spending an adventurous summer at Camp Remote: "We've got to get a hold of ourselves—there are only bears and tigers out there." There are also a search for the missing Woodstock, a river raft race, Snoopy and Woodstock in an inner tube with sail, and lots more for "Peanuts" fanciers under twelve.

The Railway Children

Britain 1971. 106 min., col. (d)(sp) Lionel Jeffries from the novel by E. Nesbit (ph) Arthur Ibbetson (m) Johnny Douglas (c) Dinah Sheridan, Jenny Agutter, Bernard Gribbins, William Mervyn, Sally Thomsett, Gary Warren. (MOD, UNI)

"Very beautiful and wonderful things do happen, and we live in the hope of them, don't we," the Old Gentleman tells the three Edwardian children in this lovely, slow-paced but charming story from E. Nesbit's children's classic, who wait out their father's mysterious absence in a Yorkshire village until everything ends happily. Not for every child, but for over-tens with a taste for sentiment and the past.

The Red Pony

Frederick Brogger 1972. 101 min., col. (d) Robert Totten (sp) Don Bishop, Robert Totten, based on John Steinbeck's story (ph) Andrew Jackson (m) Jerry Goldsmith (c) Henry Fonda, Maureen O'Hara. (PNX)

Neither one of the two films based on John Steinbeck's story of young Jody and the foal he reared and lost has captured the quality of the original, but this version (shown originally on television) is much truer to its spirit than the 1949 film directed by Lewis Milestone, which starred Robert Mitchum and Myrna Loy. The California ranch life, the birth and death of the pony, and the relationship between father and son are effectively presented.

The Rescuers

Disney 1977. 76 min., col. animation. (d) Wolfgang Reitherman, John Lounsbery, Art Stevens (sp) Based on the stories "The Rescuers" and "Miss Bianca" by Margery Sharp (m) Artie Butler (voices) Bob Newhart, Eva Gabor, Geraldine Page, Joe Flynn, Jeanette Nolan. (GEN)

More than six scriptwriters and scores of animators worked on this cartoon feature, but the redeeming factor in the overlong plot remains the imagination of Margery Sharp, on whose very popular stories, "The Rescuers" and "Miss Bianca," it is based. Two members of the mouse International Rescue Aid Society (meeting in the basement of the UN) are chosen to save the orphan Penny from the clutches of the wicked Medusa at the Devil's Bayou; and they travel on the back of the albatross Orville, (the one-bird airline service), who transports passengers in a sardine can tied to his back.

Road to Morocco

Paramount 1942. 81 min., b/w. (d) David Butler (sp) Frank Butler, Don Hartman (ph) William C. Mellor (m) Victor Young (c) Bing Crosby, Bob Hope, Dorothy Lamour, Anthony Quinn, Vladimir Sokoloff, George Givot, Monte Blue, Yvonne De Carlo. (UNI)

Bing sells Bob as a slave to Princess Dorothy Lamour. In the melee are handmaidens, Arabian chieftains, knife dancers, sausage vendors, a male and a female camel—and lots more, but chiefly Crosby and Hope singing songs by Johnny Burke and Jimmy Van Heusen: "Moonlight Becomes You," "Ain't Got a Dime to My Name," "Aladdin's Daughter," "Constantly," and "Road to Morocco."

Scaramouche

MGM 1952. 115 min., col. (d) George Sidney (sp) Ronald Millar and George Froeschel from the novel by Rafael Sabatini (c) Stewart Granger, Eleanor Parker, Mel Ferrer, Janet Leigh, Henry Wilcoxon, Nina

Foch, Robert Coote, Lewis Stone. (FNC)

"He was born with the gift of laughter and a sense that the world was mad"—the spirit of Sabatini's hero makes this a most enjoyable swashbuckler. A talented cast plays out a romance of the French Revolution, with Scaramouche (Stewart Granger) disguised as a masked clown in a traveling troupe and engaging in a brilliant duel with a Bourbon marquis (Mel Ferrer) in an opera house—the longest fencing sequence in cinema, six and a half minutes with no sound except the clash of swords.

The Scarlet Pimpernel

Britain 1934. 95 min., col. (d) Harold Young (sp) Robert Sherwood and Arthur Wimpernis from the novel by Baroness Orczy (c) Leslie Howard, Merle Oberon, Joan Gardner, Raymond Massey, Melville Cooper, Nigel Bruce, Anthony Bushell. (BUD, EMG, ROA, WHO)

With wit and grace, Leslie Howard plays Baroness Orczy's Sir Percy Blakeney, the foppish Englishman who disguises himself as the elusive "Scarlet Pimpernel" and rescues French aristocrats condemned to the guillotine during the French Revolution. Shuttling between London and Paris, he plays an exciting game of cat-and-mouse with his pursuer, Chauvelin (Raymond Massey).

The Sea Gypsies

Warners 1978. 101 min., col. (prod) Joseph C. Raffill (d)(sp) Stewart Raffill (ph) Thomas McHugh (m) Fred Steiner (c) Robert Logan, Mikki Jamison-Olsen, Heather Rattray, Shannon Taylor. (SWA)

Robert Logan (THE WILDERNESS FAMILY, ACROSS THE GREAT DIVIDE) and his party—two young daughters, a boy stowaway, an attractive lady news photographer—are wrecked in the Aleutians during a sailboat cruise around the world. The drama of survival that ensues, with lots of wild animals, is happily resolved by the arrival of the Coast Guard rescue ship. "A very agreeable children's film . . . . The scenery is spectacular" (*The New York Times*).

The Seventh Voyage of Sinbad*

Columbia 1958. 89 min., col. (d) Nathan Juran (sp) Kenneth Kolb (ph) Wilkie Cooper (spec eff) Ray Harryhausen (m) Bernard Herrmann (c) Kerwin Mathews, Kathryn Grant, Richard Eyer, Torin Thatcher. (GEN)

"One of the best monster pictures ever made for children" (*Time*) is the spectacular tale of the exploits of the legendary hero of the Arabian Nights on the island of Colossa, where he battles the Cyclops, a fire-spitting dragon, and a giant roc mother bird before saving the Princess Parisa from the magic spell of Sakurah. Ray Harryhausen (THE FIRST MEN IN THE MOON, THE THREE WORLDS OF GULLIVER) created the fantastic special effects, in which live actors and model figures are combined in "Dynamation."

The Shaggy Dog

Disney 1959. 104 min., b/w. (d) Charles Barton (sp) Bill Walsh, Lillie Hayward, suggested by Felix Salten's The Hound of Florence (ph) Edward Colman (m) Paul Smith (c) Fred MacMurray, Jean Hagen, Tommy Kirk, Annette Funicello, Tom Considine, Kevin Corcoran, Cecil Kellaway, Alexander Scourby. (GEN)

By uttering the wrong formula from an ancient museum ring, Fred MacMurray changes into a shaggy Bratislavian sheep dog. By using the right formula for kids bred on TV's situation comedy— bumbling Father, slow takes, repeated gags, obvious development—the Disney studio, in its first live-action comedy, created a mammoth box-office success in 1959, again in its re-release in 1967, and perennially in non-theatrical programs.

She Wore a Yellow Ribbon

RKO 1949. 103 min., col. (d) John Ford (sp) Frank S Nugent and Lawrence Stallings from the story "War Party" by James Warner Bellah (ph) Winton Hoch (m) Richard Hageman (c) John Wayne, Joanne Dru, John Agar, Ben Johnson, Harry Carey, Jr., Victor McLaglen, George O'Brien, Arthur Shields, Mildred Natwick. (MAC, TWY, ROA, CWF)

Thundering cavalry charges, an old cavalryman's farewell to the troops, and Monument Valley in Winton Hoch's Oscar-award photography. This was John Ford's favorite cavalry picture: "I tried to copy the Remington style . . . at least I tried to get his color and movement . . . ." Captain Nathan Brittles, in his last mission before retirement, stops the Indians' final drive to oust the whites from their territory.

Steiner (c) Brian Keith, Vera Miles, Brandon de Wilde, Walter Brennan, Ed Wynn. (GEN)

Backwoodsman Cam Calloway and his family in New England in the 1930s dream of building a bird sanctuary for the wild geese; they fight poverty and designing men to achieve it. On balance: too much Vermont syrup in an overlong Disneyish plot; excellent players and magnificent Vermont scenery and wildlife.

The Three Musketeers

MGM 1948. 126 min., col. (d) George Sidney (sp) Robert Ardrey from the novel by Alexandre Dumas (ph) Robert Planck (m) Herbert Stothart (c) Gene Kelly, Lana Turner, June Allyson, Van Heflin, Angela Lansbury, Frank Morgan, Vincent Price, Keenan Wynn, Gig Young, Robert Coote. (FNC)

Between the time, in 1921, that Douglas Fairbanks's D'Artagnan swung through the air with the greatest of ease and the present, the only first-rate film from the Dumas classic has been Richard Lester's version in 1974. However, it is too sophisticated for children, and a satisfactory, if pedestrian, alternative might be this MGM formula costume picture, which has Gene Kelly, at least, as a pleasant and acrobatic hero.

The Three Worlds of Gulliver*

Columbia 1960. 100 min., col. (d) Jack Sher (sp) Arthur Ross and Jack Sher from the novel Gulliver's Travels *by Jonathan Swift (ph) Wilkie Cooper (spec eff) Ray Harryhausen (m) Bernard Herrmann (c) Kerwin Mathews, Jo Morrow, June Thorburn, Gregoire Aslan, Basil Sydney, Peter Bull. (GEN)*

Following Swift's *Gulliver's Travels* at a distance (Gulliver's sweetheart, Elizabeth, is now a stowaway on the voyage), this adventure story is a fine showcase for Ray Harryhausen's special effects, here called "Superdynamation." To Paul V. Beckley (*New York Herald Tribune*), it seemed that "what will please the children most are the ingeniously credible shots of tiny people scampering around Gulliver's 18th century feet and a tiny Gulliver flopping about in a child's basket or dueling with a crocodile."

To Kill a Mockingbird

Universal 1962. 129 min., b/w. (d) Robert Mulligan (sp) Horton Foote from the novel by Harper Lee (ph) Russell Harlan (m) Elmer Bernstein (c) Gregory Peck, Mary Badham, Philip Alford, John Megna, Rosemary Murphy, Brock Peters, Ruth White, Alice Ghostley, Robert Duvall, William Windom. (UNI, SWA, TWY, CWF)

Seen through the eyes of six-year-old tomboy Scout, this story of a summer in 1932 in a small town in Maycomb County, Alabama, follows two motherless children and their kooky seven-year-old visitor as they learn something about their own prejudices and about their widowed father's character: Atticus Finch (Gregory Peck) defends a falsely accused black in a courtroom steaming with bigotry. For over-tens. Multiple award-winner (Cannes, Brussels, *Parents' Magazine*; Academy Awards to Peck and Horton Foote).

True Grit

Paramount 1969. 128 min., col. (d) Henry Hathaway (sp) Marguerite Roberts from the novel by Charles Portis (ph) Lucien Ballard (m) Elmer Bernstein (c) John Wayne, Glen Campbell, Kim Darby, Robert Duvall, Jeremy Slate, Dennis Hopper, Jeff Corey. (FNC)

Unlike the book, which belongs to fourteen-year-old Mattie Ross, TRUE GRIT is John Wayne's movie; his Rooster Cogburn won an Oscar. But Mattie is still the tomboy in the fairy-tale West of the 1880s, taking no guff from anyone. She helps manage Pa's Arkansas farm, hires Rooster to help her track down Pa's killer, and survives such adventures during their exciting chase as being knocked backward by gunfire blast into a rattlesnake pit.

Twelve Angry Men

United Artists 1957. 95 min., b/w. (d) Sidney Lumet (sp) Reginald Rose, based on his television play (ph) Boris Kaufman (c) Henry Fonda, E. G. Marshall, Lee J. Cobb, Ed Begley, Jack Warden, Martin Balsam, Jack Klugman, Robert Webber. (UAS)

A taut, penetrating film revealing the personal attributes of the twelve jurors who hold a boy's life in their grasp. Henry Fonda, as the logical and open-minded juror, is excellent, and the cast is full of good character actors. For older children, director Sidney Lumet (with cameraman Boris Kaufman, one of the best) has created a riveting drama from the Reginald Rose story.

The Underground Movement

BBC/WGBH-TV 1976. 59 min., col. (prod) Suzanne Gibbs (ph) Maurice Fisher, Bernard Hedges, Hugh Maynard, Jim Saunders (research) Steven Shemeld (narr) Elinor Stout (c) Tony Robinson. (WGBH)

Produced for the Public Broadcasting Service award-winning series "Nova" with the assistance of British and American scientists, this absorbing film explores the forgotten world of life underground—from badgers and foxes down to the myriad of microorganisms that make soil the most complex substrate for life on earth. Especially fascinating is the footage of the roots of trees growing and of a mole burrowing.

The War of the Worlds

Paramount 1953. 85 min., col. (prod) George Pal (d) Byron Haskin (sp) Barré Lyndon from the novel by H. G. Wells (ph) George Barnes (art) Hal Pereira, Albert Nozaki (spec eff) Gordon Jennings, Wallace Kelley, Paul Lerpae, Ivyl Burts, Jan Donela, Irmin Roberts (c) Gene Barry, Ann Robinson, Les Tremayne. (FNC)

George Pal's production of H. G. Wells's 1898 novel about the Martians' invasion of Earth, updated to include the atom bomb, won an Oscar for its special effects, among the most remarkable examples of trick photography ever created; and the machines of the "enemy" are still most ingenious and frightening sci-fi inventions.

Wee Willie Winkie*

20th Century-Fox 1937. 99 min., b/w. with tinted sequences. (d) John Ford (sp) Ernest Pascal and Julian Josephson from Rudyard Kipling's story (ph) Arthur Miller (m) Louis Silvers (c) Shirley Temple, Victor McLaglen, C. Aubrey Smith, Cesar Romero, June Lang, Constance Collier. (FNC)

In her prime at nine, Shirley is still fun, in quintessential Ford and Kipling as well as Temple. Shirley is kept busy thawing out Grandpa C. Aubrey Smith's strict regime at an 1890s British Army post in India, finding a husband for her widowed mother, keeping her gruff pal Victor McLaglen in line, and saving the regiment from war by persuading villainous Hindu rebel Cesar Romero to sign a peace treaty—all without neglecting her singing.

Yankee Doodle Dandy

Warners 1942. 126 min., b/w. (d) Michael Curtiz (sp) Robert Buckner, Edmund Joseph (ph) James Wong Howe (m)(lyr) George M. Cohan (c) James Cagney, Joan Leslie, Walter Huston, Richard Whorf, Irene Manning, George Tobias, Rosemary De Camp, Jeanne Cagney, S. Z. Sakall, Frances Langford, Eddie Foy, Jr. (UAS)

An infectious musical, with Jimmy Cagney singing and dancing his way to an Academy Award for his portrayal of the buoyant George M. Cohan. Among the legendary Cohan songs: "Yankee Doodle Dandy," "Over There," "You're a Grand Old Flag." "Give My Regards to Broadway," "Harrigan," and "So Long, Mary."

Directory of Film Companies and Distributors

Distribution information is based on James L. Limbacher's *Feature Films on 8mm, 16mm, and Videotape*, 6th ed. (New York, R. R. Bowker Company, 1979).

Since distribution rights change frequently, film users should check with the distributors' catalogs (usually free on request), as well as with the collections of local public libraries, university audiovisual centers, and foreign consulates.

Note: The directory and lists which follow have all been updated to 1980, and are more than 75% revised from the 1973 edition of *Movies for Kids*.

ABC-TV   American Broadcasting Corp.
1330 Avenue of the Americas
New York, NY 10019
(212) 581-7777

AIM   Association Instructional Materials
866 Third Ave.
New York, NY 10022
(212) 935-4210

ATL   Atlantis Productions
1252 La Granada Dr.
Thousand Oaks, CA 91360
(213) 495-2790

AUD/BRA   Audio Brandon - see MAC (Macmillan Films)

AUS   Film Australia
Australian Information Service
636 Fifth Ave.
New York, NY 10020
(212) 245-4000

BEN   Benchmark Films, Inc.
145 Scarborough Rd.
Briarcliff Manor, NY 10510
(914) 762-3838

BFA   BFA Educational Media
2211 Michigan Ave.
Santa Monica, CA 90404
(213) 829-2901

BIL   Billy Budd Films
235 E. 57th St.
New York, NY 10022
(212) 755-3968

BUD   Budget Films
4590 Santa Monica Blvd.
Los Angeles, CA 90029
(213) 680-0187

CAL   University of
California
Extension Media
Center
Berkeley, CA 94720
(415) 642-0460

CAR   Carousel Films
1501 Broadway
New York, NY 10036
(212) 279-6734

CBS-TV   Columbia
Broadcasting
System
51 W. 52nd St.
New York, NY 10019
(212) 975-4321

CCC   Cine-Craft Company
1720 W. Marshall
Portland, OR 97209
(503) 228-7484

CFS   Creative Film Society
7237 Canby Ave.
Reseda, CA 91335
(213) 881-3887

CHA   Charard Motion
Pictures
2110 E. 24th St.
Brooklyn, NY 11226
(212) 891-4339

CHU   Churchill Films
662 N. Robertson
Los Angeles, CA
90069
(213) 657-5110

CIN   Hurlock-Cine World
13 Arcadia Rd.
Old Greenwich, CT
06870
(203) 637-4319

CMC   Center for Mass
Communications
562 W. 113th St.
New York, NY 10025
(212) 865-2000

CON   Contemporary/
McGraw Hill Films
1221 Avenue of the
Americas
New York, NY 10020
(212) 997-6831

Princeton Rd.
Hightstown, NJ 08520
(609) 448-1700

COR   Coronet Films
65 E. South Water St.
Chicago, IL 60601
(312) 322-7676

CWF   Clem Williams Films
2240 Noblestown Rd.
Pittsburgh, PA 15205
(412) 921-5810

DIS   Walt Disney
Productions
800 Sonora Ave.
Glendale, CA 91201
(213) 845-3141

ECC   The Eccentric Circle
Box 4085
Greenwich, CT 06830
(203) 661-2278

EMC   Extension Media
Center - see CAL

FIM   Film Images/Radim
Films
17 W. 60th St.
New York, NY 10023
(212) 279-6653

1034 Lake St.
Oak Park, IL 60301
(312) 386-4826

4530 18th St.
San Francisco, CA
94114
(415) 431-0996

FFM   Films for the
Humanities, Inc.
Box 378
Princeton, NJ 08540

FNC   Films Incorporated
440 Park Ave. S.
New York, NY 10016
(212) 889-7940

1144 Wilmette Ave.
Wilmette, IL 60091
(312) 256-3200

476 Plasamour Dr.
Atlanta, GA 30324
(404) 873-5101

5625 Hollywood Blvd.
Hollywood, CA 90028
(213) 466-5481

GEN   General availability,
on a nonexclusive
basis, from many
national rental
sources. Also check
library and
university
collections.

GRO   Grove Press Film
Division
196 W. Houston St.
New York, NY 10014
(212) 242-4900

IFB   International Film
Bureau
332 S. Michigan Ave.
Chicago, IL 60604
(312) 427-4545

IMA   Images
2 Purdy Ave.
Rye, NY 10580
(914) 967-1102

IVY   Ivy Films/16
165 W. 46th St.
New York, NY 10036
(212) 765-3940

JAN   Janus Films
745 Fifth Ave.
New York, NY 10022
(212) 753-7100

JAS   Jason Films
2621 Palisades Ave.
Riverdale, NY 10463
(914) 884-7648

KPF   Kit Parker Films
Box 27
Carmel Valley, CA
93924
(408) 659-4131

LCA   Learning Corporation
of America
1350 Avenue of the
Americas
New York, NY 10019
(212) 397-9330

LIB   Libra Films Corp.
150 E. 58th St.
New York, NY 10022
(212) 838-7721

LUC   Lucerne Films
7 Bahama Rd.
Morris Plains, NJ
07950
(201) 538-1401

MAC   Macmillan Films/
Audio Brandon
34 MacQuesten
Pkwy. S.
Mount Vernon, NY
10550
(914) 664-5051

1619 N. Cherokee
Los Angeles, CA
90028
(213) 463-1131

3868 Piedmont Ave.
Oakland, CA 94611
(415) 658-9890

8400 Brookfield Ave.
Brookfield, IL 60513
(312) 485-3925

2512 Program Dr.
Dallas, TX 75220
(214) 357-6494

Macmillan/
Audio Brandon
Toll Free
800-527-3054

MCG   McGraw-Hill Films —
see CON
(Contemporary/
McGraw-Hill)

MEG   The Media Guild
Box 881
Solana Beach, CA
92076
(714) 755-9191

MMA   Museum of Modern
Art Film Dept.
11 W. 53rd St.
New York, NY 10019
(212) 956-4209

MMM   Mass Media
Ministries
1720 Chouteau Ave.
St. Louis, MO 63103
(314) 436-0418

MOD   Modern Sound
Pictures
1402 Howard St.
Omaha, NB 68102
(402) 341-8476

MOG   Mogull's
235 W. 46th St.
New York, NY 10036
(212) 757-1411

NBC-TV   NBC Educational
Enterprises
30 Rockefeller Plaza
New York, NY 10020
(212) 664-4444

NFB   National Film Board
of Canada
1251 Avenue of the
Americas
New York, NY 10020
(212) 586-2400

NGA   National Gallery of
Art
Extension Services
Washington, DC
20565
(202) 737-4215

NGE   National Geographic
Educational
Services
Dept. 2025
(Audiovisual)
17th & M Sts., NW
Washington, DC
20036
(202) 857-7000

NLC   New Line Cinema
121 University Pl.
New York, NY 10003
(212) 674-7460

NYF   New Yorker Films
16 W. 61st. St.
New York, NY 10023
(212) 247-6110

NYU   New York University
Film Library
26 Washington Pl.
New York, NY 10003
(212) 598-2250

PAR   Paramount Pictures
Corp. Non-
Theatrical
5451 Marathon St.
Hollywood, CA 90038
(213) 874-7330

PBS-TV   Public Broadcasting
Service
15 W. 51st St.
New York, NY 10019
(212) 489-0945

PER   Perspective Films
369 W. Erie St.
Chicago, IL 60610
(312) 332-7676

PIC Pictura Films
111 Eighth Ave.
New York, NY 10011
(212) 691-1730

PNX Phoenix Films
267 W. 25th St.
New York, NY 10001
(212) 684-5910

PRU Productions
Unlimited
1301 Avenue of the
Americas
New York, NY 10020
(212) 541-6770

PYR Pyramid Films
Box 1048
Santa Monica, CA
90406
(213) 828-7577

REM Rembrandt Films
267 W. 25th St.
New York, NY 10001
(212) 675-5330

ROA Roa's Films
1696 W. Astor St.
Milwaukee, WI 53202
(414) 271-0861

SAL Salzburg Enterprises
98 Cutter Hill Rd.
Great Neck, NY 11021
(516) 487-4515

SAN Sanrio
Communications
1505 Vine
Hollywood, CA 90028
(213) 462-7248

SCO Scotia American
600 Madison Ave.
New York, NY 10021
(212) 758-4775

SCR Screenscope, Inc.
1022 Wilson Blvd.
Arlington, VA 22209
(703) 527-3555

SOH SoHo Cinema, Ltd.
225 Lafayette St.
New York, NY 10012
(212) 966-1416

STE Sterling Educational
Films
241 E. 34th St.
New York, NY 10016
(212) 683-6300

SWA Swank Motion
Pictures
393 Front St.
Hempstead, NY 11550
(516) 538-6500

220 Forbes Rd.
Braintree, MA 02184
(617) 848-8300

7926 Jones Branch Dr.
McLean, VA 22101
(703) 821-1040

1200 Roosevelt Rd.
Glen Ellyn, IL 60137
(312) 629-9004

201 S. Jefferson Ave.
Saint Louis, MO
63103
(314) 534-6300

4111 Director's Row
Houston, TX 77092
(713) 683-8222

6767 Forest Lawn Dr.
Hollywood, CA 90068
(213) 851-6300

TIM Time/Life Multimedia
100 Eisenhower Dr.
Paramus, NJ 07652
(201) 843-4545

TWF Trans-World Films
332 S. Michigan Ave.
Chicago, IL 60604
(312) 922-1530

TWY   Twyman Films
329 Salem Ave.
Dayton, OH 45401
(513) 222-4014
Toll Free:
800-543-9594

UAS   United Artists/16
729 Seventh Ave.
New York, NY 10019
(212) 575-4715

UNF   United Films
1425 S. Main
Tulsa, OK 74119
(918) 584-6491

UNI   Universal 16
445 Park Ave.
New York, NY 10022
(212) 759-7500

425 N. Michigan Ave.
Chicago, IL 60611
(312) 822-0513

205 Walton St.
Atlanta, GA 30303
(404) 523-5081

810 S. St. Paul
Dallas, TX 75201
(214) 741-3164

2001 S. Vermont Ave.
Los Angeles, CA
90007
(213) 731-2151

WCF   Westcoast Films
25 Lusk St.
San Francisco, CA
94107
(415) 362-4700

WGBH-TV   WGBH Distribution
125 Western Ave.
Boston, MA 02134
(617) 492-2777

WHO   Wholesome Film
Center
20 Melrose St.
Boston, MA 02116
(617) 426-0155

WIL   Willoughby-Peerless
110 W. 32nd St.
New York, NY 10001
(212) 564-1600

WOM   Wombat Productions
77 Tarrytown Rd.
White Plains, NY
10607
(914) 428-6220

WOR   World Northal
1 Dag Hammarskjold
Plaza
New York, NY 10017
(212) 223-8169

WRS   Walter Reade 16
241 E. 34th St.
New York, NY 10016
(212) 683-6300

XER   Xerox Films
245 Long Hill Rd.
Middletown, CT
06457
(203) 347-7251

ZPH   Zipporah Films
54 Lewis Wharf
Boston, MA 02110
(617) 742-6680

Organizations

A selected list of organizations providing useful information on matters involving children and movies or television.

Action for Children's Television
(ACT)
46 Austin St.
Newtonville, MA 02160

American Center of Films for Children
Division of Cinema
University of Southern California
University Park
Los Angeles, CA 90007

The American Film Institute
National Education Services
John F. Kennedy Center for the Performing Arts
Washington, DC 20566

Center for Understanding Media, Inc.
66 Fifth Ave.
New York, NY 10011

Chicago Children's Film Center
Facets Multimedia Inc.
1517 W. Fullerton Ave.
Chicago, IL 60614

Department of Audiovisual Instruction
National Education Association
1201 16th St., N.W.
Washington, DC 20036

Educational Film Library Association (EFLA)
43 W. 61st St.
New York, NY 10023

Media Center for Children/Children's Film Theater
43 W. 61st St.
New York, NY 10023

Museum of Modern Art
Film Study Center
11 W. 53rd St.
New York, NY 10019

National Film Information Service
Academy of Motion Picture Arts and Sciences
Margaret Herrick Library
8949 Wilshire Blvd.
Beverly Hills, CA 90211

National Screen Education Committee
15 Trowbridge St.
Cambridge, MA 02138

New York Public Library/Donnell
Library
Video/Film Study Center
20 W. 53rd St.
New York, NY 10019

New York Public Library/Lincoln
Center Theatre Collection
111 Amsterdam Ave.
New York, NY 10023

North West Film Study Center
Portland Art Museum
Southwest Park and Madison
Portland, OR 97205

Television Information Office
Library
745 Fifth Ave.
New York, NY 10022

100 Good Books About Film

Agee, James. *Agee on Film.* Vol. 1, *Reviews and Comments.* New York: McDowell, Obolensky, 1958-1960. New York: Grosset & Dunlap.

Alpert, Hollis. *The Dream and the Dreamers.* New York: Macmillan, 1962.

Artel, Linda, and Wengraf, Susan. *Positive Images: A Guide to Nonsexist Films for Children.* San Francisco: Booklegger Press, 1976.

Balázs, Béla. *Theory of the Film: Character and Growth of a New Art.* New York: Dover, 1970.

Baldwin, James. *The Devil Finds Work.* New York: Dial, 1976.

Barnouw, Erik. *Documentary: A History of the Non-Fiction Film.* New York: Oxford University Press, 1974.

Baxter, John. *Science Fiction in the Cinema.* New York: Barnes, 1970.

Bazin, André. *What Is Cinema?* 2 Vols. Berkeley: University of California Press, 1967, 1971.

Boyle, Donald. *Toms, Coons, Mulattoes, Mammies and Bucks.* New York: Viking, 1974.

Braudy, Leo. *The World in a Frame: What We See in Films.* Garden City, N.Y.: Anchor/Doubleday, 1977.

Calder-Marshall, Arthur. *The Innocent Eye: The Life of Robert J. Flaherty.* London: W. H. Allen, 1963; Baltimore: Penguin, 1966.

Capra, Frank. *The Name Above the Title.* New York: Macmillan, 1971; New York: Bantam, 1972.

Clarens, Carlos. *An Illustrated History of Horror Films.* New York: Putnam, 1967; New York: Capricorn, 1968.

Cocteau, Jean. *Beauty and the Beast-Diary of a Film.* New York: Dover, 1972.

Corliss, Richard. *Talking Pictures: Screenwriters in the American Cinema, 1927-1930.* Woodstock, N.Y.: Overlook Press, 1974; Baltimore: Penguin, 1975.

Cowie, Peter, ed. *A Concise History of the Cinema.* 2 vols. New York: Barnes, 1971.

Crist, Judith. *The Private Eye, The Cowboy, and the Very Naked Girl: The Movies from Cleo to Clyde.* Chicago: Holt, 1968.

Crowther, Bosley. *The Great Films: Fifty Golden Years of Motion Pictures.* New York: Putnam, 1967.

Denby, David, ed. *Awake in the Dark: An Anthology of American Film Criticism, 1915 to the Present.* New York: Vintage, 1977.

Edgar, Patricia. *Children and Screen Violence.* Lawrence, Me.: University of Queensland Press, 1977.

Eisenstein, Sergei M. *Film Form.* New York: Harcourt, Brace, 1949.
——. *The Film Sense.* New York: Harcourt, Brace, 1947.
Everson, William K. *The Art of W. C. Fields.* New York: Bobbs-Merrill, 1967.
——. *The Bad Guys: A Pictorial History of the Movie Villain.* Secaucus, N. J.: Citadel, 1964.
Fenin, George N., and William K. Everson. *The Western: From Silents to the Seventies.* New York: Grossman, 1973. Baltimore: Penguin. 1974.
Friedlander, Madeline S. *Leading Film Discussions.* New York: League of Women Voters, 1972.
Gaffney, Maureen. *More Films Kids Like: A Catalog of Short Films for Children.* Chicago: American Library Association, 1977.
Geduld, Harry M., ed. *Film Makers on Film Making.* Bloomington: Indiana University Press, 1967.
Gelmis, Joseph. *The Film Director as Superstar.* Garden City, N. Y.: Doubleday, 1970.
Gessner, Robert. *The Moving Image: A Guide to Cinematic Literacy.* New York: Dutton, 1968.
Gilliatt, Penelope. *Unholy Fools.* New York: Viking, 1973.
Goldstein, Ruth M., and Edith Zornow. *The Screen Image of Youth: Movies About Children and Adolescents.* New York: Scarecrow Press, 1980.
Griffith, Richard, and Arthur Mayer. *The Movies,* rev. ed. New York: Simon and Schuster, 1970.
Hall, Stuart, et al. *Film Teaching.* London: British Film Institute, 1968.
Halliwell, Leslie. *The Filmgoer's Companion,* 6th ed. New York: Hill & Wang, 1977.
Haskell, Molly. *From Reverence to Rape: The Treatment of Women in the Movies.* New York: Holt, 1974. Baltimore: Penguin, 1974.
Higham, Charles, and Joel Greenberg. *The Celluloid Muse: Hollywood Directors Speak.* New York: New American Library, 1969. New York: Signet, 1972.
Houston, Penelope. *The Contemporary Cinema.* Baltimore: Penguin, 1971.
Huff, Theodore. *Charlie Chaplin.* New York: Henry Schuman, 1951. New York: Arno, 1972.
Huss, Roy, and Norman Silverstein. *The Film Experience: Elements of Motion Picture Art.* New York: Harper & Row, 1968.
Jacobs, Lewis, ed. *The Documentary Tradition: From Nanook to Woodstock.* New York: Hopkinson and Blake, 1971.
——. *The Emergence of Film Art.* New York: Hopkinson and Blake, 1969.
——. *The Movies as Medium.* New York: Farrar, Straus & Giroux, 1970. New York: Octagon, 1973.
——. *The Rise of the American Film.* New York: Harcourt, Brace, 1939. New York: Teachers College, 1968.
Kael, Pauline. *Deeper into Movies.* Boston: Little, Brown, 1973.
——. *Going Steady.* Boston: Little, Brown, 1970.

———. *I Lost It At the Movies*. Boston: Little, Brown, 1965. New York: Bantam, 1976.

———. *Kiss Kiss Bang Bang*. Boston: Little, Brown 1968. New York: Bantam, 1976.

———. *Reeling*. Boston: Little, Brown, 1976. New York: Warner, 1977.

Kauffmann, Stanley, ed., with Bruce Hanstell. *American Film Criticism from the Beginnings to 'Citizen Kane.'* New York: Liveright, 1972.

———. *Figures of Light: Film Criticism and Comment*. New York: Harper & Row, 1971. New York: Colophon, 1972.

———. *Living Images: Film Comment and Criticism*. New York: Harper & Row, 1975.

———. *A World on Film*. New York: Harper & Row, 1966. Westport: Greenwood, 1975.

Kay, Karyn, and Gerald Peary. *Women and the Cinema: A Critical Anthology*. New York: Dutton, 1976.

Kaye, Evelyn. *The Family Guide to Children's Television*. (Action for Children's Television). New York: Pantheon, 1974.

Kerr, Walter. *The Silent Clowns*. New York: Knopf, 1975.

Knight, Arthur. *The Liveliest Art: A Panoramic History of the Movies*, rev. ed. New York: Macmillan, 1978.

Leyda, Jay. *Voices of Film Experience, 1894 to the Present*. New York: Macmillan, 1977.

Lindgren, Ernest. *The Art of Film*. 2nd ed., New York: Macmillan, 1963.

MacCann, Richard Dyer, ed. *Film and Society*. New York: Scribner, 1964.

Madsen, Axel. *The New Hollywood: American Movies in the Seventies*. New York: Crowell, 1975.

Maland, Charles J. *American Visions: The Films of Chaplin, Ford, Capra, and Welles, 1936-1941*. New York: Arno, 1977.

Mallery, David. *Film in the Life of the School*. Boston: National Association of Independent Schools, 1968.

Manvell, Roger, and Lewis Jacobs, eds. *The International Film Encyclopedia*. New York: Crown, 1972.

Manvell, Roger. *Experiment in the Film*. London: Grey Walls Press, 1949. New York: Arno, 1970.

Mayer, Arthur. *Merely Colossal: The Story of the Movies from the Long Chase to the Chaise Longue*. New York: Simon and Schuster, 1953.

Maynard, Richard A. *The Celluloid Curriculum: How to Use Movies in the Classroom*. New York: Hayden, 1971.

Monaco, James. *How to Read a Film: The Art, Technology, Language, History, and Theory of Film and Media*. New York: Oxford University Press, 1977.

Murray, Edward. *Nine American Film Critics*. New York: Ungar, 1975.

Nichols, Bill, ed. *Movies and Methods*. Berkeley: University of California Press, 1976.

O'Connor, John E., and Martin A. Jackson. *American History/American Film: Interpreting the Hollywood Image*. Foreword by Arthur M. Schlesinger, Jr. New York: Ungar, 1979.

Patterson, Lindsay, comp. *Black Films and Film-Makers: A Comprehensive Anthology from Stereotype to Superhero.* New York: Dodd, 1975.

Peary, Gerald, and Roger Shatzkin, eds. *The Modern American Novel and the Movies.* New York: Ungar, 1979.

Ramsaye, Terry. *A Million and One Nights: A History of the Motion Picture,* 2 vols. New York: Simon and Schuster, 1926; 1 vol. ed., 1964.

Reilly, Adam. *Harold Lloyd: The King of Daredevil Comedy.* New York: Macmillan, 1977.

Renoir, Jean. *My Life and My Films.* New York: Atheneum, 1974.

Rhode, Eric. *Tower of Babel: Speculations on the Cinema.* Philadelphia: Chilton, 1967.

Rice, Susan. *Films Kids Like: A Catalog of Short Films for Children.* Chicago: American Library Association, 1973.

Robinson, William R., ed. *Man and the Movies.* Baton Rouge: Louisiana State University Press, 1967. Baltimore: Penguin, 1969.

Rohmer, Eric, and Claude Chabrol. *Hitchcock: The First Forty-Four Films.* Transl. by Stanley Hochman. New York: Ungar, 1979.

Ross, Lillian. *Picture.* New York: Rinehart, 1952. Garden City, New York: Doubleday, Dolphin.

Sarris, Andrew. *The American Cinema: Directors and Directions, 1929-1968.* New York: Dutton, 1968.

Schickel, Richard. *The Disney Version: The Life, Times, Art, and Commerce of Walt Disney.* New York: Simon and Schuster, 1968. New York: Avon, 1969.

——. *Harold Lloyd: The Shape of Laughter.* Boston: New York Graphic Society, 1974.

Schillaci, Anthony, and John M. Culkin, eds. *Films Deliver.* New York: Citation, 1970.

Sheridan, Marion C., with Harold H. Owen, Jr., Ken Macrorie, and Fred Marcus. *The Motion Picture and the Teaching of English.* New York: Appleton-Century-Crofts, 1965.

Simon, John. *Private Screenings.* New York: Macmillan, 1967; New York: Berkley.

Sklar, Robert. *Movie-Made America.* New York: Random House, 1975; New York: Vintage, 1976.

Stephenson, Ralph and J. R. Debrix. *The Cinema As Art.* Baltimore: Penguin, 1965.

Talbot, Daniel, ed. *Film: An Anthology,* 2nd ed. Berkeley: University of California Press, 1966.

Taylor, John Russell. *Directors and Directions: Cinema for the Seventies.* New York: Hill & Wang, 1975.

Thompson, Howard, ed. *The New York Times Guide to Movies on TV.* Chicago: Quadrangle, 1971.

Truffault, Francois. *The Films in My Life.* New York: Simon and Schuster, 1978.

Tyler, Parker. *Classics of the Foreign Film.* Secaucus, N. J.: Citadel, 1962.

——. *The Hollywood Hallucination.* New York: Simon and Schuster, 1970. Louisville: Touchstone Books, 1970.

UNESCO, ed. *The Influence of the Cinema on Children and Adolescents.* Westport: Greenwood reprint, 1961.

Vogel, Amos. *Film As a Subversive Art.* New York: Random House, 1976.

Walker, Alexander. *Sex in the Movies: The Celluloid Sacrifice.* Baltimore: Penguin, 1970.

Warshow, Robert. *The Immediate Experience.* Garden City, N.Y.: Anchor, 1964.

Weinberg, Herman G. *Saint Cinema: Writings on Film, 1929-1970.* New York: 2nd ed., rev., Ungar, 1980.

Weiner, Janet. *How To Organize and Run a Film Society.* New York: Macmillan, 1973.

White, David Manning, and Richard Averson. *The Celluloid Weapon: Social Comment in the American Film.* Boston: Beacon, 1972.

Wright, Basil. *The Long View.* New York: Knopf, 1974.

A Selected List of Film and Television Periodicals

"Factfile #1, *Film and TV Periodicals in English*," containing more than 160 annotated listings, indexed by subject matter and general interest, may be obtained from the National Education Services of The American Film Institute ($3.00 nonmembers; $2.00 members) at the address below.

American Film
The American Film Institute
J. F. Kennedy Center for the Performing Arts
Washington, DC 20566
10 issues a year. $15/year.

Audiovisual Instruction
1126 16th St., N.W.
Washington, DC 20036
10 issues a year. $18/year.

Cinéaste
333 Sixth Ave.
New York, NY 10014
Quarterly. $4/year.

Cinema Journal
17 W. College St.
Iowa City, IA 52242
2 issues a year. $4/year.

Cinema Papers
143 Therry St.
Melbourne, Victoria 3000
Australia
Quarterly. $7/year.

Film & Broadcasting Review
Office for Film & Broadcasting of the U.S. Catholic Conference
1011 First Ave.
New York, NY 10022
Bimonthly. $10/year.

Film Comment
Film Society of Lincoln Center
1865 Broadway
New York, NY 10023
6 issues a year. $10/year.

Film Culture
G.P.O. 1499
New York, NY 10001
Irregularly published. $8/4 issues.

Film Library Quarterly
Film Library Information Council
Box 348, Radio City Station
New York, NY 10019
Quarterly. $10/year.

Film News
250 W. 57th St.
Suite 1527
New York, NY 10019
5 issues a year. $7/year.

Film Quarterly
University of California Press
Berkeley, CA 94702
Quarterly. $6/year.

Filmfacts
University of Southern California
P.O. Box 69610, West Station
Los Angeles, CA 90069
Bimonthly. $40/year.

260

Films and Filming
75 Victoria St.
London, SW1, England
Monthly. $16.10/year.

Films in Review
210 E. 68th St.
New York, NY 10021
10 issues a year. $10.50/year.

Focus on Film
136-148 Tooley St.
London, SE1, England
Quarterly. $7/year.

Journal of Popular Film
Bowling Green State University
101 University Hall
Bowling Green, OH 43404
Quarterly. $5/year.

*Journal of the University Film
    Association*
Temple University
Philadelphia, PA 19122
Quarterly. $6/year.

Jump Cut
P.O. Box 865
Berkeley, CA 94701
Quarterly. $4/6 issues.

Literature/Film Quarterly
Salisbury State College
Salisbury, MD 21801
Quarterly. $6/year.

Mass Media Newsletter
Mass Media Ministries
2116 N. Charles St.
Baltimore, MD 21218
20 issues a year. $12/year.

Media & Methods
401 N. Broad St.
Philadelphia, PA 19108
9 issues a year. $9/year.

Millimeter
12 E. 46th St.
New York, NY 10017
Monthly. $10/year.

Monthly Film Bulletin
British Film Institute
81 Dean St.
London, W1V 6AA, England
Monthly. $11/year.

Quarterly Review of Film Studies
430 Manville Rd.
Pleasantville, NY 10570
Quarterly. $14/year.

Sight and Sound
British Film Institute
Eastern News Distributors
111 Eighth Ave.
New York, NY 10011
Quarterly. $12/year.

Sightlines
Educational Film Library Association
43 W. 61st St.
New York, NY 10023
Quarterly. $15/year.

Take One
P.O. Box 1778, Station B
Montreal H3B 3L3, Quebec
Canada
Monthly. $6/year.

Teachers Guides to Television
699 Madison Ave.
New York, NY 10021
Twice yearly. $4/year.

Televisions
Washington Community Video
    Center
P.O. Box 21068
Washington, DC 20009
Quarterly. $10/10 issues.

*University Film Study Center
    Newsletter*
Box 275
Cambridge, MA 02138
Bimonthly. $10/year.

Variety
154 W. 46th St.
New York, NY 10036
Weekly. $30/year.

Wide Angle
Ohio University Department of Film
Box 388
Athens, OH 45701
Quarterly. $6.50/year.

TITLE INDEX TO FILMS

E = Entertainment Feature
D = Documentary
F = Featurette
S = Supplement
CFF = Children's Film Foundation
CM = Chaplin Mutual Comedies
* = For Under-8's

Abe Lincoln in Illinois (E) 13
Absent-Minded Professor, The (E) * 13
Across the Great Divide (S) 211
Adventure in the Hopfields (CFF) 198
Adventurer, The (CM) * 191
Adventures of Chico, The (S) * 211
Adventures of Huckleberry Finn, The (S) 211
Adventures of Robin Hood, The (E) * 14
Adventures of Robinson Crusoe, The (E) 14
Adventures of Sherlock Holmes, The (S) 212
Adventures of the Wilderness Family, The (S) * 212
Adventures of Tom Sawyer, The (E) * 15
African Lion, The (S) (D) 12
African Queen, The (E) 15
Alice's Adventures in Wonderland (E) 16
All Creatures Great and Small (S) 213
All Things Bright and Beautiful (S) 213
Almost Angels (S) 213
Amazing Cosmic Awareness of Duffy Moon, The (F) 171
Amazing Grace (E) (D) 17
Anchors Aweigh (S) 214
And Now Miguel (E) 17

Animal Crackers (S) 214
Anoop and the Elephant (CFF), 199
Around the World in 80 Days (E) 18
Arsenic and Old Lace (E) 19
Autobiography of Miss Jane Pittman, The (E) 19

Bad News Bears, The (E) 20
Bambi (E) * 21
Bank Dick, The (E) 21
Battle for the Planet of the Apes (E) 132
Bears and I, The (S) * 214
Beau Geste (S) 215
Beauty and the Beast (E) 22
Bedknobs and Broomsticks (S) 215
Behind the Screen (CM) * 191
Bellboy, The (E) * 22
Beneath the Planet of the Apes (E) 133
Ben-Hur (S) 23
Benji (E) * 23
Bethune (S) (D) 215
Beware, Beware, My Beauty Fair (F) * 171
Big Henry and the Polka Dot Kid (F) 171
Big Store, The (E) * 25
Bighorn! (E) (D) 24
Billy Budd (E) 25
Bim (F) * 172
Biscuit Eater, The (E) * 26
Black Beauty (E) * 26
Black Stallion, The (E) 27
Blind Bird (F) * 172
Blow Your Own Trumpet (CFF) 199
Blue Bird, The (S) 216
Blue Water, White Death (E) (D) 28
Bolero (F) (D) 173
Born Free (E) * 28
Boy Named Charlie Brown, A (E) * 29
Boy of Two Worlds (S) 216

263

RUTH M. GOLDSTEIN, a pioneer teacher of film in New York City, has published teaching aids on films and plays, wrote film catalogs for Brandon Films during the '50s and '60s, and is a regular reviewer of 16 mm feature films for *Film News* Magazine. She now lives in Florida.

EDITH ZORNOW went from radio to films as manager of the Film Library for Brandon Films. An Emmy-winning television producer for the Public Broadcasting station in New York City, she is now film producer at the Children's Television Workshop, responsible for *Sesame Street* and other programs.